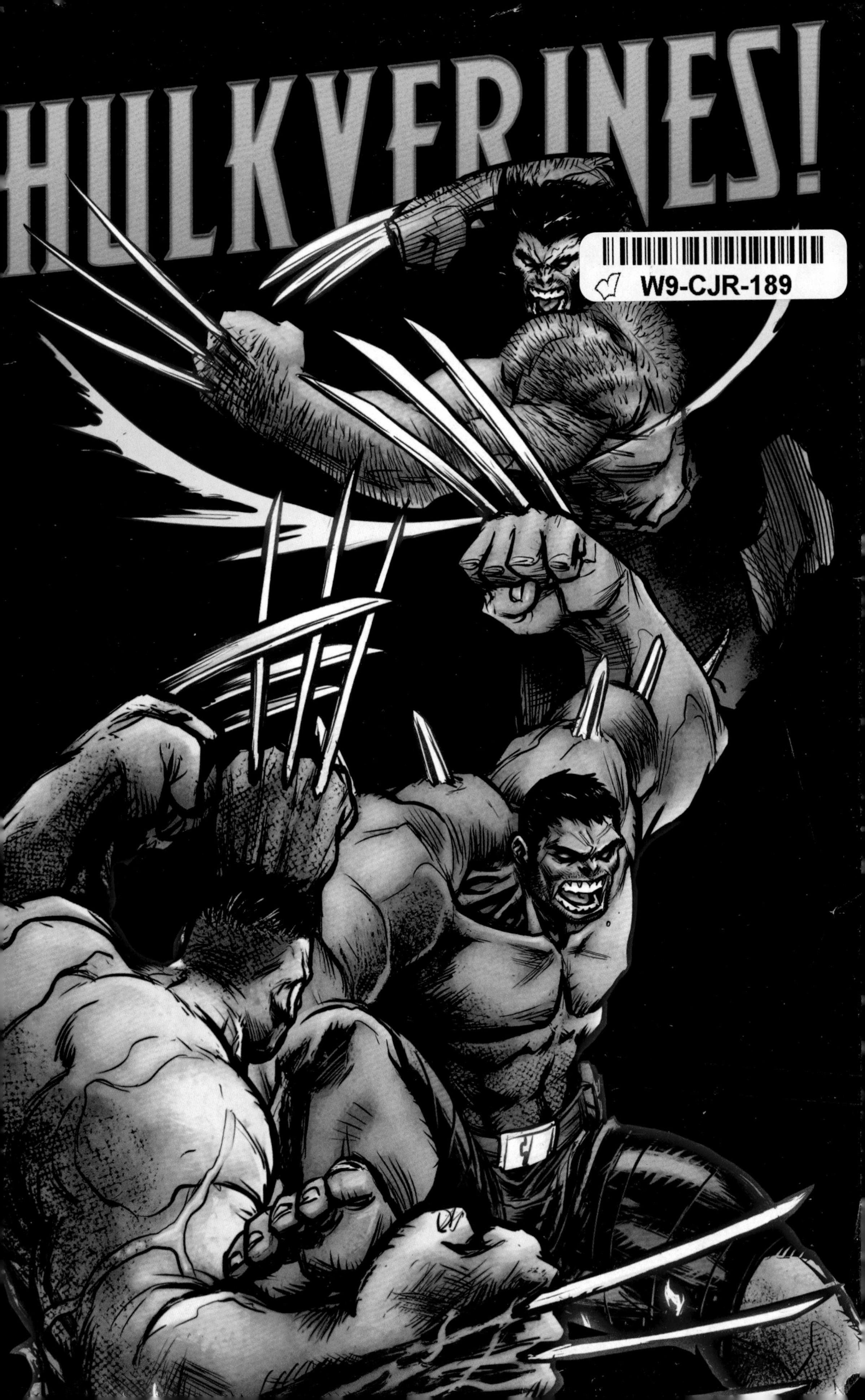
HULKVERINES!

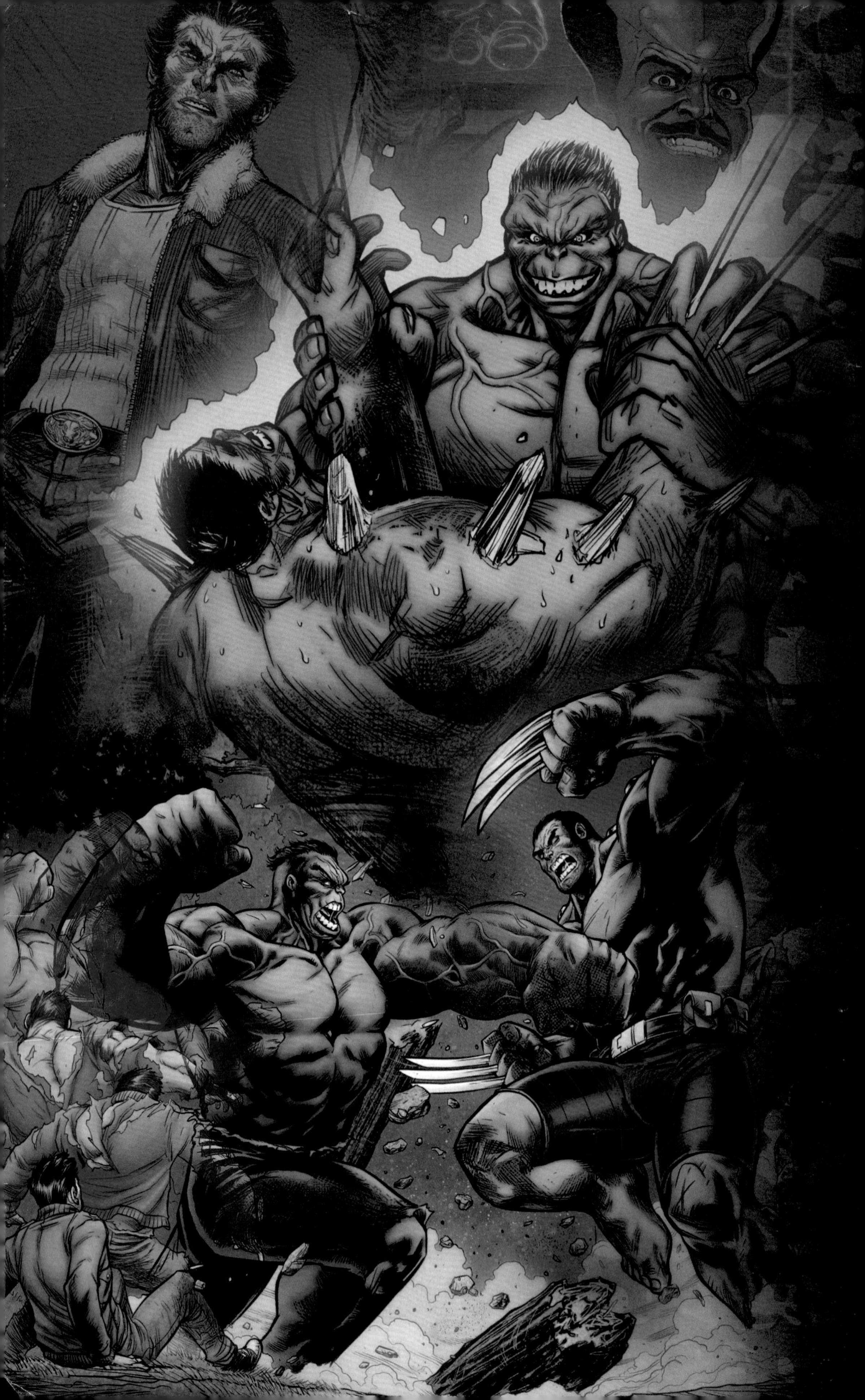

HULKVERINES!

GREG PAK
WRITER

ARIO ANINDITO (#1 & 3)
& **GUIU VILANOVA** (#2)
ARTISTS

MORRY HOLLOWELL (#1-3)
WITH **ANDREW CROSSLEY** (#1) & **CHRIS SOTOMAYOR** (#2)
COLOR ARTISTS

VC'S JOE CARAMAGNA
LETTERER

GREG LAND & **FRANK D'ARMATA** (#1);
GREG LAND, JAY LEISTEN & **FRANK D'ARMATA** (#2-3)
COVER ARTISTS

SARAH BRUNSTAD
ASSOCIATE EDITOR

WIL MOSS
EDITOR

TOM BREVOORT
EXECUTIVE EDITOR

COLLECTION EDITOR **MARK D. BEAZLEY** ■ ASSISTANT EDITOR **CAITLIN O'CONNELL**
ASSOCIATE MANAGING EDITOR **KATERI WOODY** ■ SENIOR EDITOR, SPECIAL PROJECTS **JENNIFER GRÜNWALD**
VP PRODUCTION & SPECIAL PROJECTS **JEFF YOUNGQUIST** ■ BOOK DESIGNER **STACIE ZUCKER**

SVP PRINT, SALES & MARKETING **DAVID GABRIEL** ■ DIRECTOR, LICENSED PUBLISHING **SVEN LARSEN**
EDITOR IN CHIEF **C.B. CEBULSKI** ■ CHIEF CREATIVE OFFICER **JOE QUESADA**
PRESIDENT **DAN BUCKLEY** ■ EXECUTIVE PRODUCER **ALAN FINE**

HULKVERINES. Contains material originally published in magazine form as HULKVERINES #1-3 and THE TOTALLY AWESOME HULK #22. First printing 2019. ISBN 978-1-302-91835-4. Published by MARVEL WORLDWIDE, INC., a subsidiary of MARVEL ENTERTAINMENT, LLC. OFFICE OF PUBLICATION: 135 West 50th Street, New York, NY 10020. © 2019 MARVEL No similarity between any of the names, characters, persons, and/or institutions in this magazine with those of any living or dead person or institution is intended, and any such similarity which may exist is purely coincidental. **Printed in Canada.** DAN BUCKLEY, President, Marvel Entertainment; JOHN NEE, Publisher; JOE QUESADA, Chief Creative Officer; TOM BREVOORT, SVP of Publishing; DAVID BOGART, Associate Publisher & SVP of Talent Affairs; DAVID GABRIEL, SVP of Sales & Marketing, Publishing; JEFF YOUNGQUIST, VP of Production & Special Projects; DAN CARR, Executive Director of Publishing Technology; ALEX MORALES, Director of Publishing Operations; DAN EDINGTON, Managing Editor; SUSAN CRESPI, Production Manager; STAN LEE, Chairman Emeritus. For information regarding advertising in Marvel Comics or on Marvel.com, please contact Vit DeBellis, Custom Solutions & Integrated Advertising Manager, at vdebellis@marvel.com. For Marvel subscription inquiries, please call 888-511-5480. **Manufactured between 4/19/2019 and 5/21/2019 by SOLISCO PRINTERS, SCOTT, QC, CANADA.**

10 9 8 7 6 5 4 3 2 1

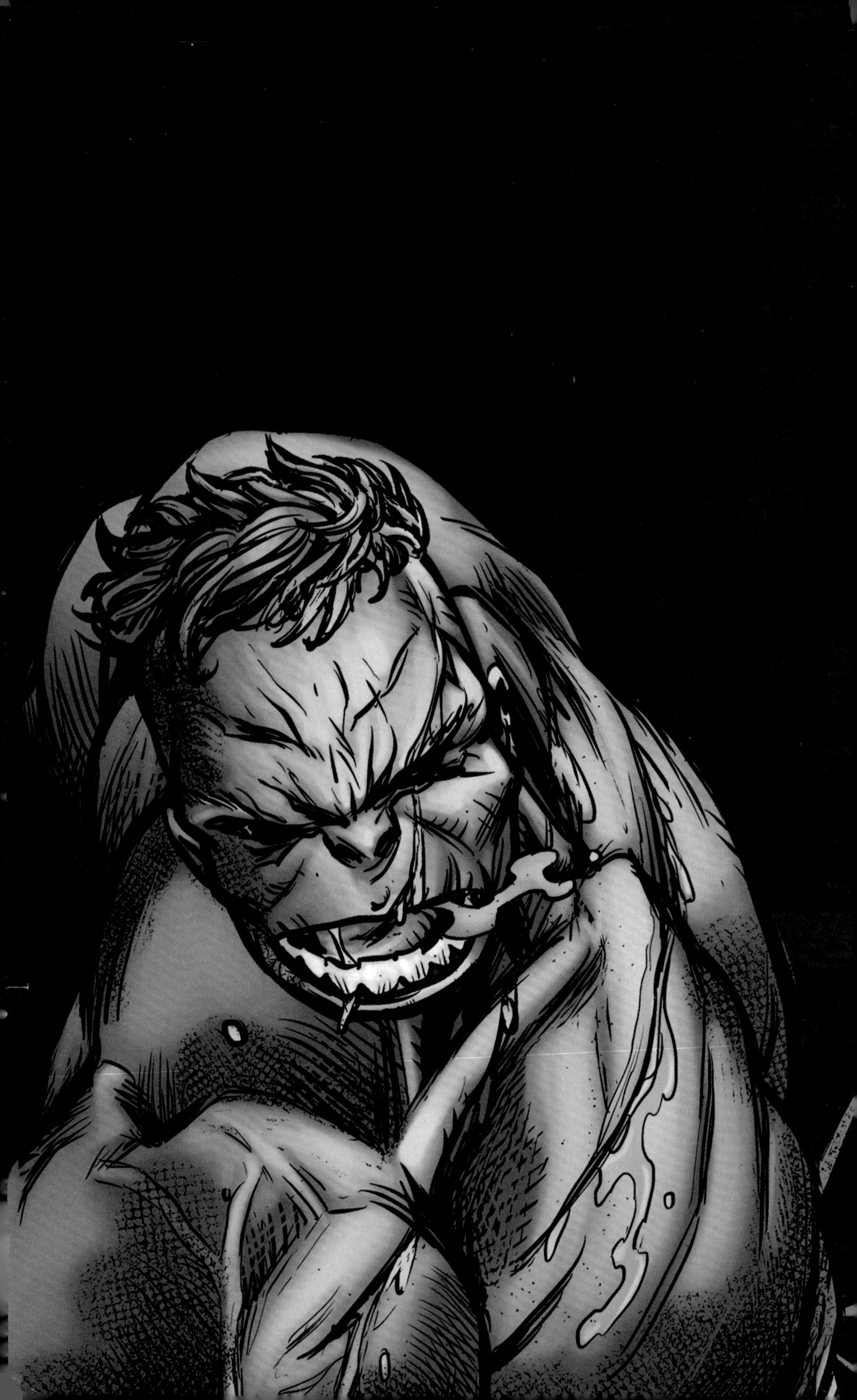

Intending to build the perfect killing machine, the Weapon X Program transformed an ordinary soldier named Clay Cortez into a Hulk-Wolverine hybrid, complete with nanotech Adamantium in his skeleton, gamma energy in his blood and healing abilities. But this soldier has had enough of death.

They tried to create a weapon. Instead they created the most dangerous hero on the planet: Weapon H.

Clay and his wife, Sonia, recently became millionaires after Dario Agger, the unscrupulous C.E.O. of the Roxxon Corporation, was forced to pay them for extricating a team of Roxxon employees from a monster-filled portal on Weirdworld. But in the process, they destroyed a priceless energy source that would have made Roxxon the premier energy provider for the entire planet. And Agger wants revenge.

Weapon H promised that if anyone ever hurt his family, he would come after Agger himself. But he forgot to specify that no one should harm him. Now Agger's set in motion a series of events that will upend Weapon H's whole world...

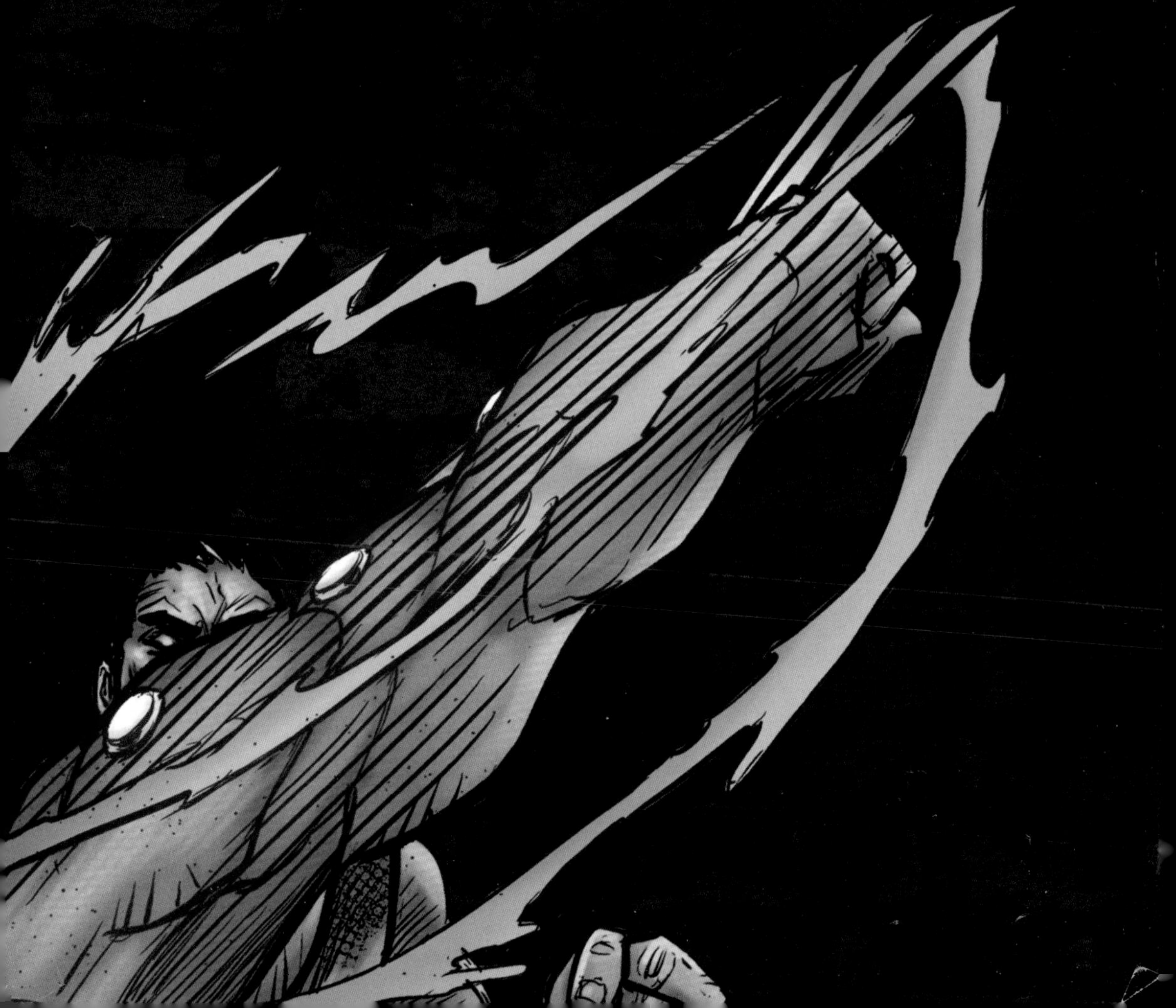

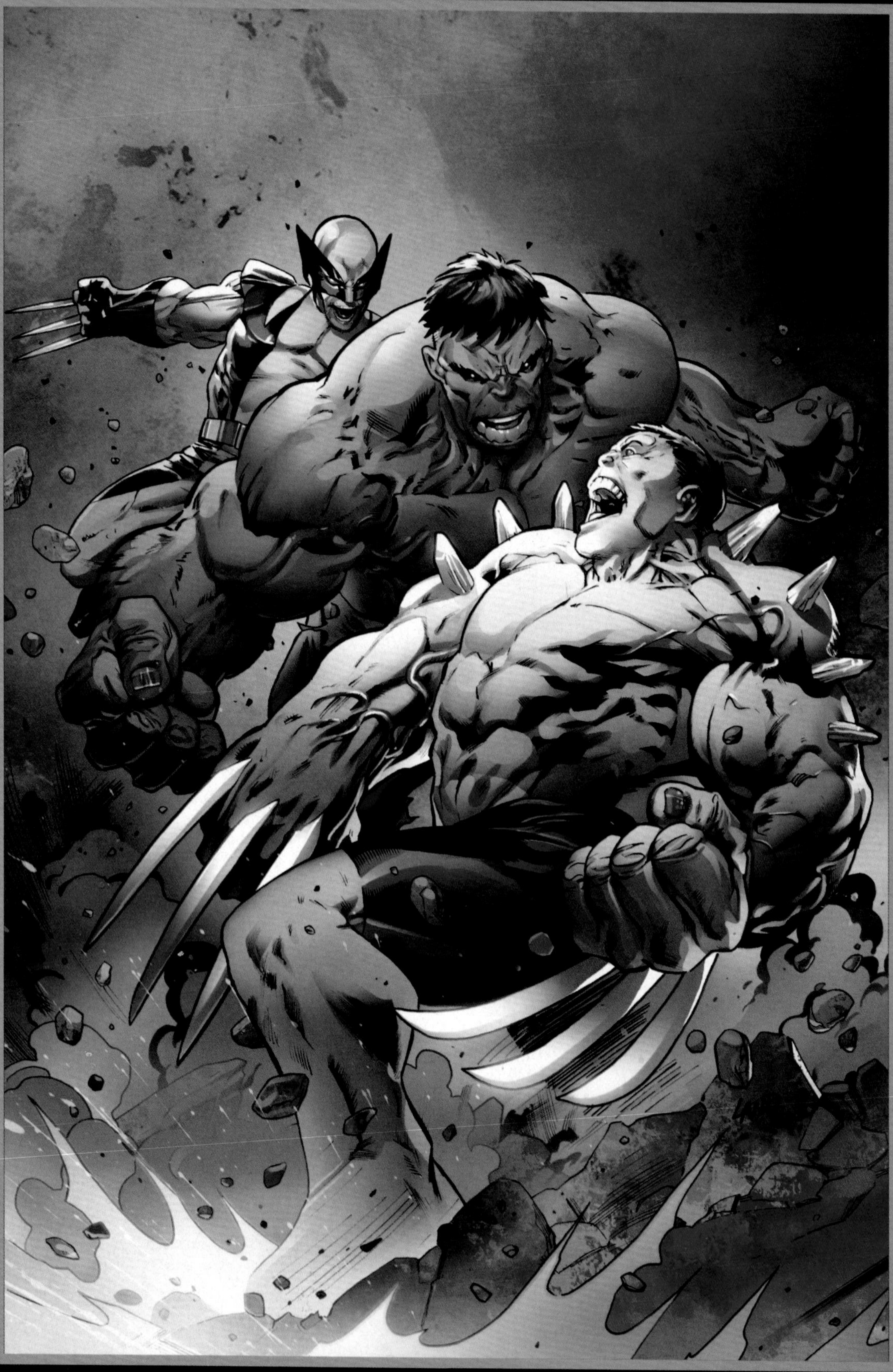

1

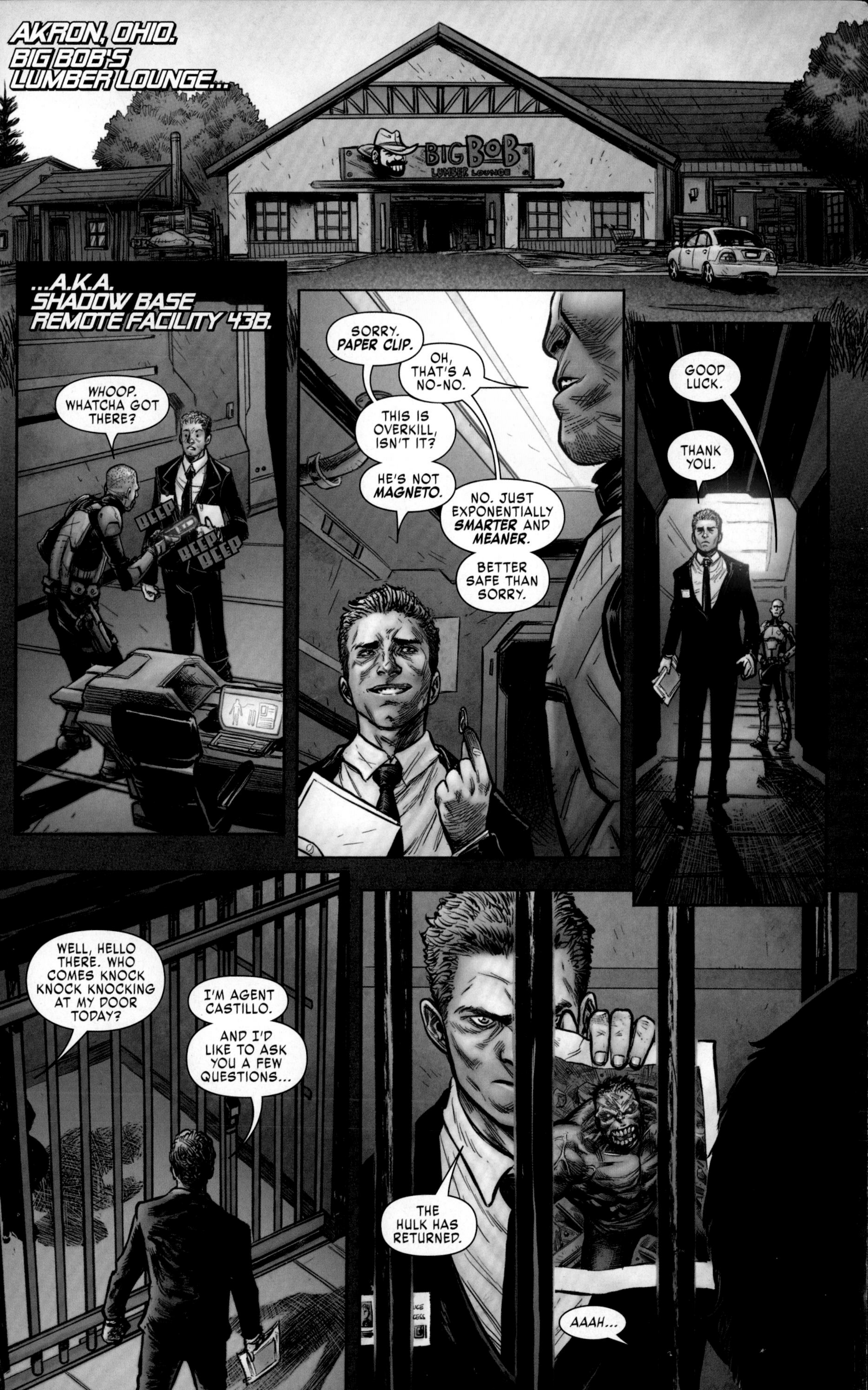
AKRON, OHIO. BIG BOB'S LUMBER LOUNGE...
BIG BOB LUMBER LOUNGE
...A.K.A. SHADOW BASE REMOTE FACILITY 43B.
WHOOP. WHATCHA GOT THERE?
BEEP BEEP BEEP
SORRY. PAPER CLIP.
OH, THAT'S A NO-NO.
THIS IS OVERKILL, ISN'T IT?
HE'S NOT MAGNETO.
NO. JUST EXPONENTIALLY SMARTER AND MEANER.
BETTER SAFE THAN SORRY.
GOOD LUCK.
THANK YOU.
WELL, HELLO THERE. WHO COMES KNOCK KNOCK KNOCKING AT MY DOOR TODAY?
I'M AGENT CASTILLO.
AND I'D LIKE TO ASK YOU A FEW QUESTIONS...
THE HULK HAS RETURNED.
AAAH...

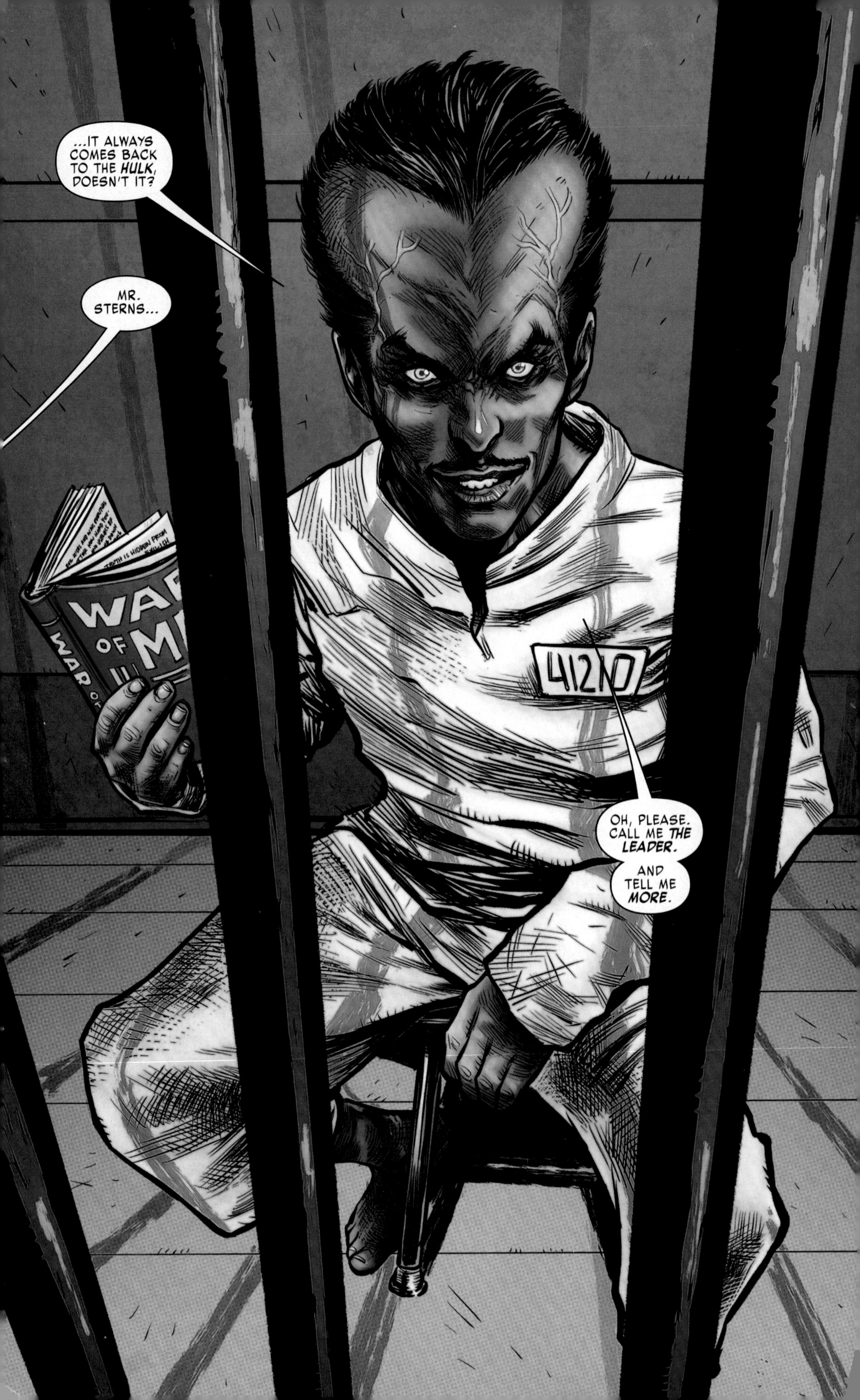
...IT ALWAYS COMES BACK TO THE HULK, DOESN'T IT?
MR. STERNS...
41210
OH, PLEASE. CALL ME THE LEADER.
AND TELL ME MORE.

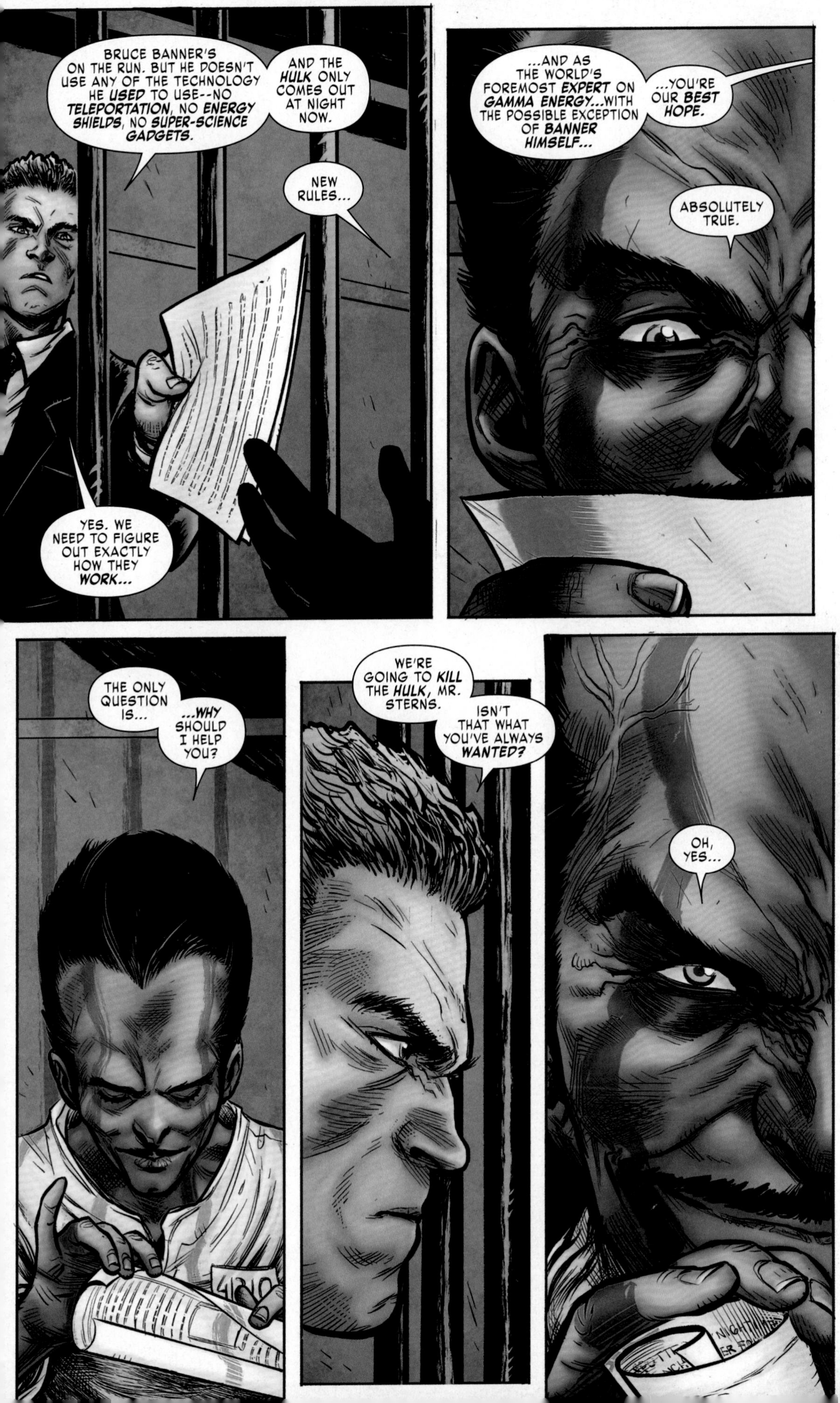
BRUCE BANNER'S ON THE RUN. BUT HE DOESN'T USE ANY OF THE TECHNOLOGY HE USED TO USE--NO TELEPORTATION, NO ENERGY SHIELDS, NO SUPER-SCIENCE GADGETS.
AND THE HULK ONLY COMES OUT AT NIGHT NOW.
NEW RULES...
YES. WE NEED TO FIGURE OUT EXACTLY HOW THEY WORK...
...AND AS THE WORLD'S FOREMOST EXPERT ON GAMMA ENERGY...WITH THE POSSIBLE EXCEPTION OF BANNER HIMSELF...
...YOU'RE OUR BEST HOPE.
ABSOLUTELY TRUE.
THE ONLY QUESTION IS...
...WHY SHOULD I HELP YOU?
WE'RE GOING TO KILL THE HULK, MR. STERNS.
ISN'T THAT WHAT YOU'VE ALWAYS WANTED?
OH, YES...

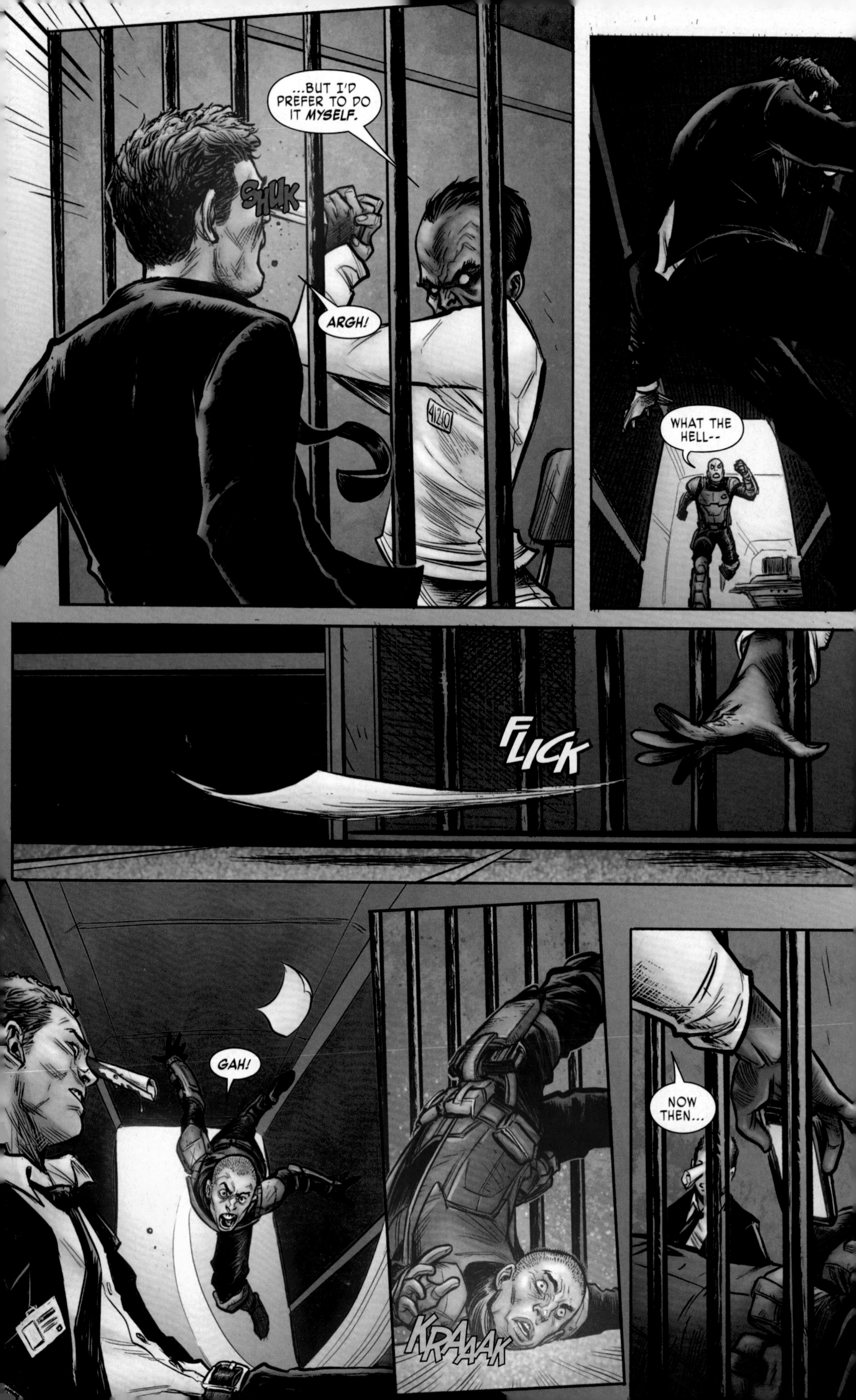
...BUT I'D PREFER TO DO IT MYSELF.
SHUK
ARGH!
41210
WHAT THE HELL--
FLICK
GAH!
KRAAAAK
NOW THEN...

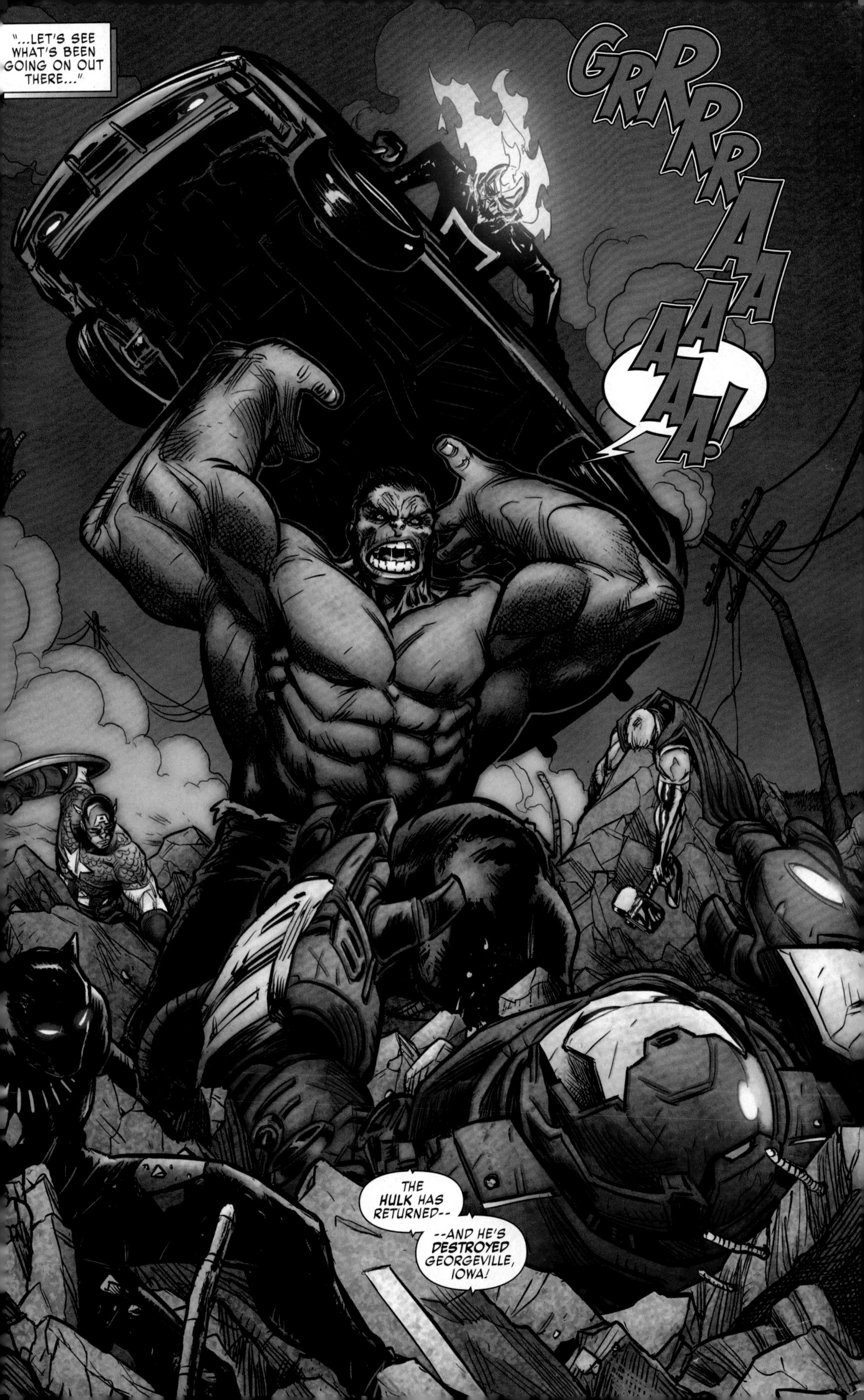
"...LET'S SEE WHAT'S BEEN GOING ON OUT THERE..."
GRRRRAAAAAAA!
THE HULK HAS RETURNED--
--AND HE'S DESTROYED GEORGEVILLE, IOWA!

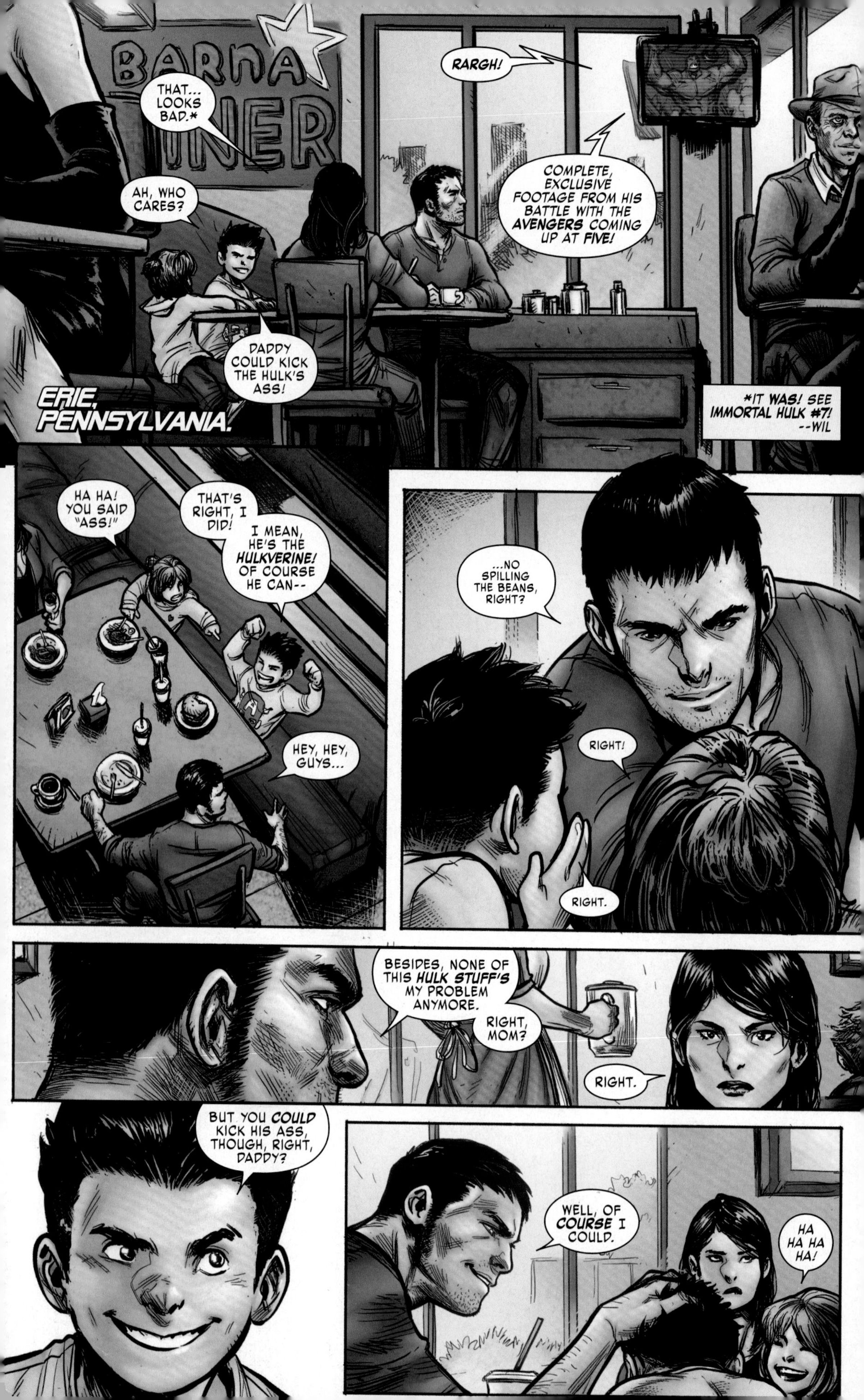
RARGH!
THAT... LOOKS BAD.*
COMPLETE, EXCLUSIVE FOOTAGE FROM HIS BATTLE WITH THE AVENGERS COMING UP AT FIVE!
AH, WHO CARES?
DADDY COULD KICK THE HULK'S ASS!
ERIE, PENNSYLVANIA.
*IT WAS! SEE IMMORTAL HULK #7! --WIL
HA HA! YOU SAID "ASS!"
THAT'S RIGHT, I DID!
I MEAN, HE'S THE HULKVERINE! OF COURSE HE CAN--
HEY, HEY, GUYS...
...NO SPILLING THE BEANS, RIGHT?
RIGHT!
RIGHT.
BESIDES, NONE OF THIS HULK STUFF'S MY PROBLEM ANYMORE.
RIGHT, MOM?
RIGHT.
BUT YOU COULD KICK HIS ASS, THOUGH, RIGHT, DADDY?
WELL, OF COURSE I COULD.
HA HA HA HA!

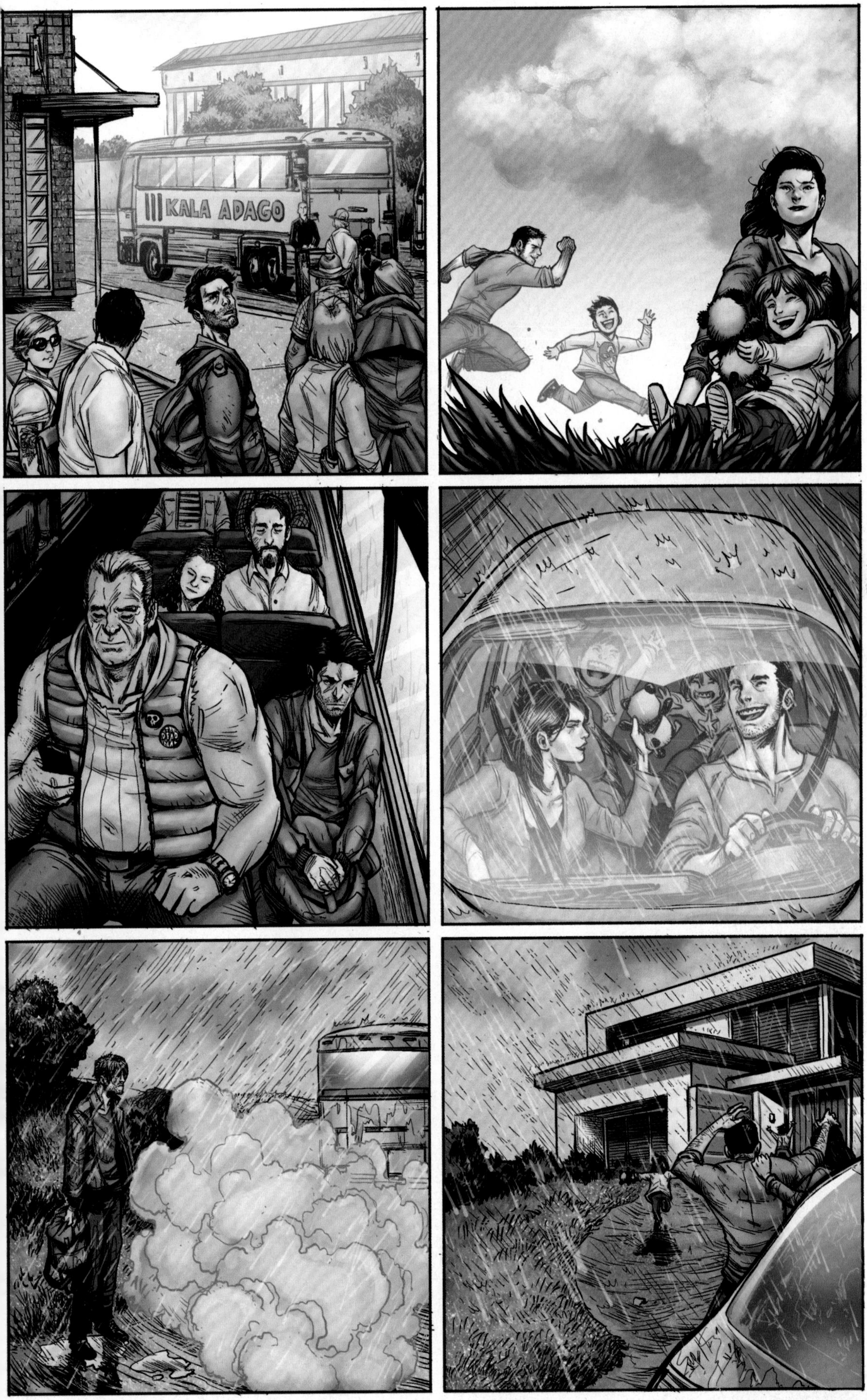
KALA ADAGO

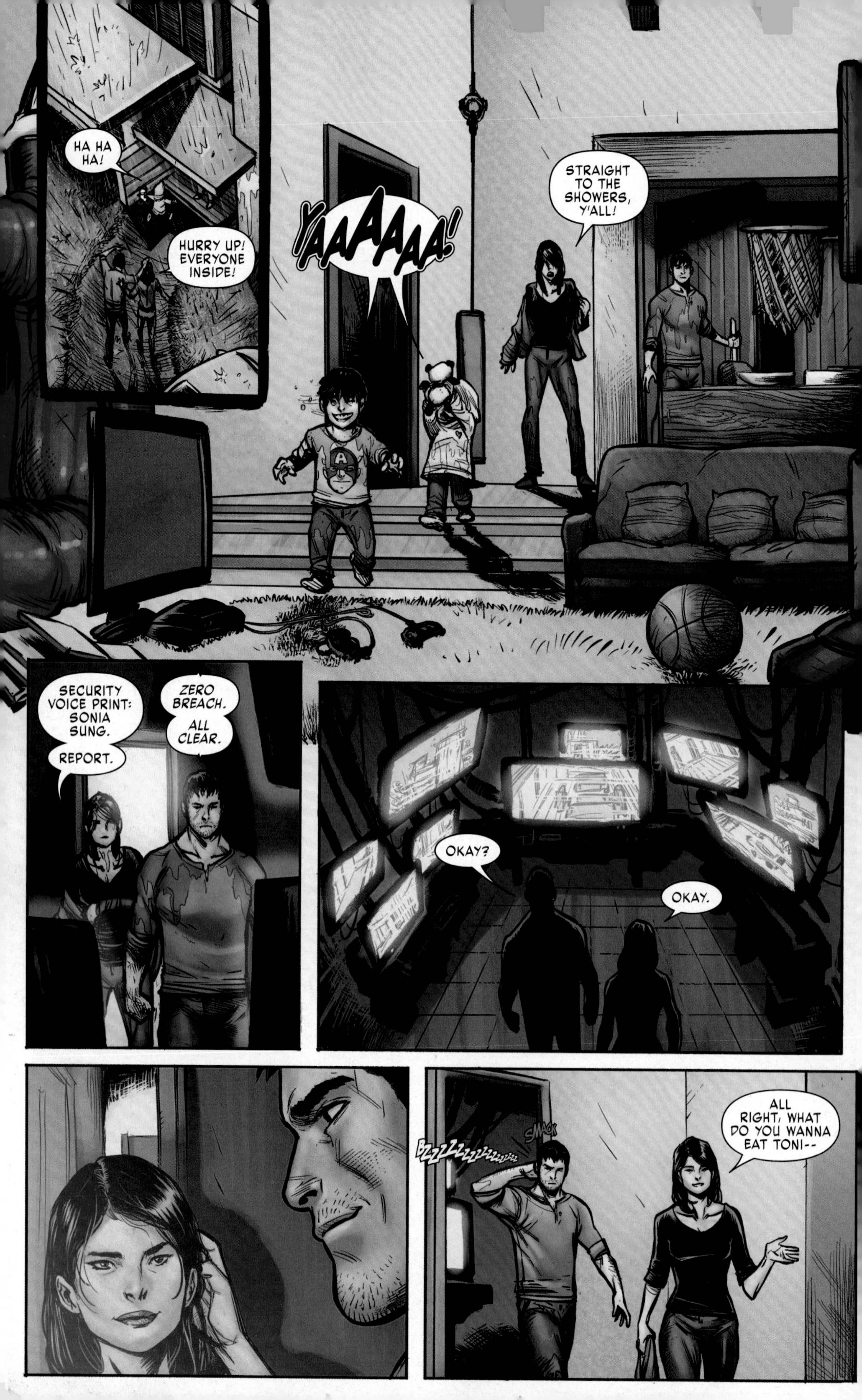
HA HA HA!
HURRY UP! EVERYONE INSIDE!
YAAAAAA!
STRAIGHT TO THE SHOWERS, Y'ALL!
SECURITY VOICE PRINT: SONIA SUNG.
REPORT.
ZERO BREACH. ALL CLEAR.
OKAY?
OKAY.
BZZZZZZZZZZZZZZZ
SMACK
ALL RIGHT, WHAT DO YOU WANNA EAT TONI--

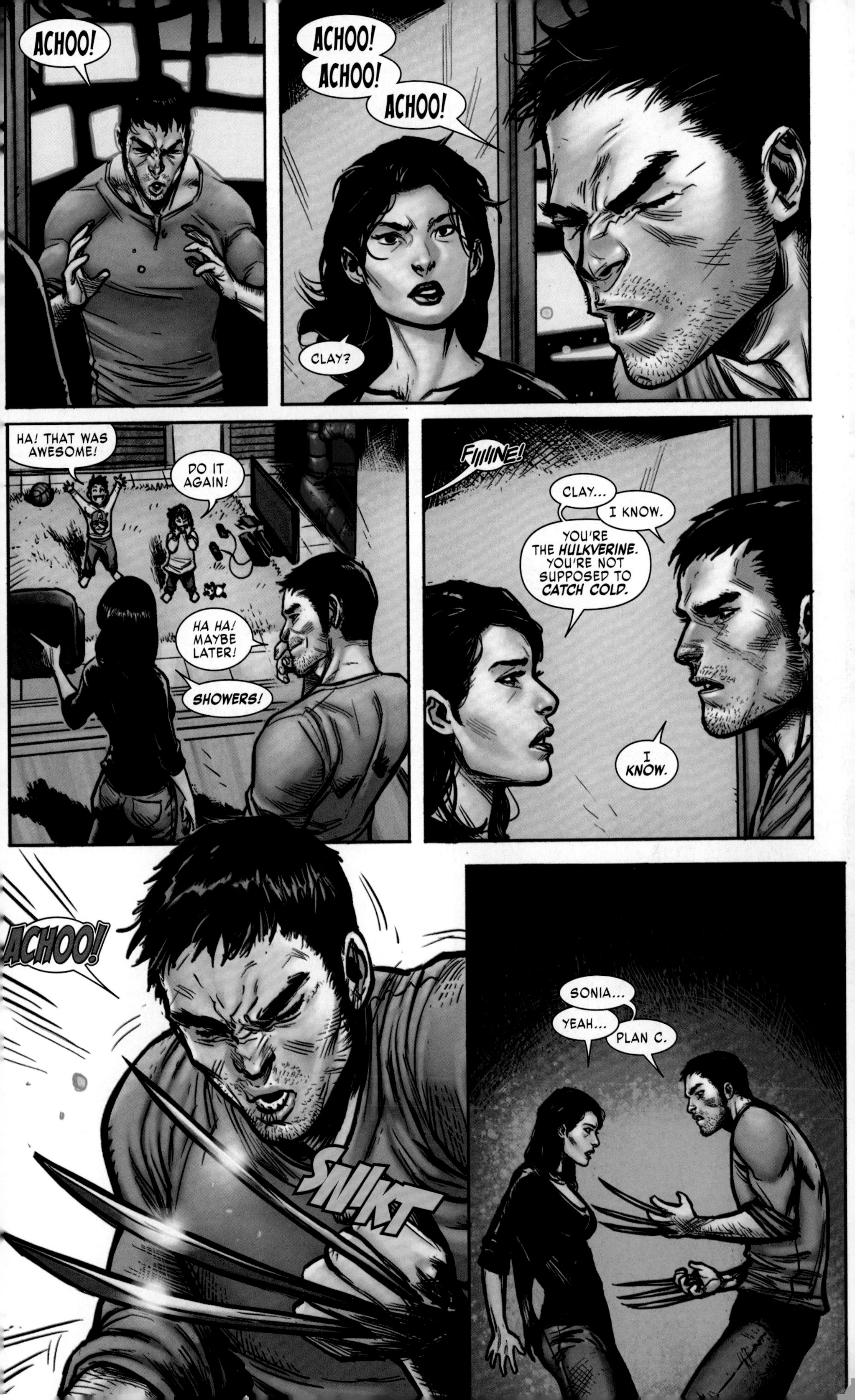

ACHOO!
ACHOO! ACHOO! ACHOO!
CLAY?
HA! THAT WAS AWESOME!
DO IT AGAIN!
HA HA! MAYBE LATER!
SHOWERS!
FIIIINE!
CLAY...
I KNOW.
YOU'RE THE HULKVERINE. YOU'RE NOT SUPPOSED TO CATCH COLD.
I KNOW.
ACHOO!
SNIKT
SONIA...
YEAH...
PLAN C.

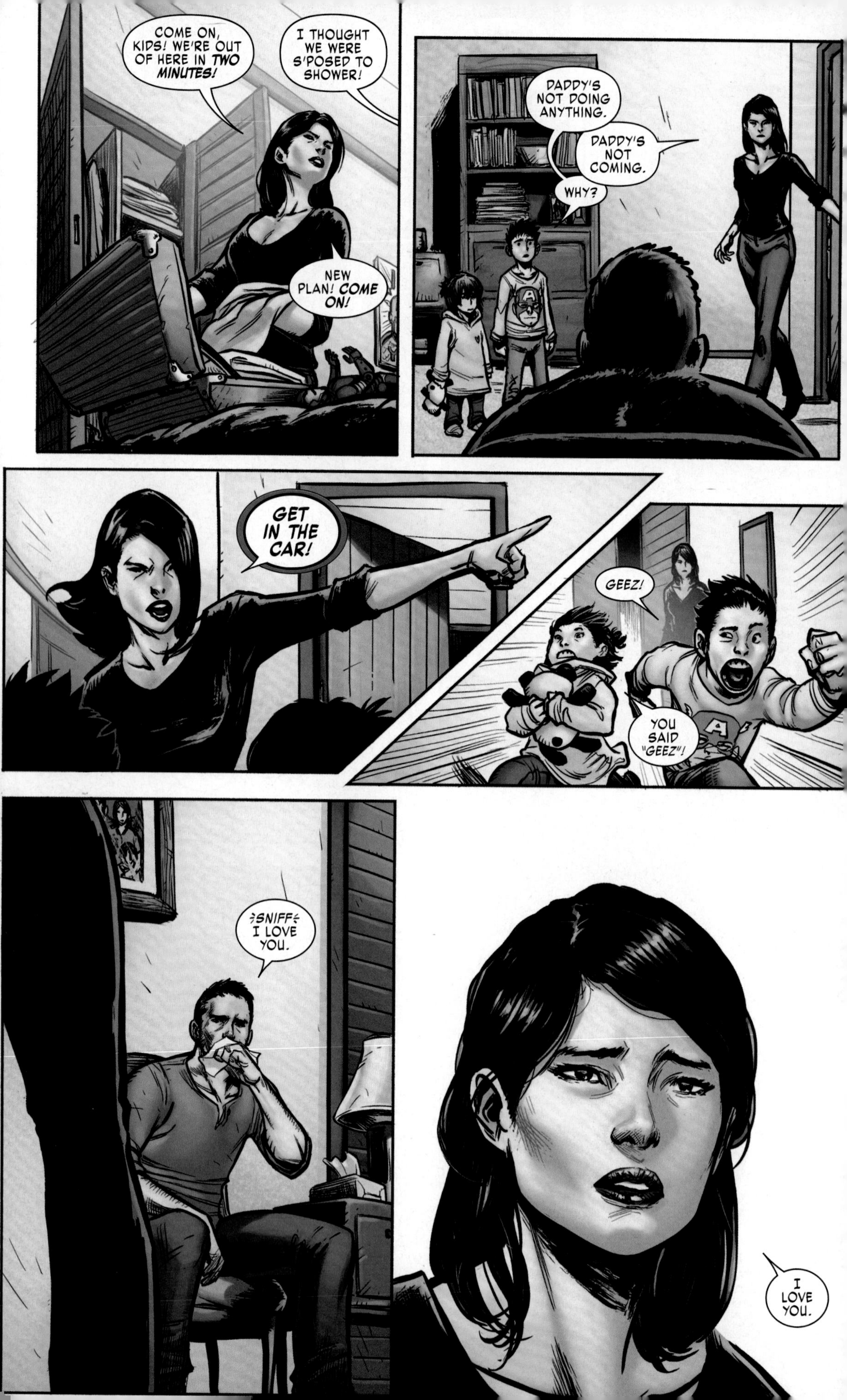
COME ON, KIDS! WE'RE OUT OF HERE IN *TWO MINUTES!*
I THOUGHT WE WERE S'POSED TO SHOWER!
NEW PLAN! *COME ON!*
DADDY'S NOT DOING ANYTHING.
DADDY'S NOT COMING.
WHY?
GET IN THE CAR!
GEEZ!
YOU SAID "GEEZ"!
SNIFF I LOVE YOU.
I LOVE YOU.

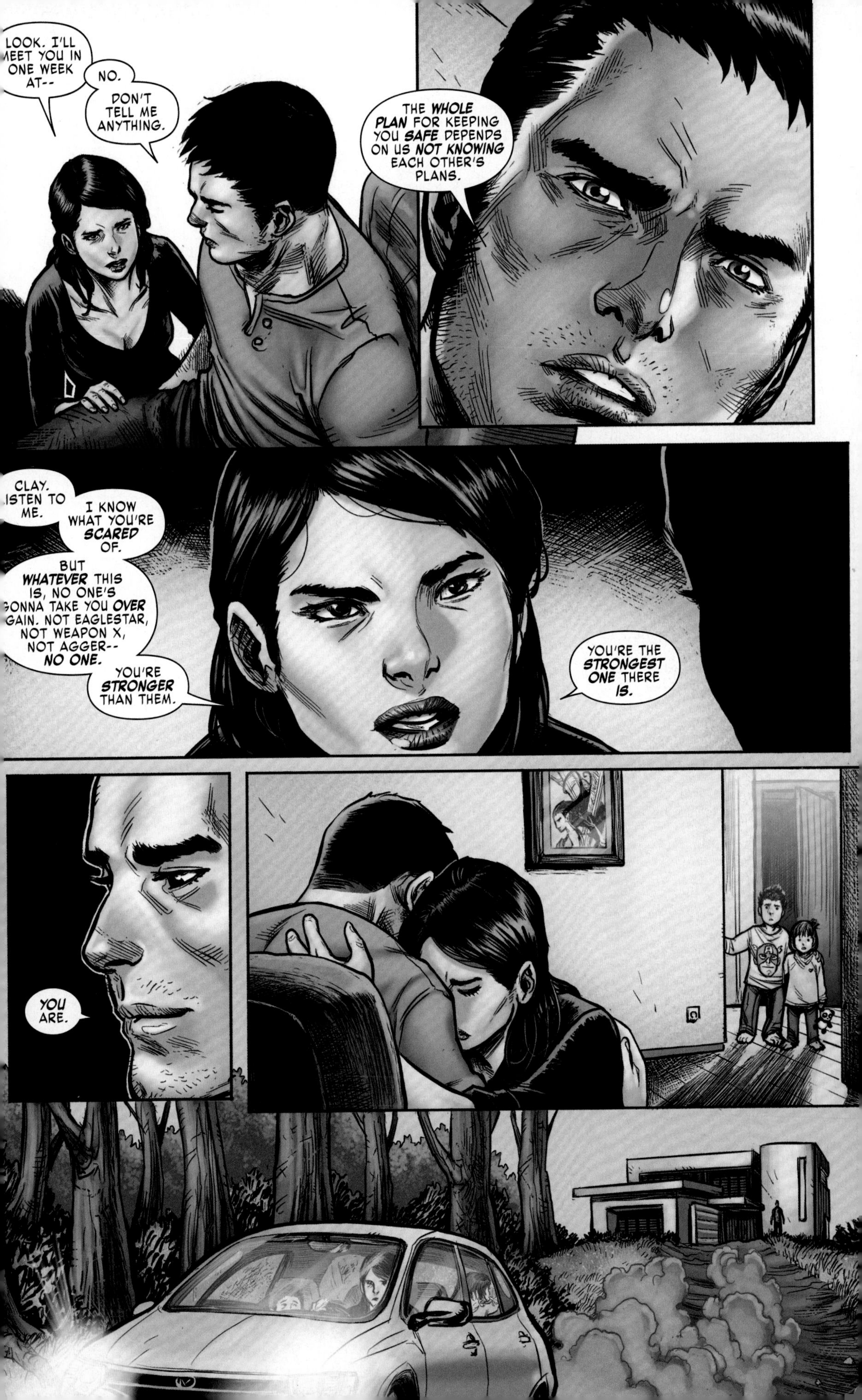
LOOK. I'LL MEET YOU IN ONE WEEK AT--
NO.
DON'T TELL ME ANYTHING.
THE WHOLE PLAN FOR KEEPING YOU SAFE DEPENDS ON US NOT KNOWING EACH OTHER'S PLANS.
CLAY. LISTEN TO ME.
I KNOW WHAT YOU'RE SCARED OF.
BUT WHATEVER THIS IS, NO ONE'S GONNA TAKE YOU OVER AGAIN. NOT EAGLESTAR, NOT WEAPON X, NOT AGGER-- NO ONE.
YOU'RE STRONGER THAN THEM.
YOU'RE THE STRONGEST ONE THERE IS.
YOU ARE.

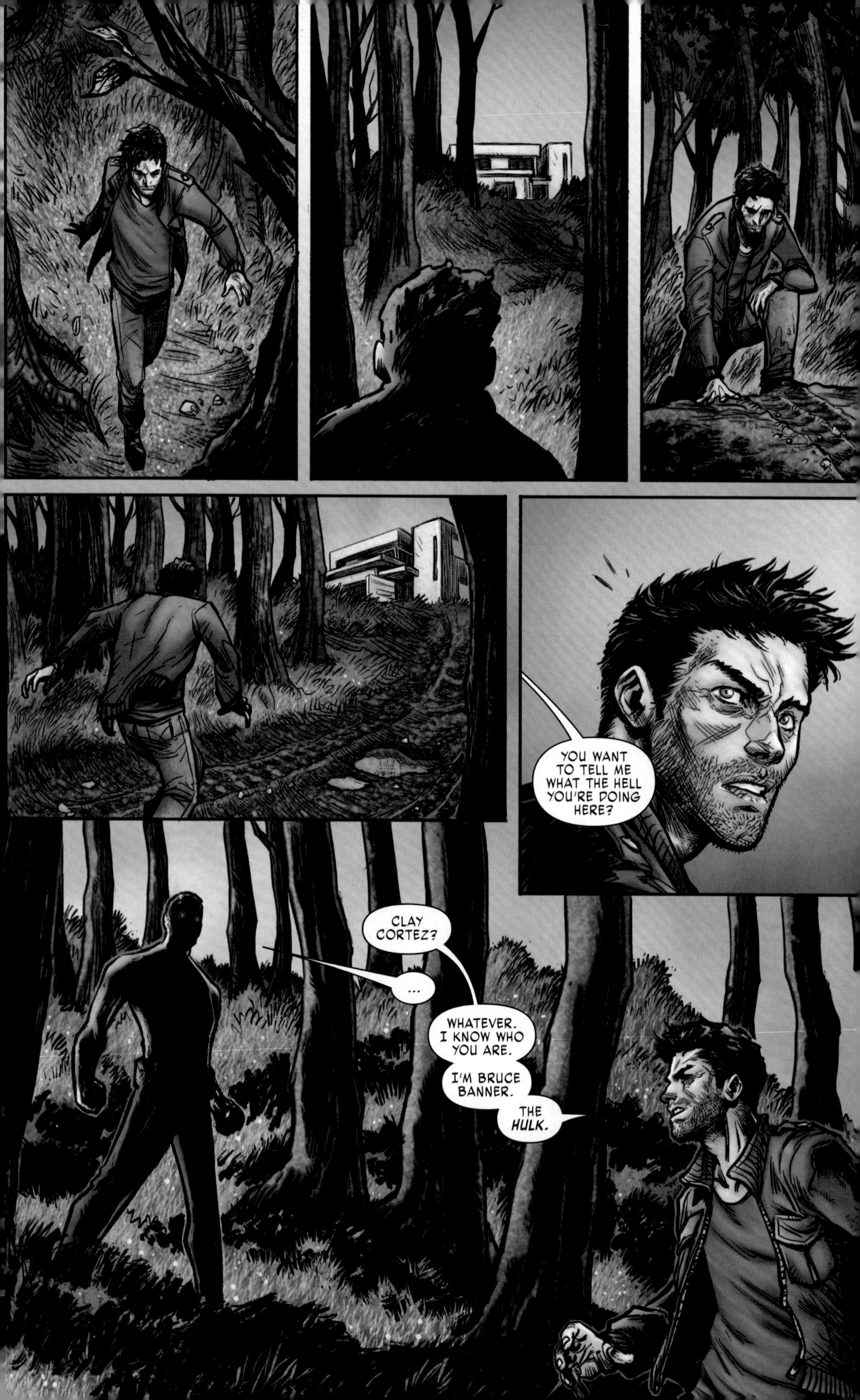
YOU WANT TO TELL ME WHAT THE HELL YOU'RE DOING HERE?
CLAY CORTEZ?
...
WHATEVER. I KNOW WHO YOU ARE.
I'M BRUCE BANNER.
THE *HULK*.

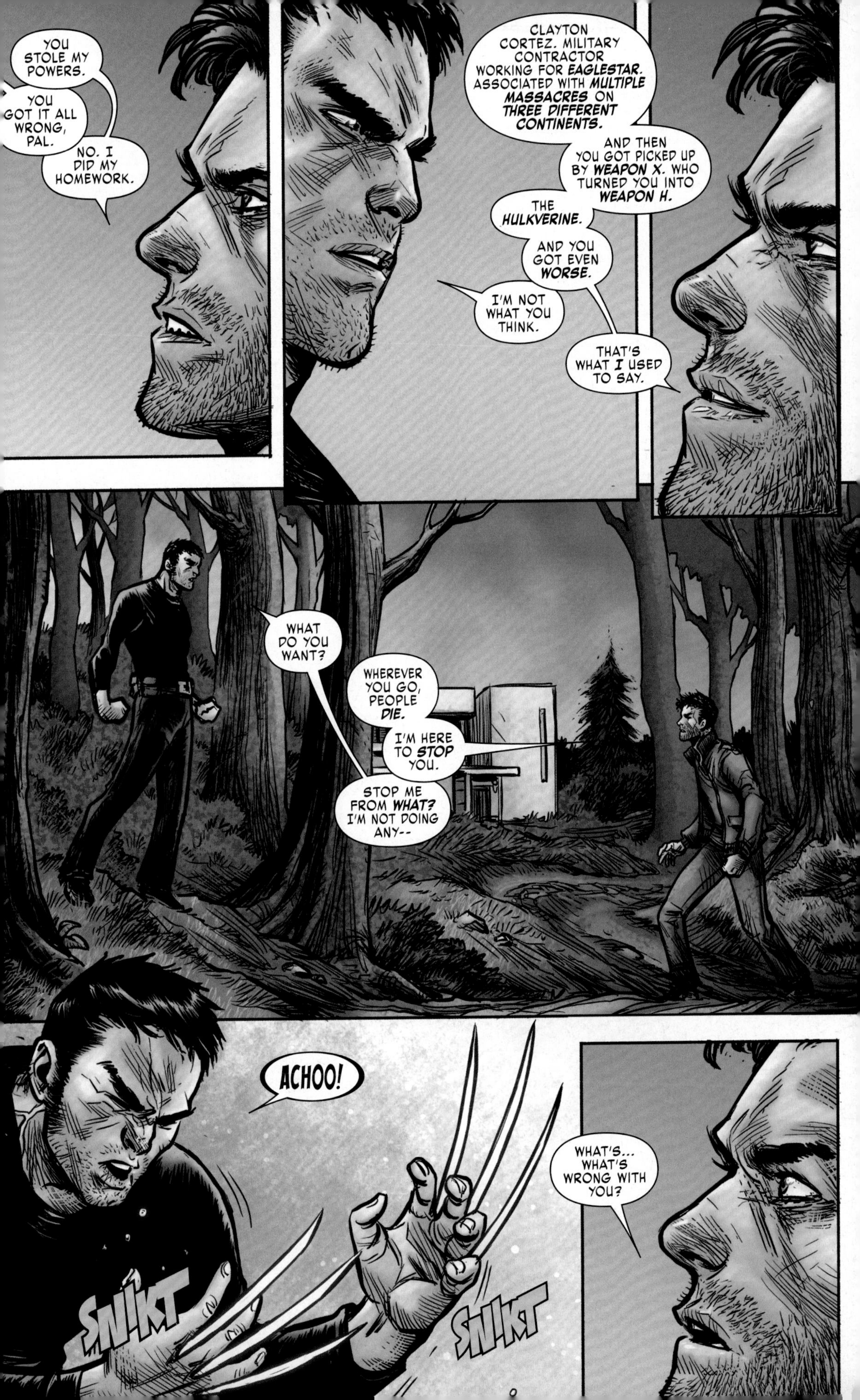
YOU STOLE MY POWERS.
YOU GOT IT ALL WRONG, PAL.
NO. I DID MY HOMEWORK.
CLAYTON CORTEZ. MILITARY CONTRACTOR WORKING FOR EAGLESTAR. ASSOCIATED WITH MULTIPLE MASSACRES ON THREE DIFFERENT CONTINENTS.
AND THEN YOU GOT PICKED UP BY WEAPON X. WHO TURNED YOU INTO WEAPON H.
THE HULKVERINE.
AND YOU GOT EVEN WORSE.
I'M NOT WHAT YOU THINK.
THAT'S WHAT I USED TO SAY.
WHAT DO YOU WANT?
WHEREVER YOU GO, PEOPLE DIE.
I'M HERE TO STOP YOU.
STOP ME FROM WHAT? I'M NOT DOING ANY--
ACHOO!
SNIKT
SNIKT
WHAT'S... WHAT'S WRONG WITH YOU?

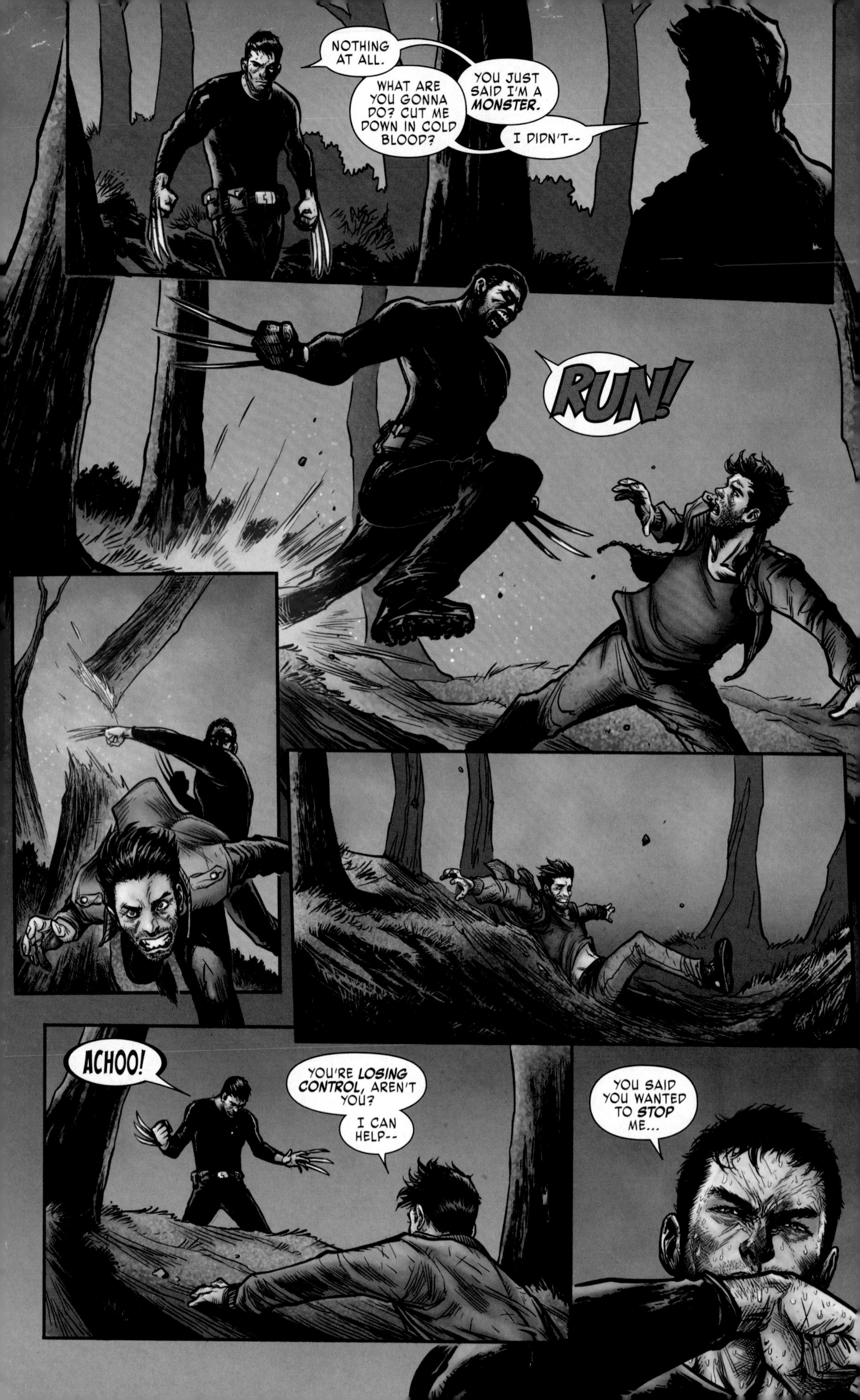

NOTHING AT ALL.
WHAT ARE YOU GONNA DO? CUT ME DOWN IN COLD BLOOD?
YOU JUST SAID I'M A MONSTER.
I DIDN'T--
RUN!
ACHOO!
YOU'RE LOSING CONTROL, AREN'T YOU?
I CAN HELP--
YOU SAID YOU WANTED TO STOP ME...

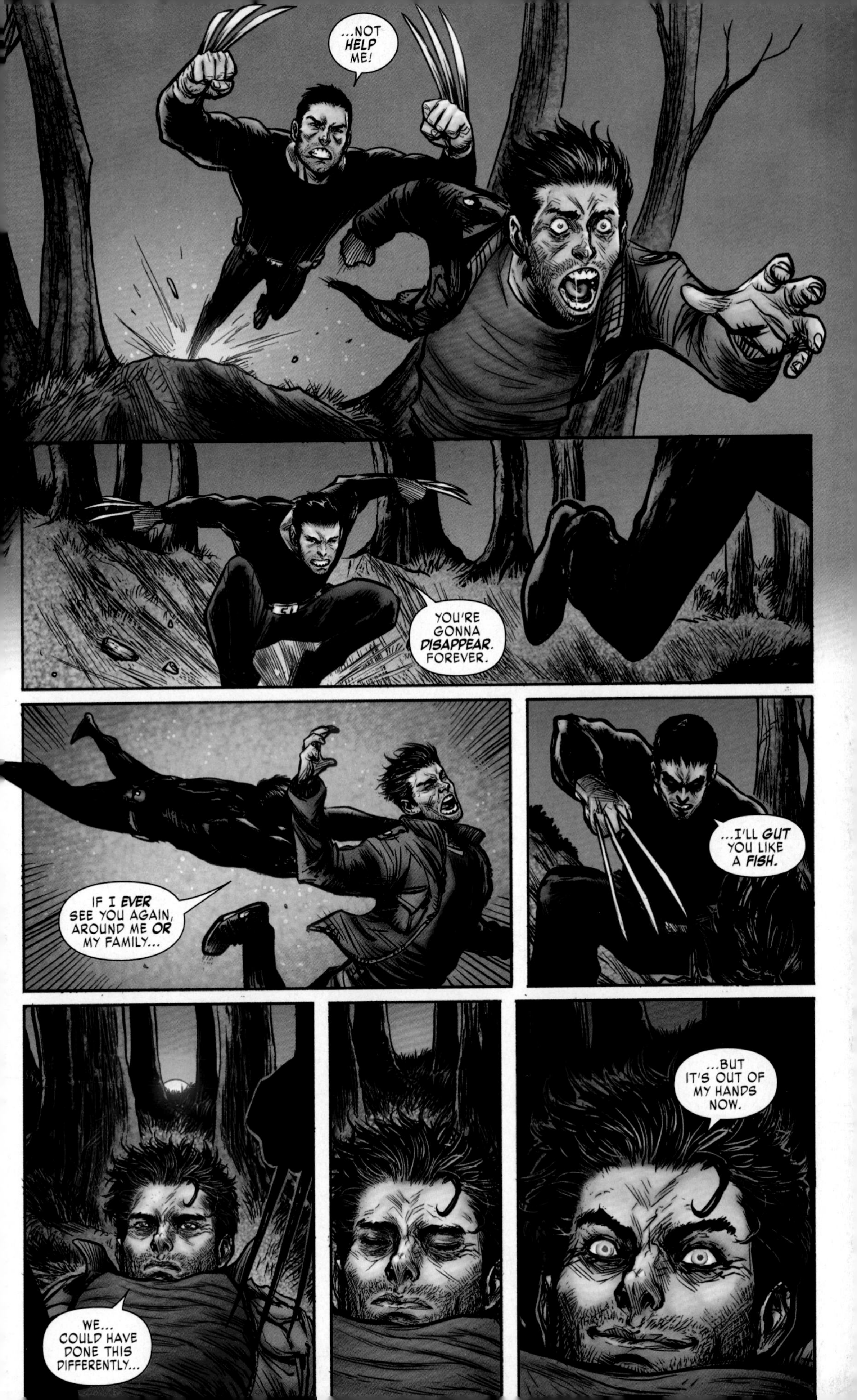
...NOT HELP ME!
YOU'RE GONNA DISAPPEAR. FOREVER.
IF I EVER SEE YOU AGAIN, AROUND ME OR MY FAMILY...
...I'LL GUT YOU LIKE A FISH.
WE... COULD HAVE DONE THIS DIFFERENTLY...
...BUT IT'S OUT OF MY HANDS NOW.

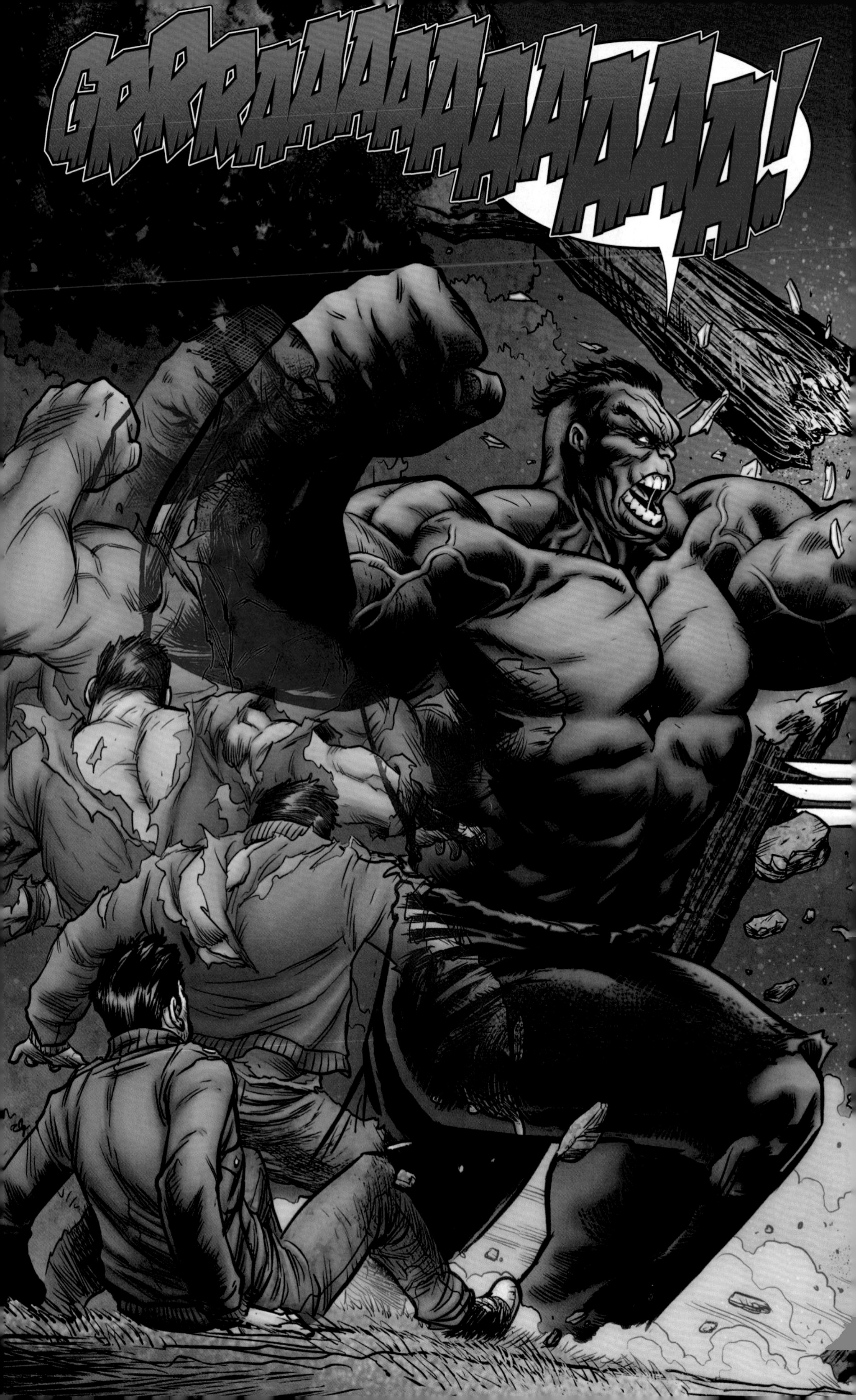
GRRRAAAAAAAAAAA!

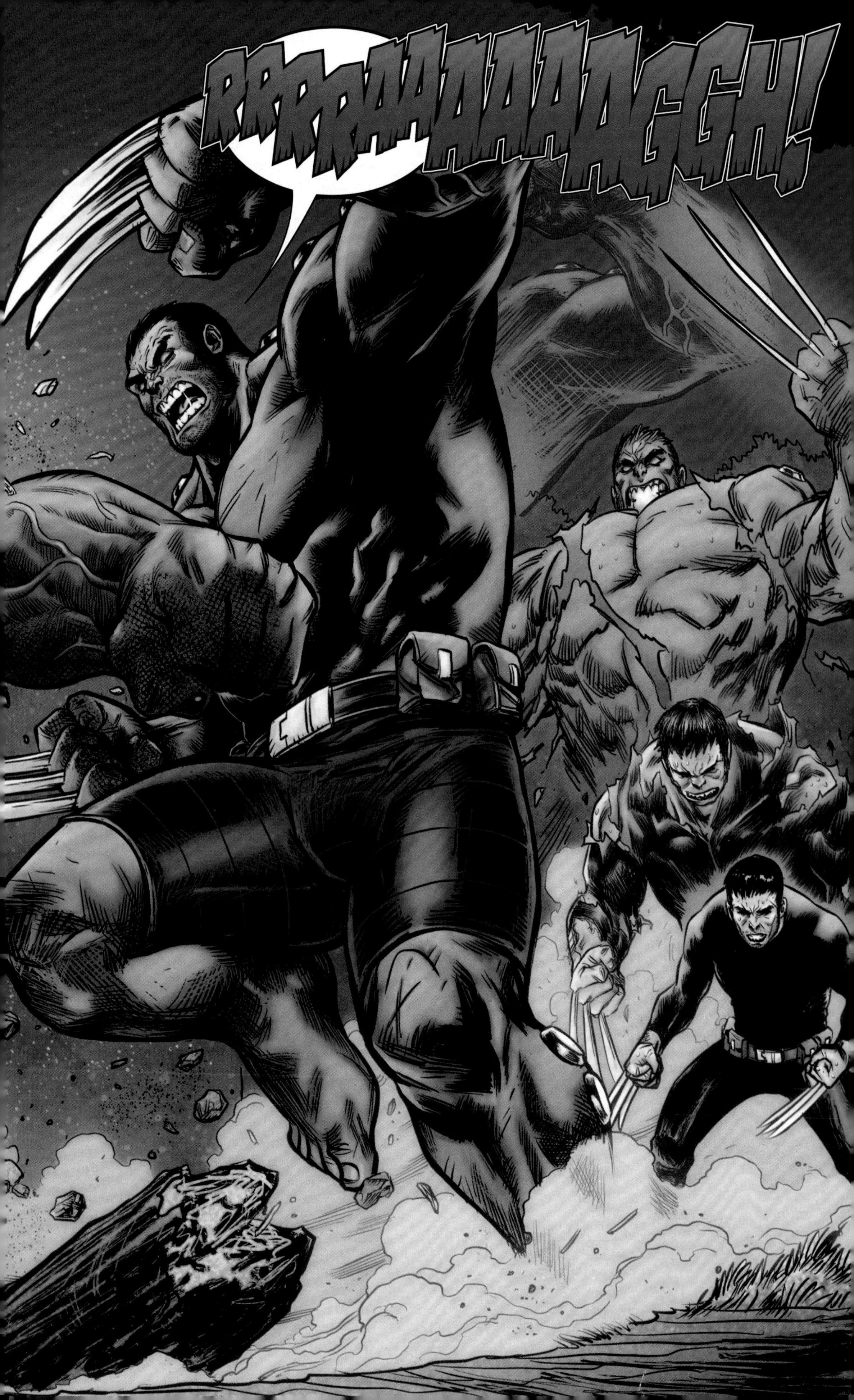
RRRRAAAAAAAGH!

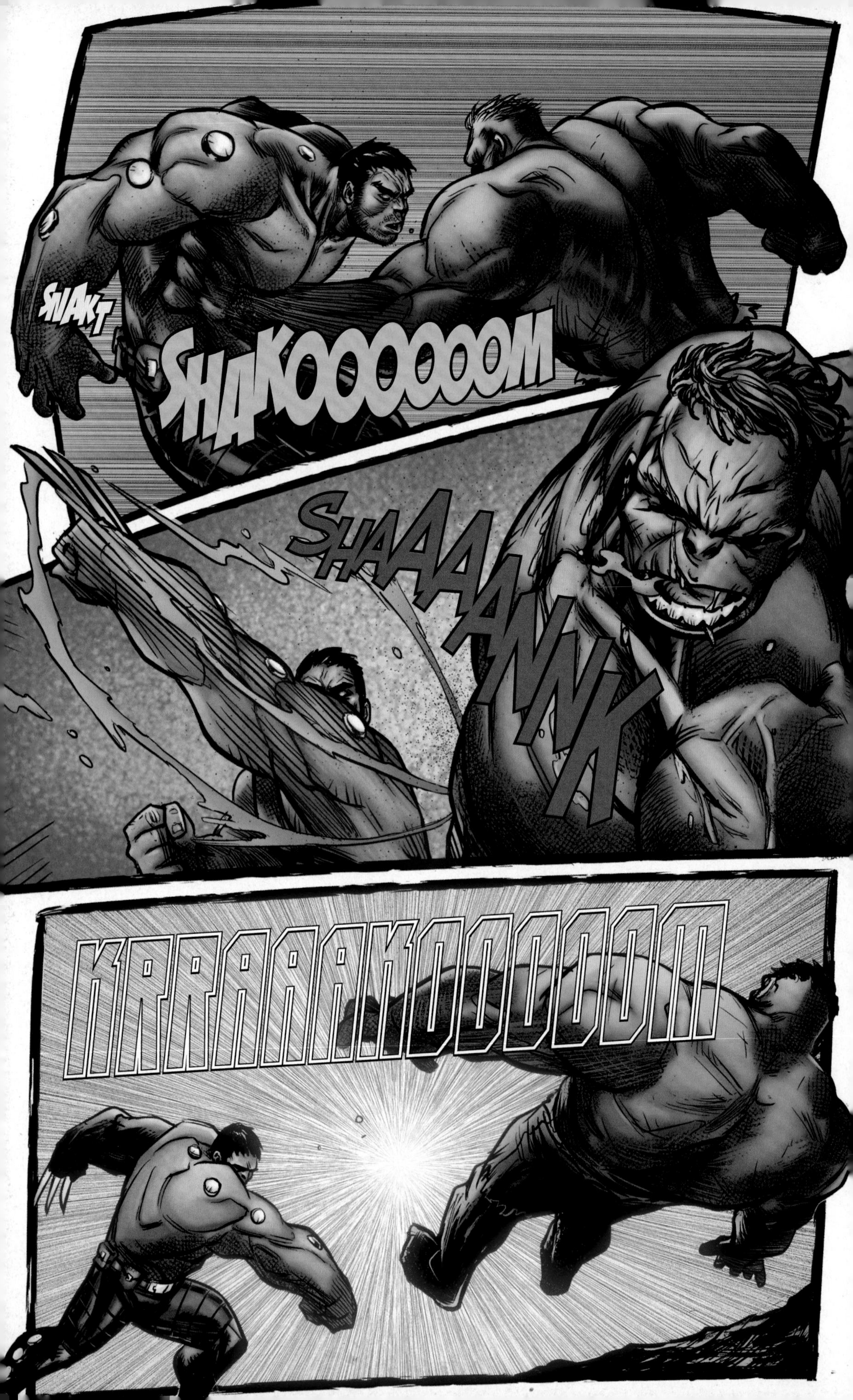
SNAKT
SHAKOOOOOOM
SHAAAAANNK
KRRAAAAKOOOOOOM

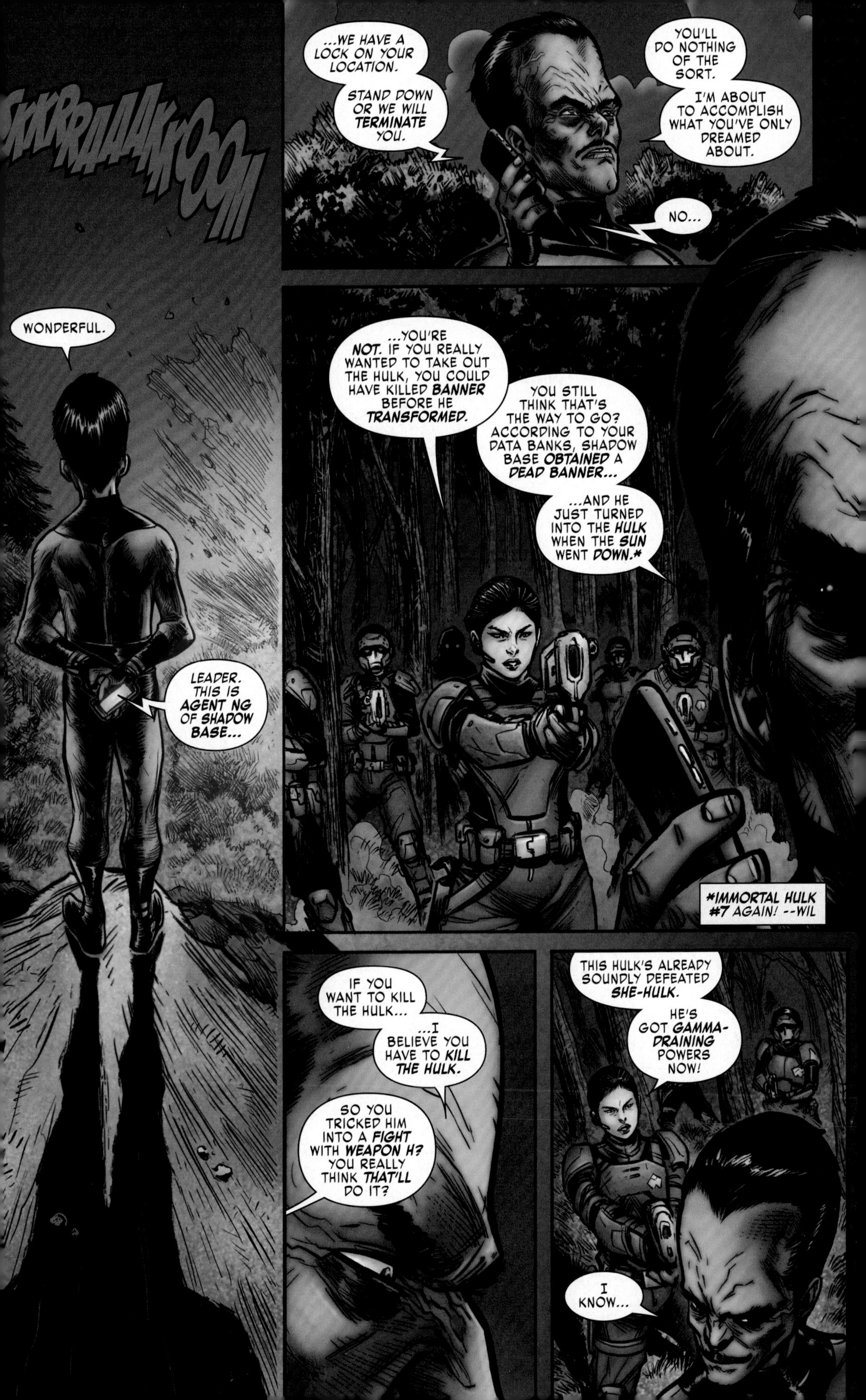
SKKRRAAAKKOOM
WONDERFUL.
LEADER. THIS IS AGENT NG OF SHADOW BASE...
...WE HAVE A LOCK ON YOUR LOCATION.
STAND DOWN OR WE WILL TERMINATE YOU.
YOU'LL DO NOTHING OF THE SORT.
I'M ABOUT TO ACCOMPLISH WHAT YOU'VE ONLY DREAMED ABOUT.
NO...
...YOU'RE NOT. IF YOU REALLY WANTED TO TAKE OUT THE HULK, YOU COULD HAVE KILLED BANNER BEFORE HE TRANSFORMED.
YOU STILL THINK THAT'S THE WAY TO GO? ACCORDING TO YOUR DATA BANKS, SHADOW BASE OBTAINED A DEAD BANNER...
...AND HE JUST TURNED INTO THE HULK WHEN THE SUN WENT DOWN.*
*IMMORTAL HULK #7 AGAIN! --WIL
IF YOU WANT TO KILL THE HULK...
...I BELIEVE YOU HAVE TO KILL THE HULK.
SO YOU TRICKED HIM INTO A FIGHT WITH WEAPON H? YOU REALLY THINK THAT'LL DO IT?
THIS HULK'S ALREADY SOUNDLY DEFEATED SHE-HULK.
HE'S GOT GAMMA-DRAINING POWERS NOW!
I KNOW...

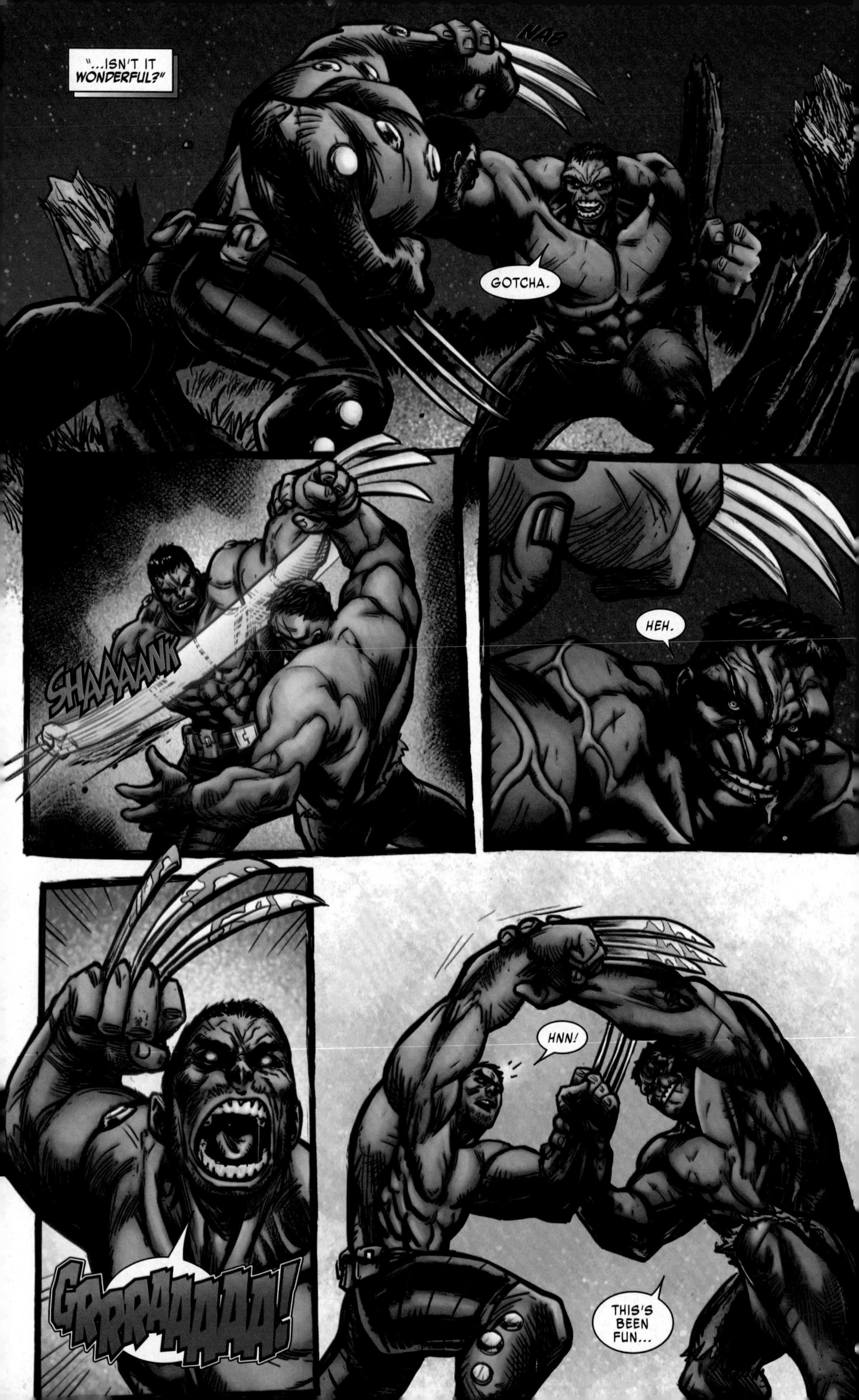
"...ISN'T IT WONDERFUL?"
NAB
GOTCHA.
SHAAAANK
HEH.
GRRRAAAAA!
HNN!
THIS'S BEEN FUN...

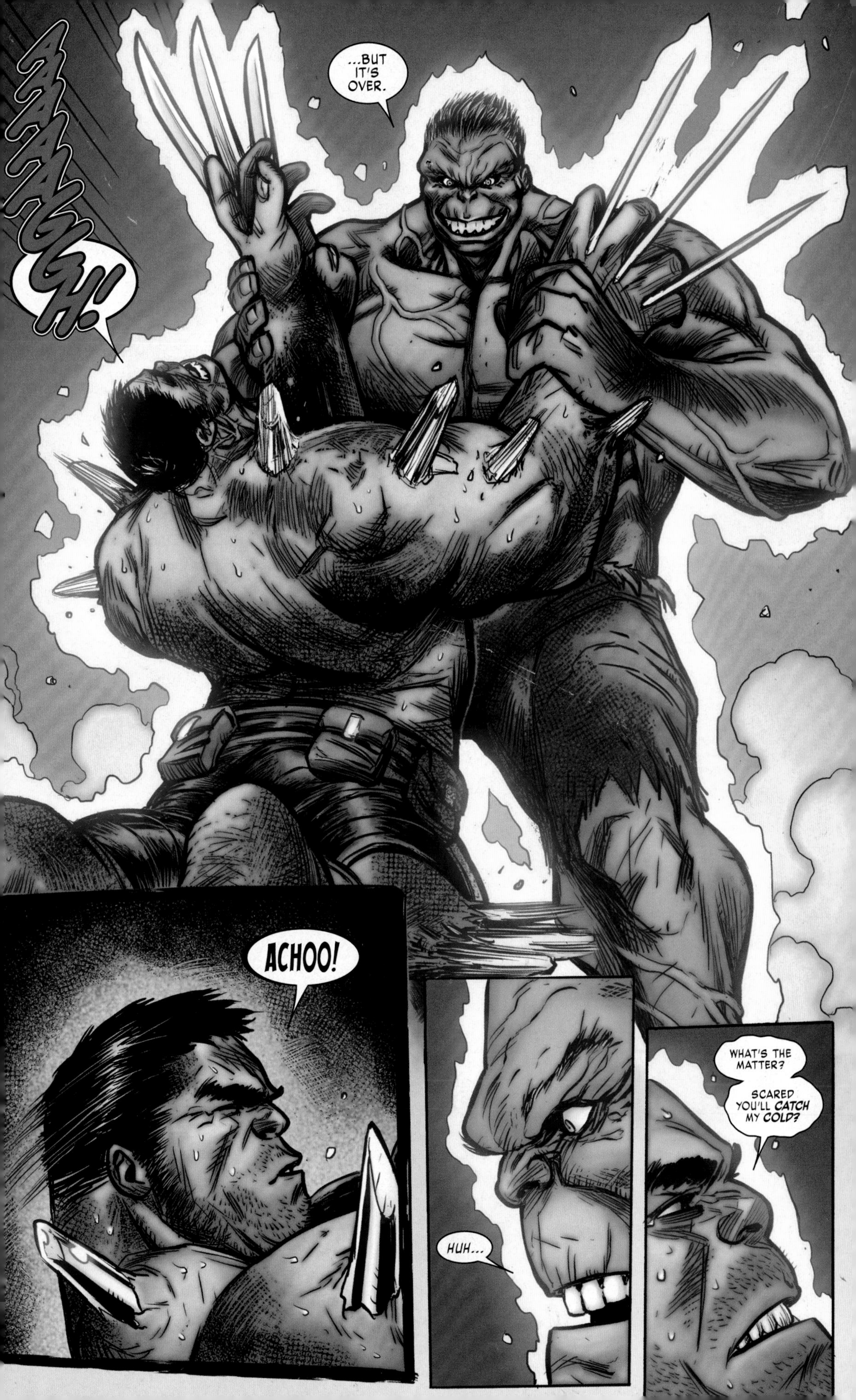
AAAAGGH!
...BUT IT'S OVER.
ACHOO!
HUH...
WHAT'S THE MATTER?
SCARED YOU'LL CATCH MY COLD?

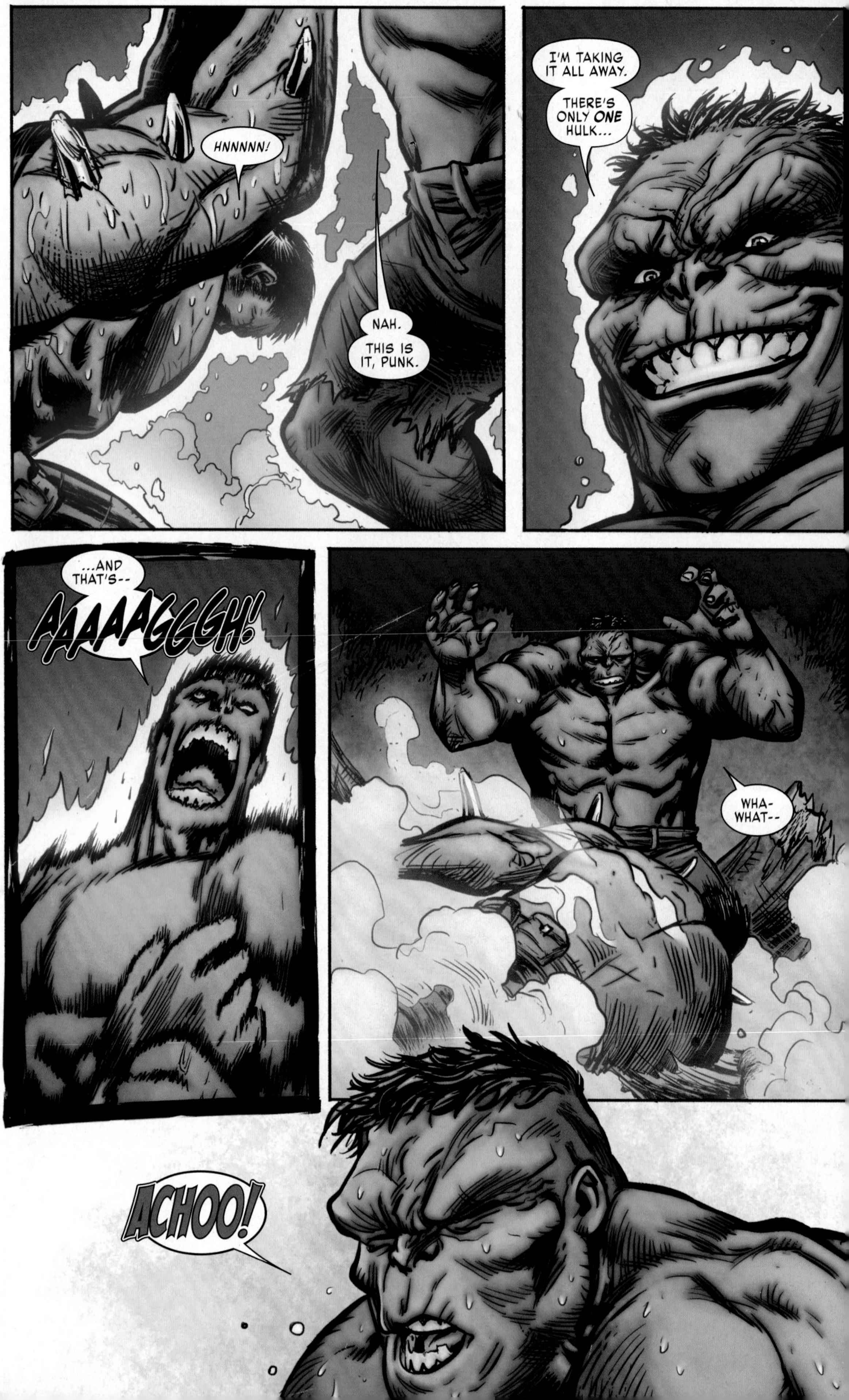
HNNNNN!
NAH.
THIS IS IT, PUNK.
I'M TAKING IT ALL AWAY.
THERE'S ONLY ONE HULK...
...AND THAT'S--
AAAAAGGGH!
WHA-WHAT--
ACHOO!

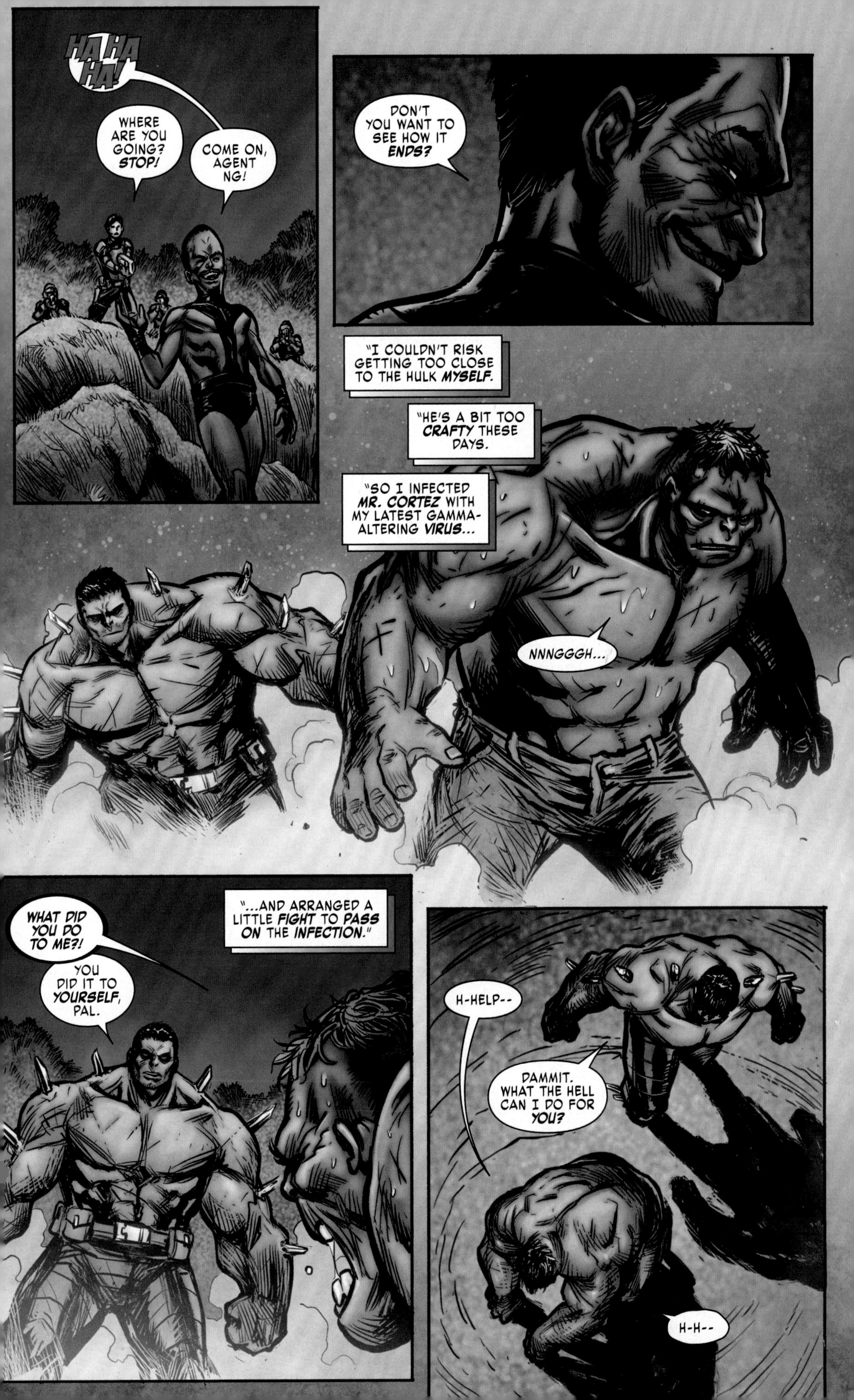
HA HA HA!
WHERE ARE YOU GOING? STOP!
COME ON, AGENT NG!
DON'T YOU WANT TO SEE HOW IT ENDS?
"I COULDN'T RISK GETTING TOO CLOSE TO THE HULK MYSELF.
"HE'S A BIT TOO CRAFTY THESE DAYS.
"SO I INFECTED MR. CORTEZ WITH MY LATEST GAMMA-ALTERING VIRUS...
NNNGGGH...
"...AND ARRANGED A LITTLE FIGHT TO PASS ON THE INFECTION."
WHAT DID YOU DO TO ME?!
YOU DID IT TO YOURSELF, PAL.
H-HELP--
DAMMIT. WHAT THE HELL CAN I DO FOR YOU?
H-H--

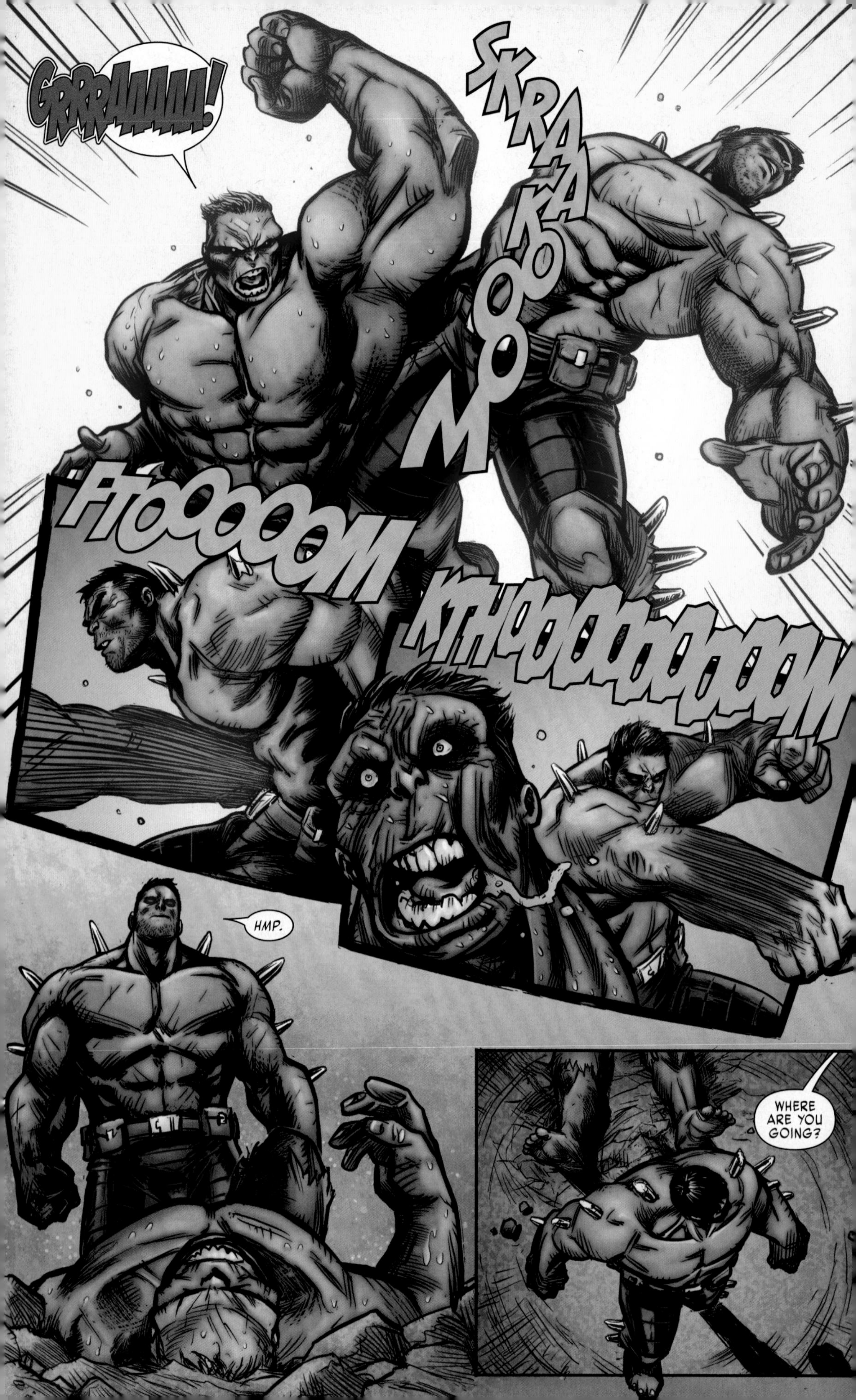
GRRRAAAAA!
SKRAAKOOOOM
FTOOOOOM
KTHOOOOOOOOOM
HMP.
WHERE ARE YOU GOING?

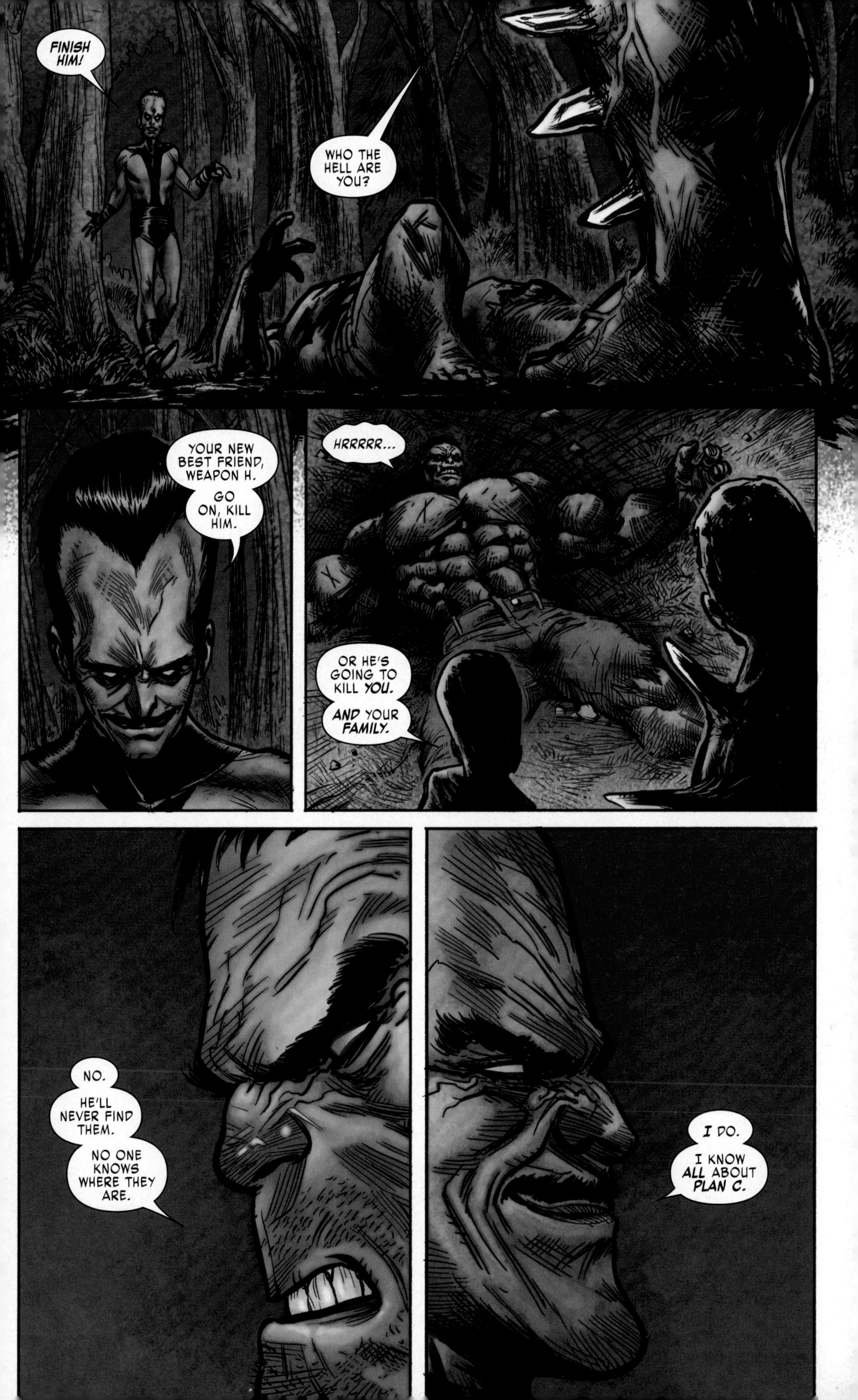
FINISH HIM!
WHO THE HELL ARE YOU?
YOUR NEW BEST FRIEND, WEAPON H.
GO ON, KILL HIM.
HRRRRR...
OR HE'S GOING TO KILL YOU.
AND YOUR FAMILY.
NO.
HE'LL NEVER FIND THEM.
NO ONE KNOWS WHERE THEY ARE.
I DO.
I KNOW ALL ABOUT PLAN C.

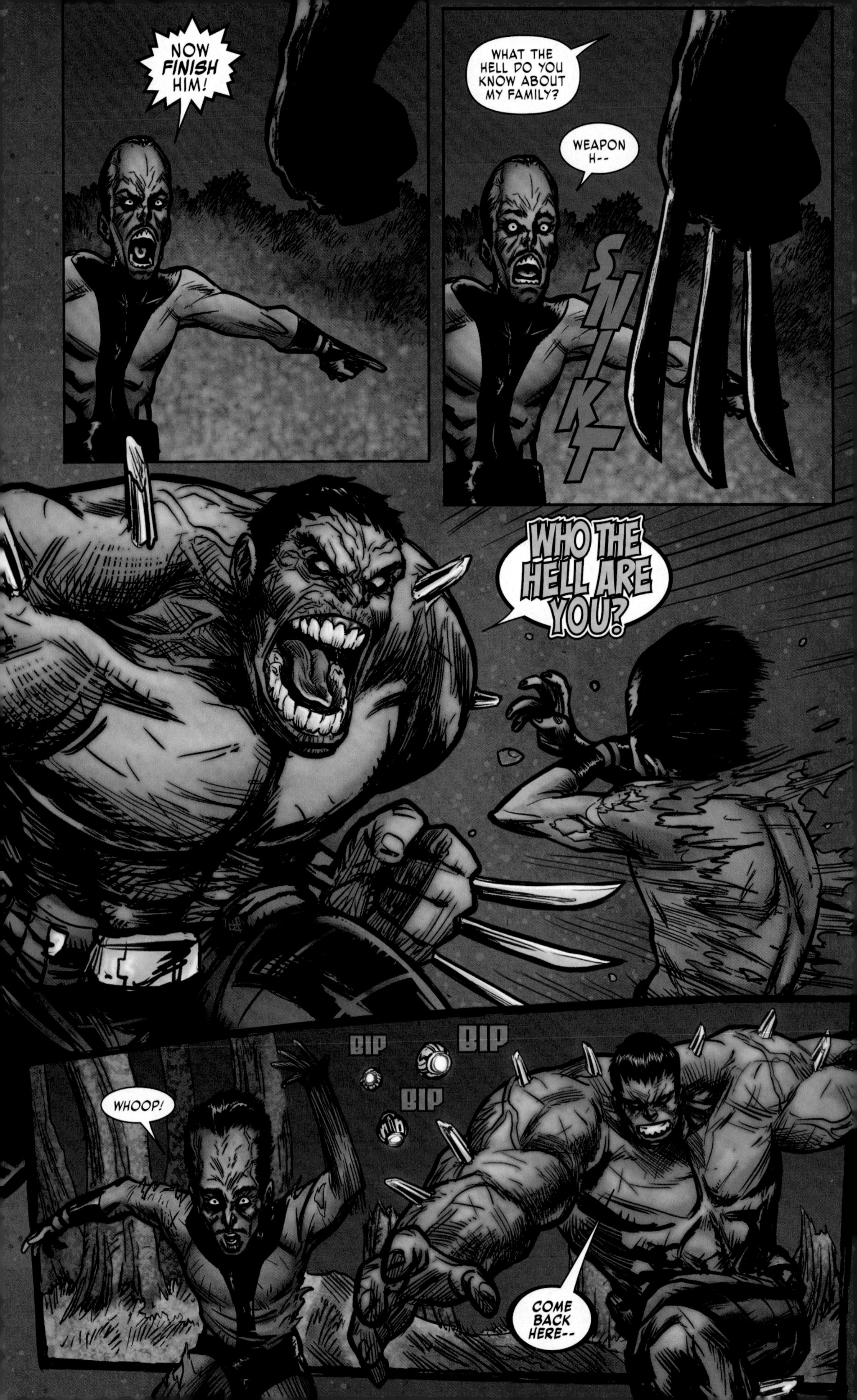
NOW FINISH HIM!
WHAT THE HELL DO YOU KNOW ABOUT MY FAMILY?
WEAPON H--
SNIKT
WHO THE HELL ARE YOU?
BIP
BIP
BIP
WHOOP!
COME BACK HERE--

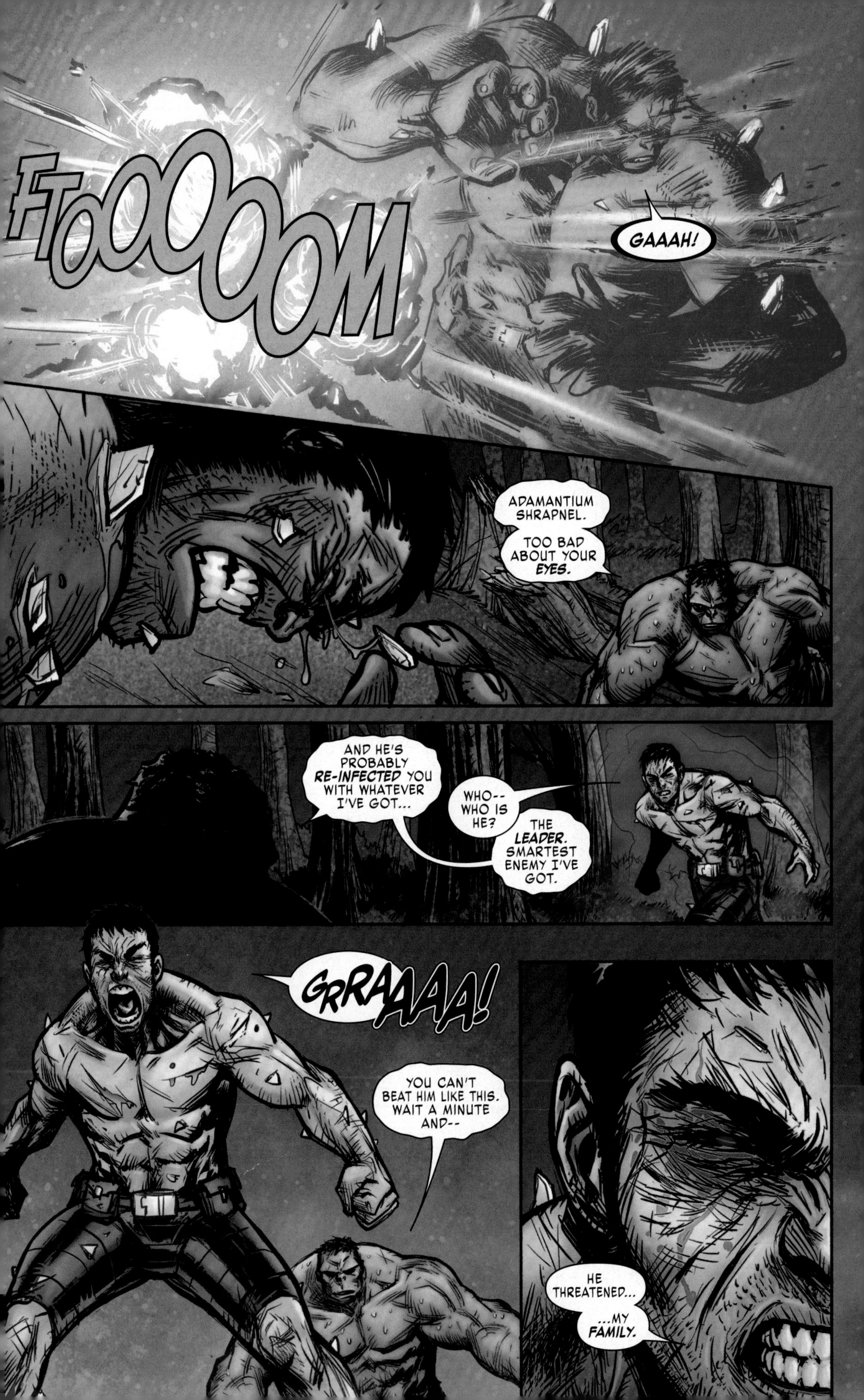
FTOOOOOOM
GAAAH!
ADAMANTIUM SHRAPNEL.
TOO BAD ABOUT YOUR EYES.
AND HE'S PROBABLY RE-INFECTED YOU WITH WHATEVER I'VE GOT...
WHO-- WHO IS HE?
THE LEADER. SMARTEST ENEMY I'VE GOT.
GRRAAAAA!
YOU CAN'T BEAT HIM LIKE THIS. WAIT A MINUTE AND--
HE THREATENED...
...MY FAMILY.

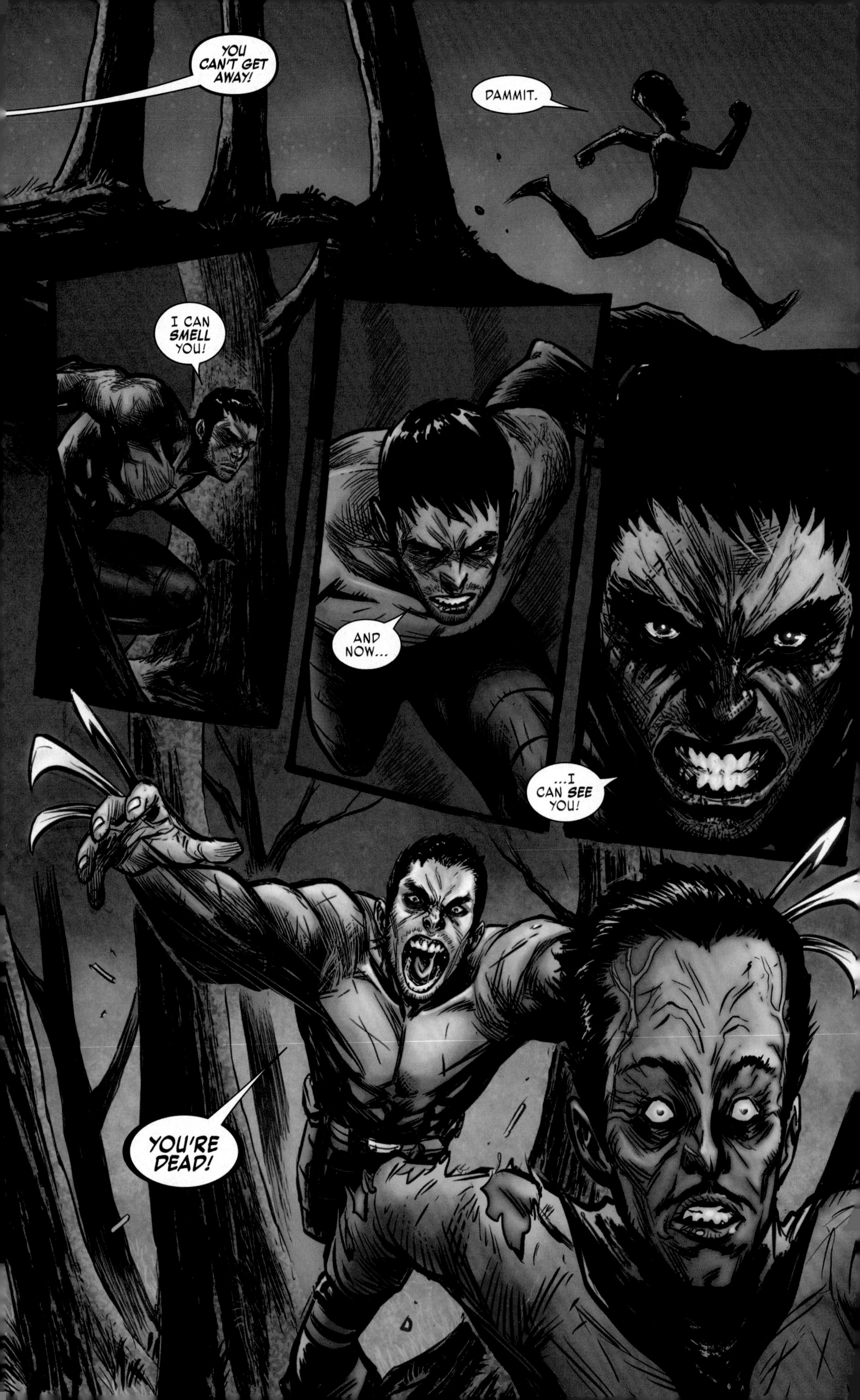
YOU CAN'T GET AWAY!
DAMMIT.
I CAN SMELL YOU!
AND NOW...
...I CAN SEE YOU!
YOU'RE DEAD!

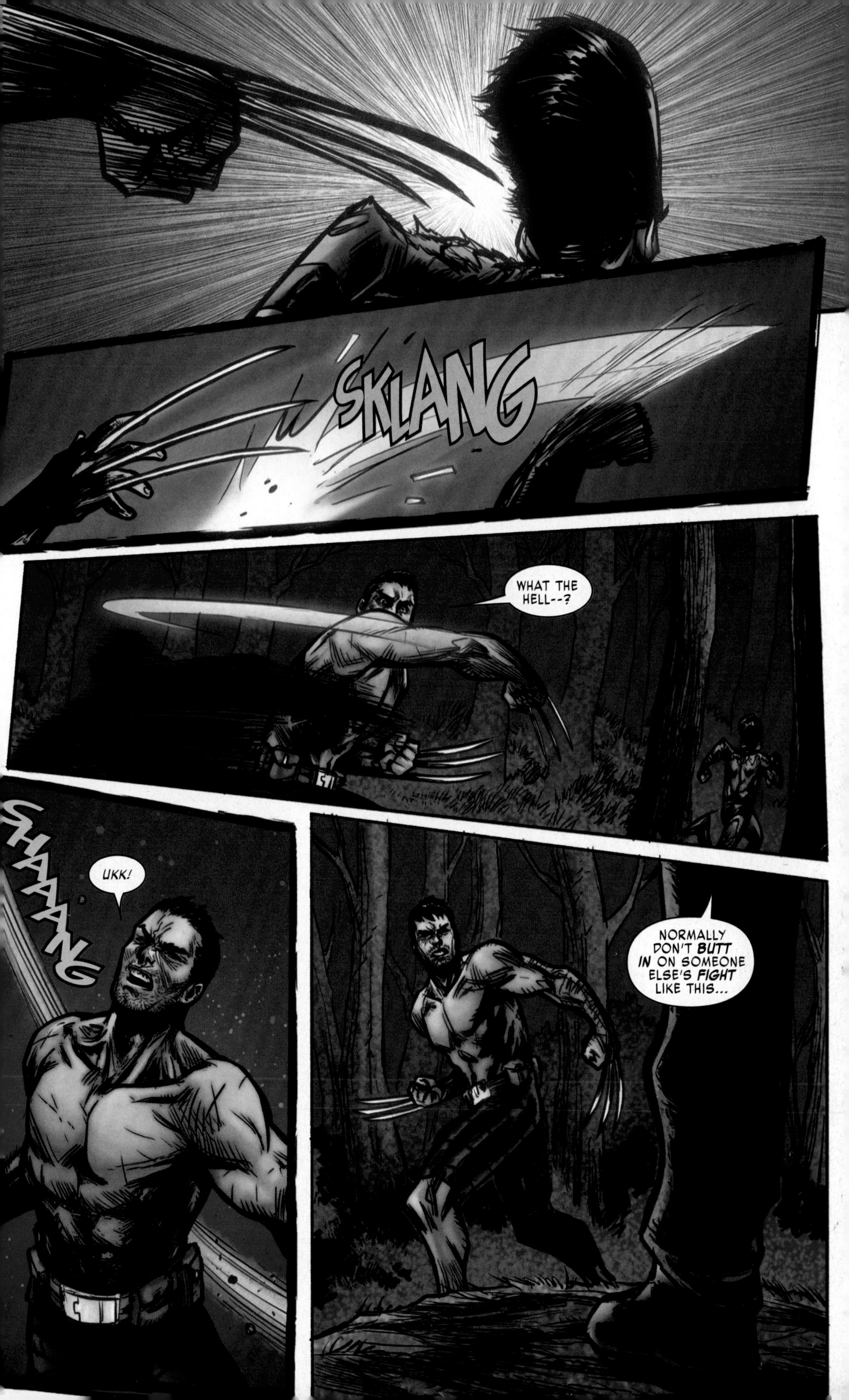
SKLANG
WHAT THE HELL--?
SHAAANG
UKK!
NORMALLY DON'T BUTT IN ON SOMEONE ELSE'S FIGHT LIKE THIS...

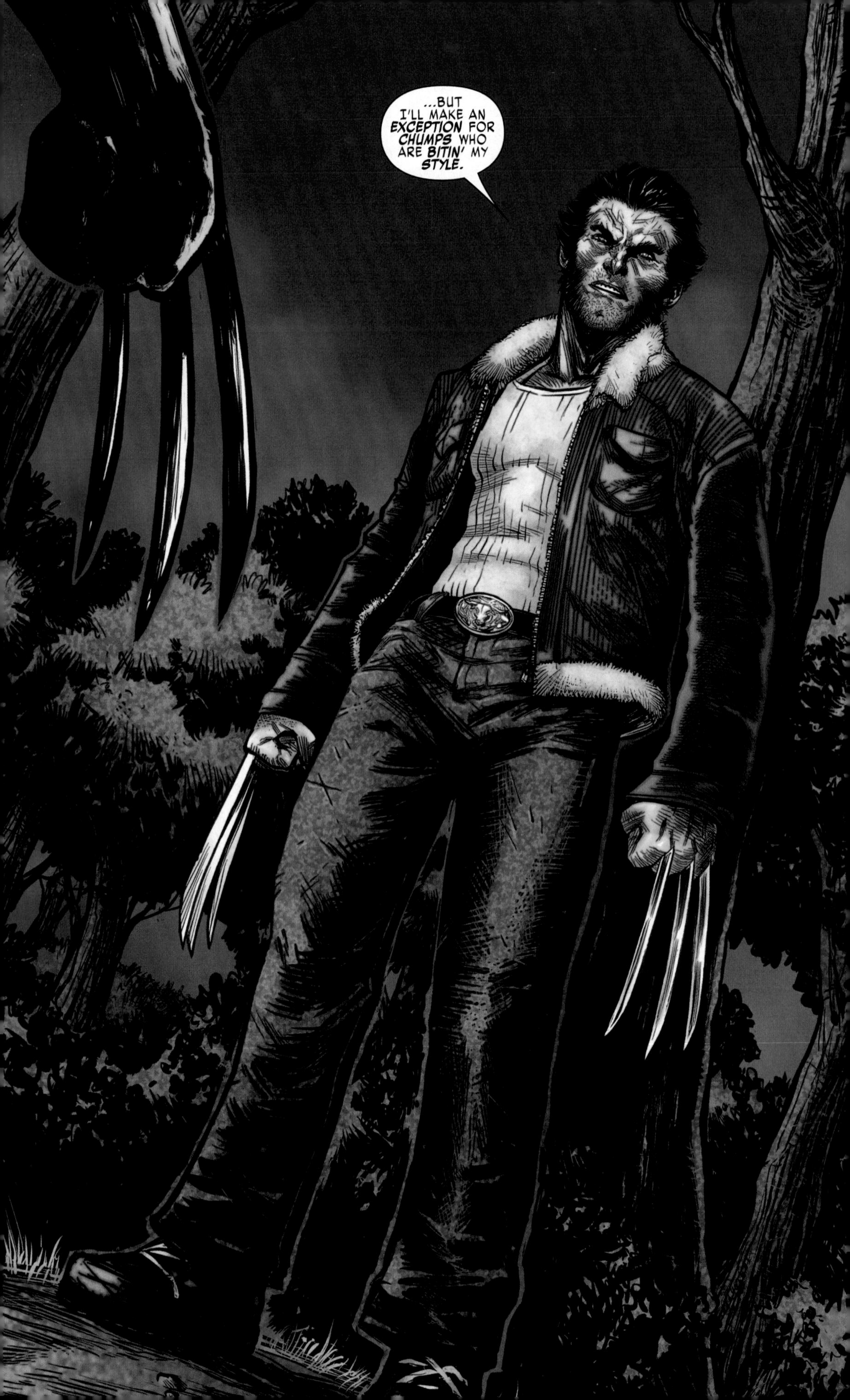
...BUT I'LL MAKE AN EXCEPTION FOR CHUMPS WHO ARE BITIN' MY STYLE.

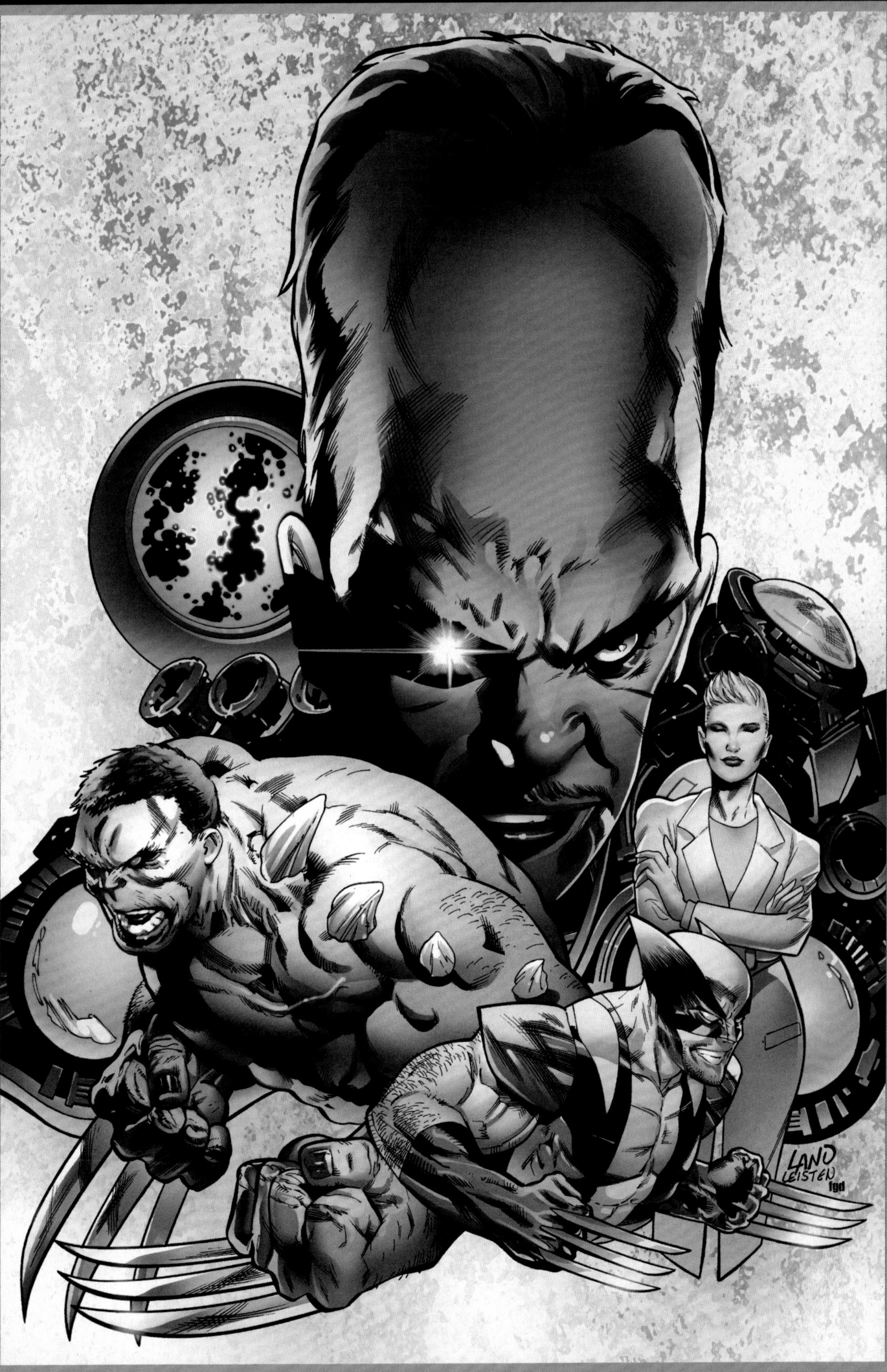
LAND
LEISTEN
fgd

2

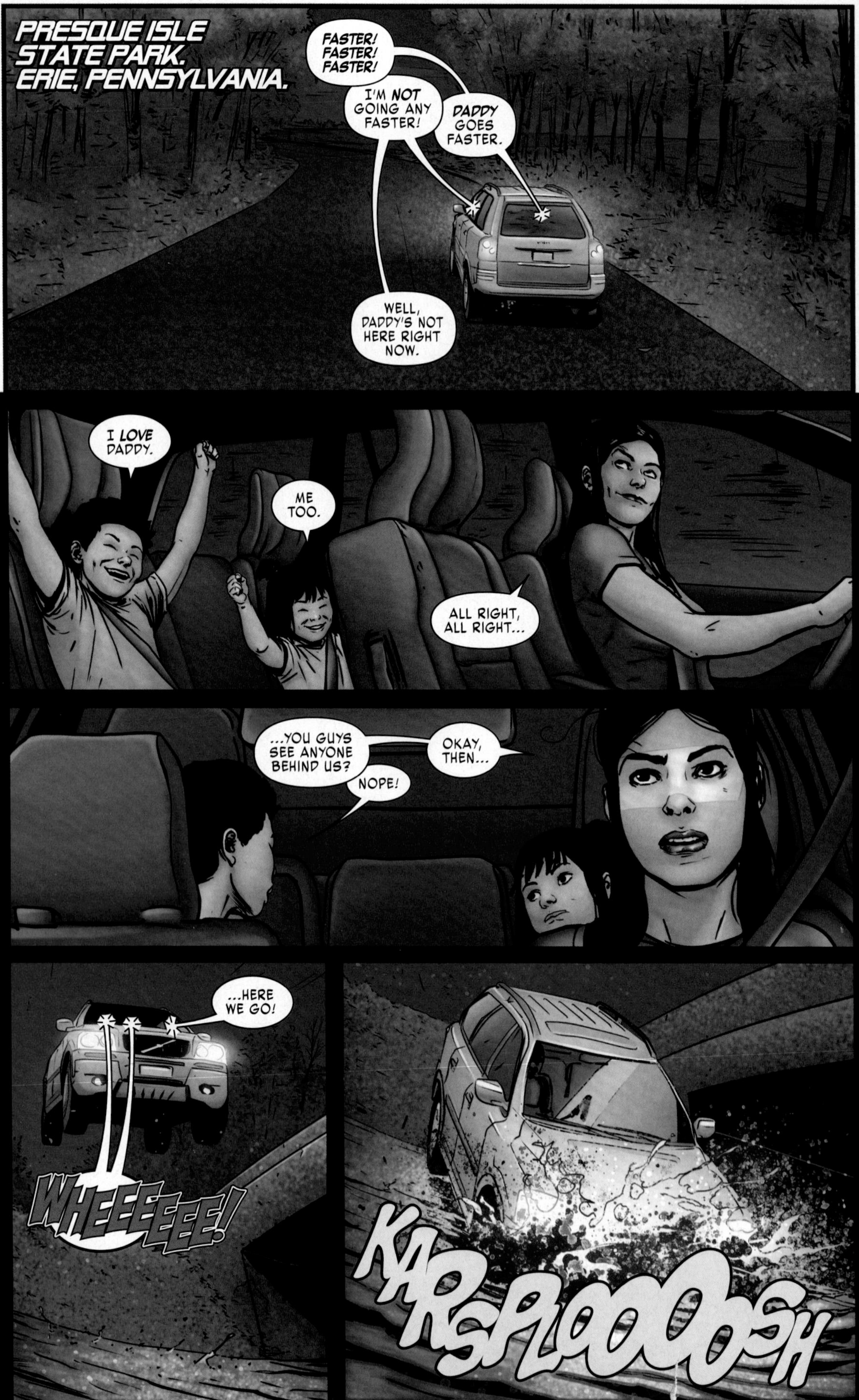
PRESQUE ISLE STATE PARK. ERIE, PENNSYLVANIA.
FASTER! FASTER! FASTER!
I'M NOT GOING ANY FASTER!
DADDY GOES FASTER.
WELL, DADDY'S NOT HERE RIGHT NOW.
I LOVE DADDY.
ME TOO.
ALL RIGHT, ALL RIGHT...
OKAY, THEN...
...YOU GUYS SEE ANYONE BEHIND US?
NOPE!
...HERE WE GO!
WHEEEEEEE!
KARSPLOOOOSH

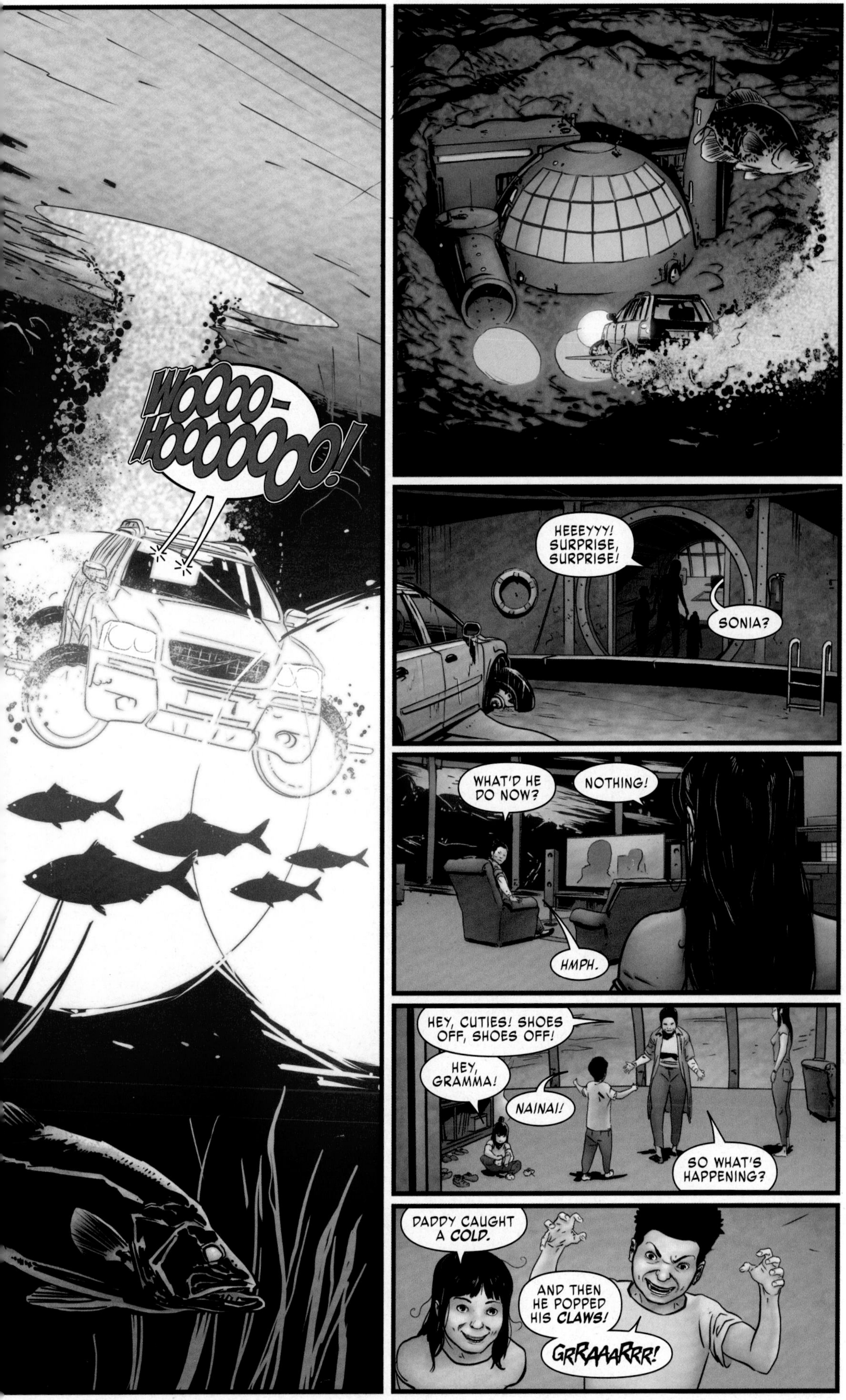
WOOOO-HOOOOOOO!
HEEEYYY! SURPRISE, SURPRISE!
SONIA?
WHAT'D HE DO NOW?
NOTHING!
HMPH.
HEY, CUTIES! SHOES OFF, SHOES OFF!
HEY, GRAMMA!
NAINAI!
SO WHAT'S HAPPENING?
DADDY CAUGHT A COLD.
AND THEN HE POPPED HIS CLAWS!
GRRAAARRR!

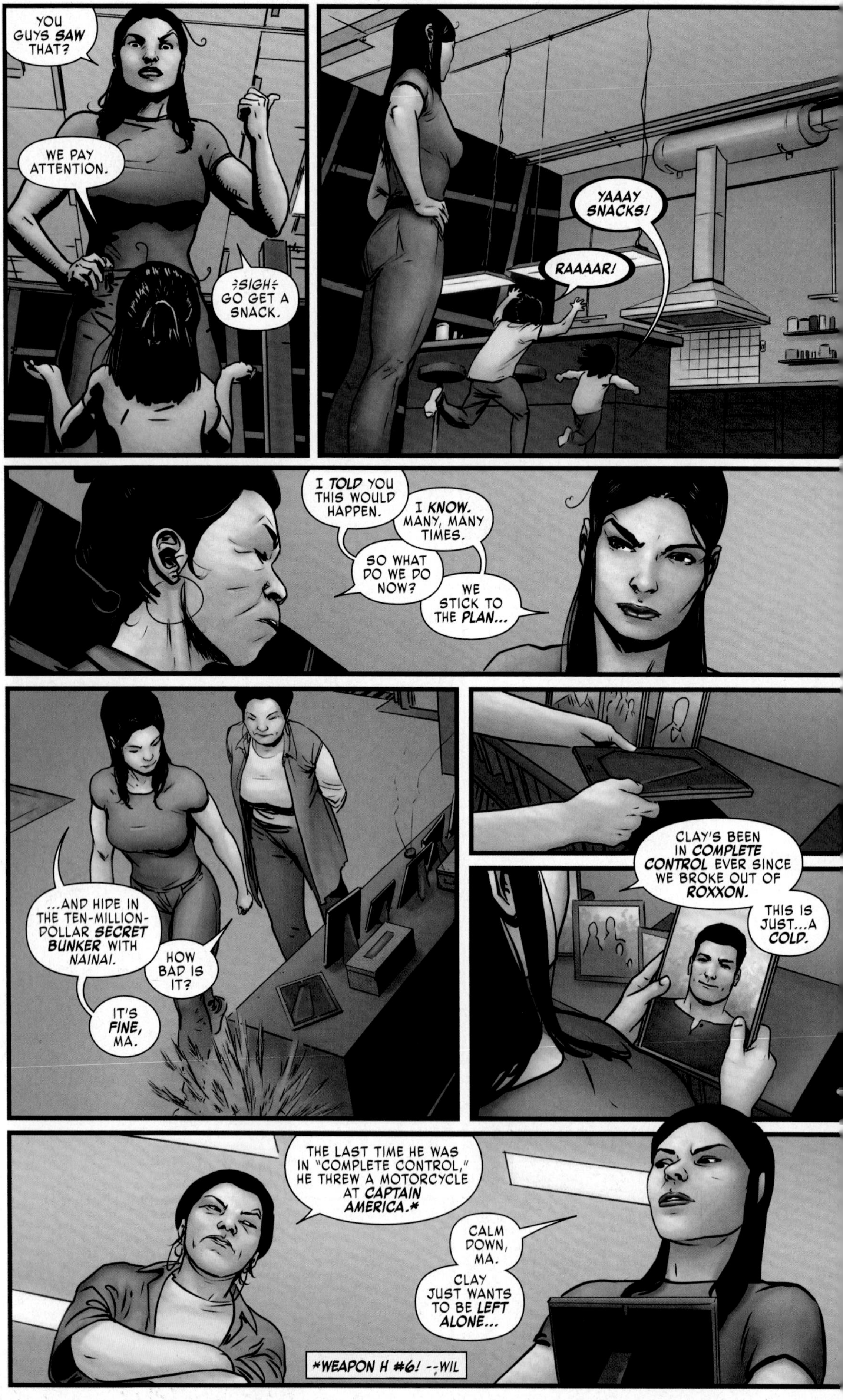
YOU GUYS SAW THAT?
WE PAY ATTENTION.
⁼SIGH⁼ GO GET A SNACK.
YAAAY SNACKS!
RAAAAR!
I TOLD YOU THIS WOULD HAPPEN.
I KNOW. MANY, MANY TIMES.
SO WHAT DO WE DO NOW?
WE STICK TO THE PLAN...
...AND HIDE IN THE TEN-MILLION-DOLLAR SECRET BUNKER WITH NAINAI.
HOW BAD IS IT?
IT'S FINE, MA.
CLAY'S BEEN IN COMPLETE CONTROL EVER SINCE WE BROKE OUT OF ROXXON.
THIS IS JUST...A COLD.
THE LAST TIME HE WAS IN "COMPLETE CONTROL," HE THREW A MOTORCYCLE AT CAPTAIN AMERICA.*
CALM DOWN, MA.
CLAY JUST WANTS TO BE LEFT ALONE...
*WEAPON H #6! --WIL

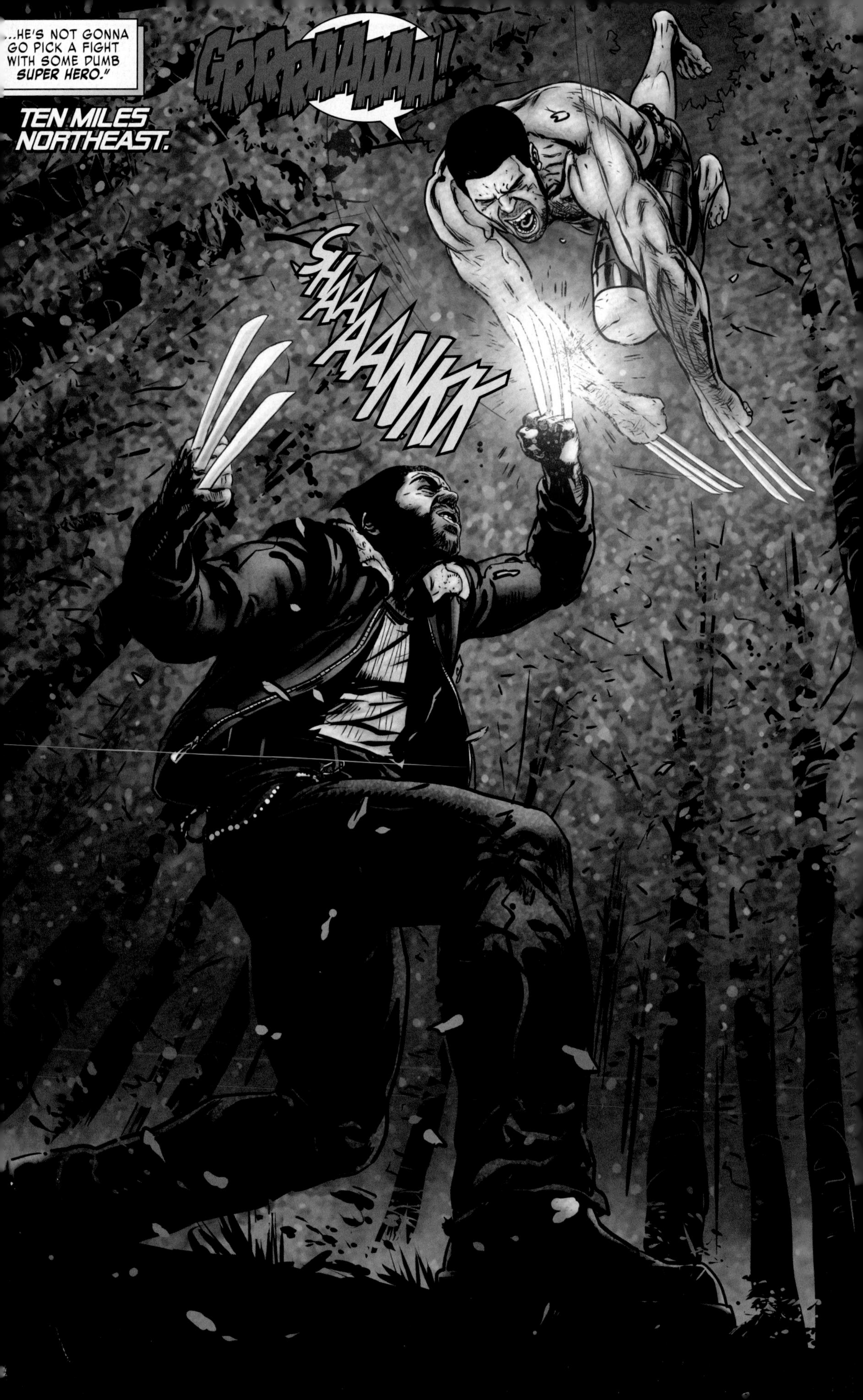

...HE'S NOT GONNA GO PICK A FIGHT WITH SOME DUMB SUPER HERO."
GRRRAAAAA!
TEN MILES NORTHEAST.
SHAAAANKK

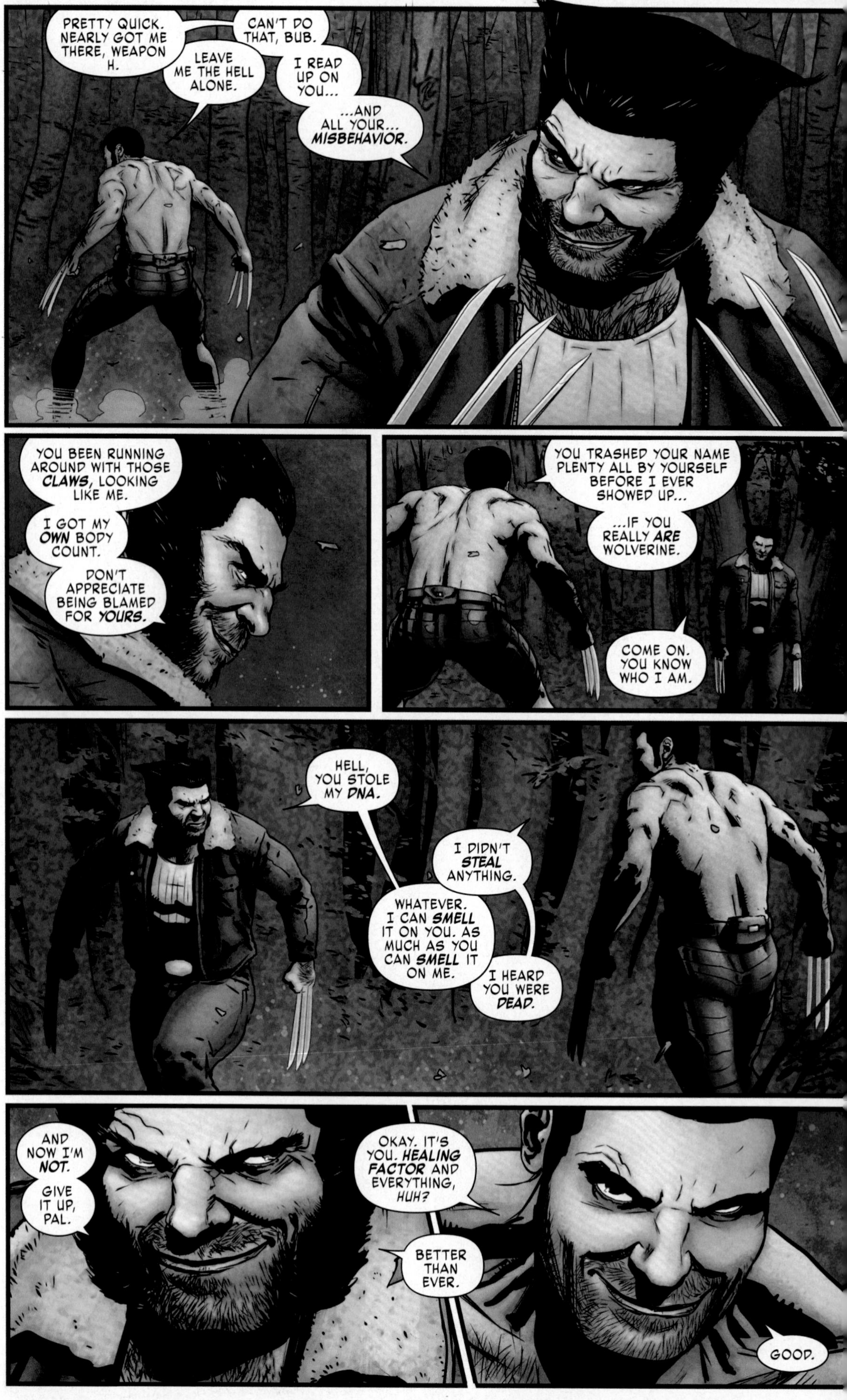
PRETTY QUICK. NEARLY GOT ME THERE, WEAPON H.
LEAVE ME THE HELL ALONE.
CAN'T DO THAT, BUB.
I READ UP ON YOU...
...AND ALL YOUR... MISBEHAVIOR.
YOU BEEN RUNNING AROUND WITH THOSE CLAWS, LOOKING LIKE ME.
I GOT MY OWN BODY COUNT.
DON'T APPRECIATE BEING BLAMED FOR YOURS.
YOU TRASHED YOUR NAME PLENTY ALL BY YOURSELF BEFORE I EVER SHOWED UP...
...IF YOU REALLY ARE WOLVERINE.
COME ON. YOU KNOW WHO I AM.
HELL, YOU STOLE MY DNA.
I DIDN'T STEAL ANYTHING.
WHATEVER. I CAN SMELL IT ON YOU. AS MUCH AS YOU CAN SMELL IT ON ME.
I HEARD YOU WERE DEAD.
AND NOW I'M NOT.
GIVE IT UP, PAL.
OKAY. IT'S YOU. HEALING FACTOR AND EVERYTHING, HUH?
BETTER THAN EVER.
GOOD.

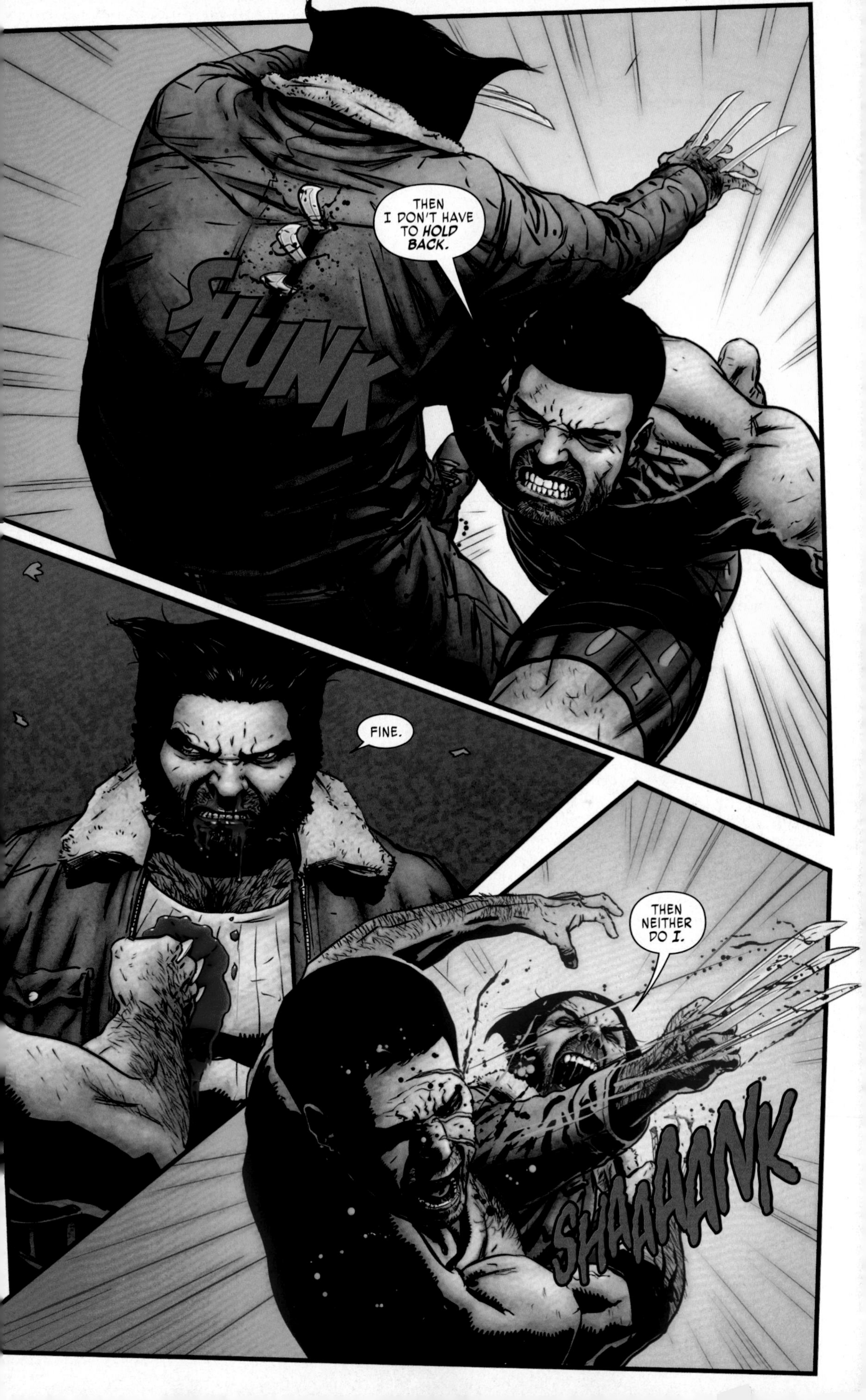
THEN I DON'T HAVE TO HOLD BACK.
SHUNK
FINE.
THEN NEITHER DO I.
SHAAAANK

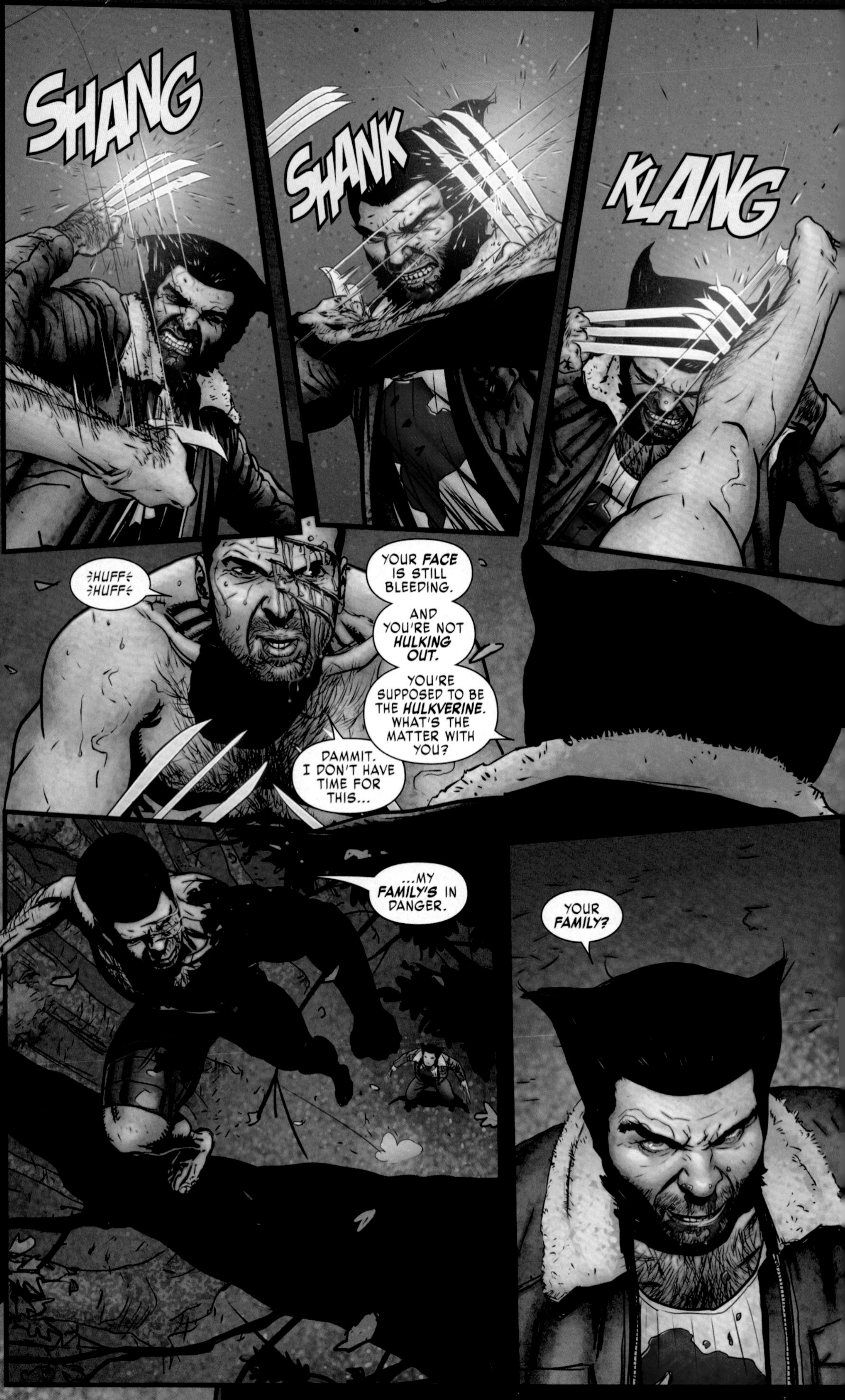
SHANG
SHANK
KLANG
HUFF HUFF
YOUR FACE IS STILL BLEEDING.
AND YOU'RE NOT HULKING OUT.
YOU'RE SUPPOSED TO BE THE HULKVERINE. WHAT'S THE MATTER WITH YOU?
DAMMIT. I DON'T HAVE TIME FOR THIS...
...MY FAMILY'S IN DANGER.
YOUR FAMILY?

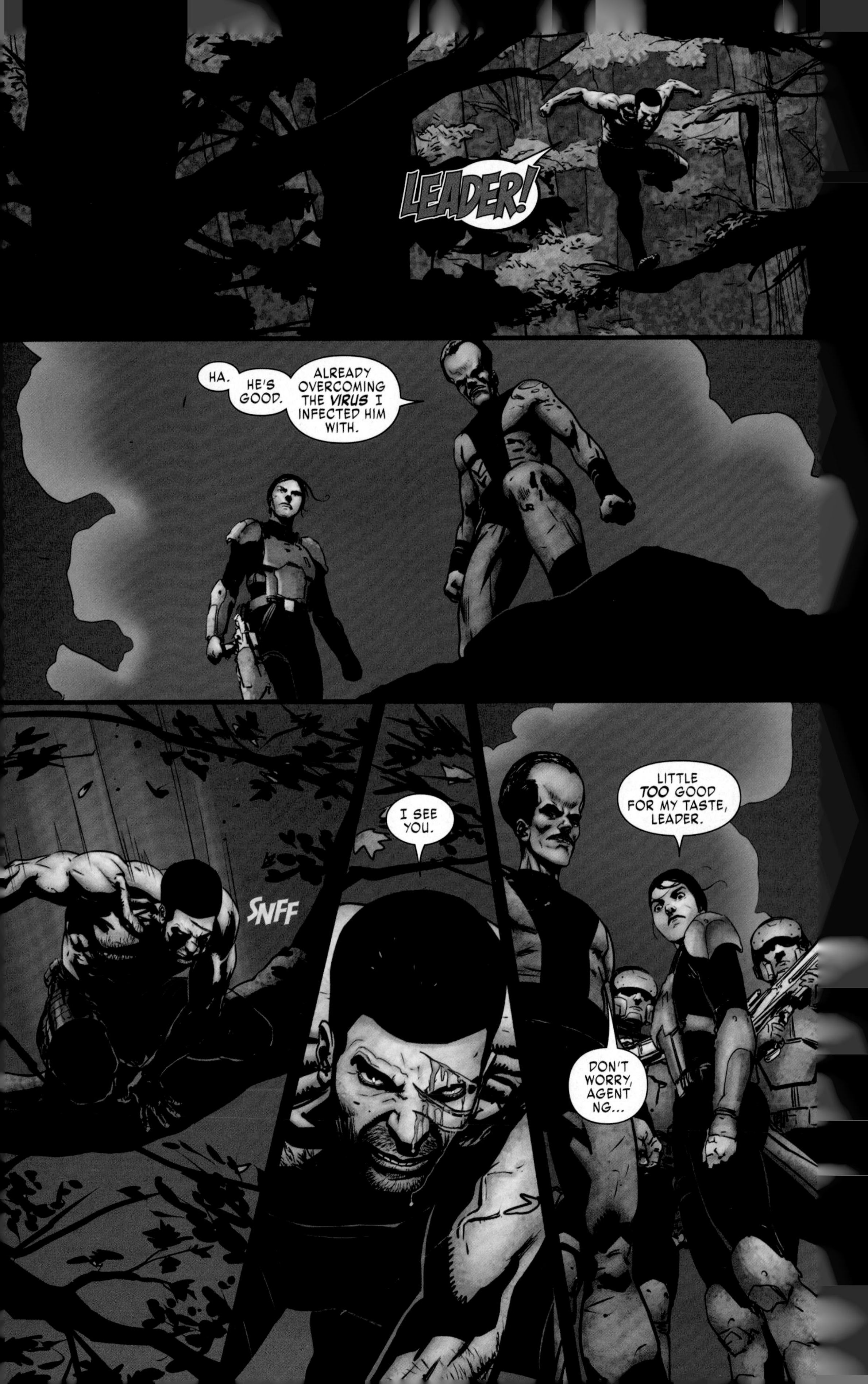
LEADER!
HA.
HE'S GOOD.
ALREADY OVERCOMING THE VIRUS I INFECTED HIM WITH.
SNFF
I SEE YOU.
LITTLE TOO GOOD FOR MY TASTE, LEADER.
DON'T WORRY, AGENT NG...

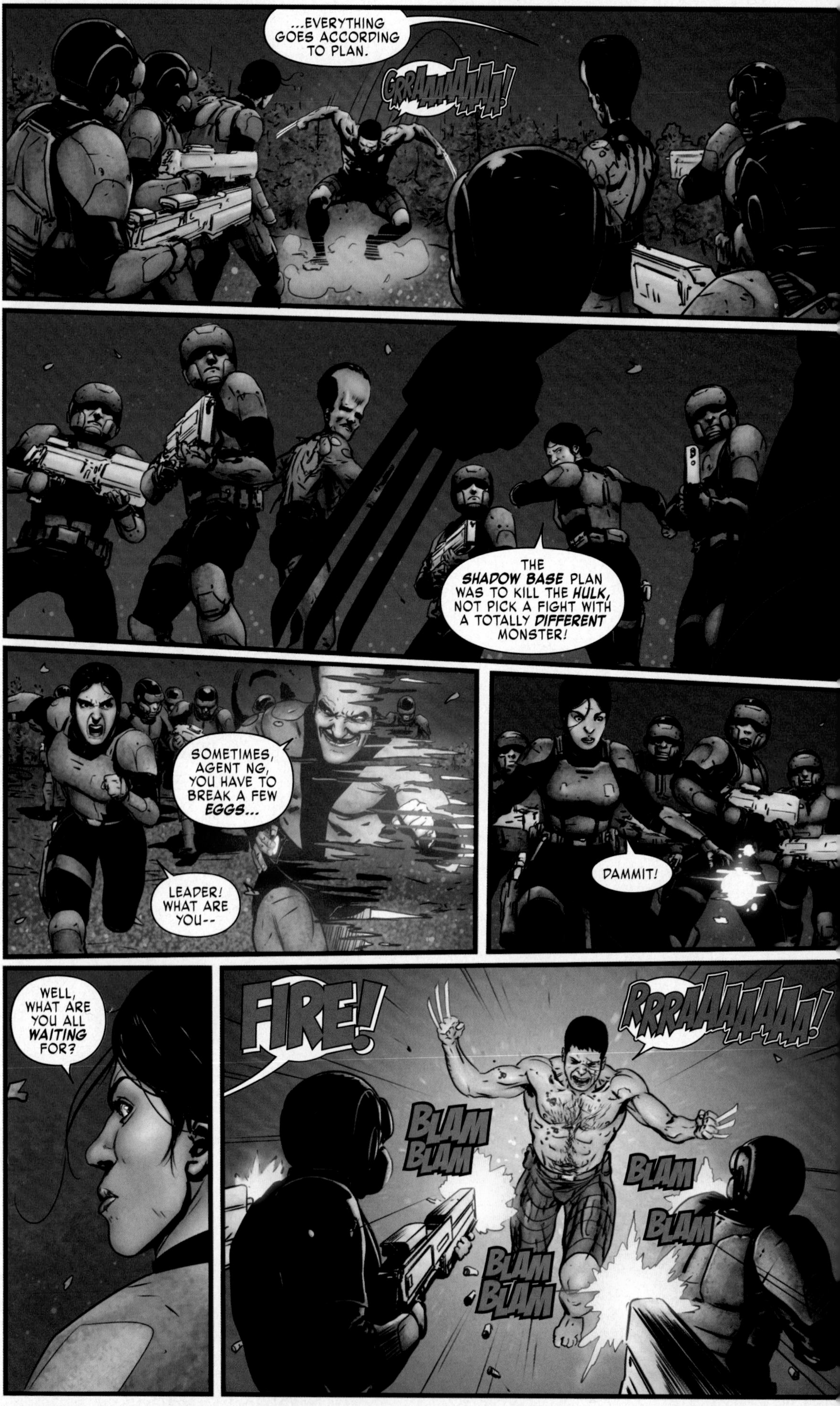
...EVERYTHING GOES ACCORDING TO PLAN.
GRRAAAAAAA!
THE SHADOW BASE PLAN WAS TO KILL THE HULK, NOT PICK A FIGHT WITH A TOTALLY DIFFERENT MONSTER!
SOMETIMES, AGENT NG, YOU HAVE TO BREAK A FEW EGGS...
LEADER! WHAT ARE YOU--
DAMMIT!
WELL, WHAT ARE YOU ALL WAITING FOR?
FIRE!
RRRAAAAAAA!
BLAM BLAM
BLAM
BLAM
BLAM BLAM

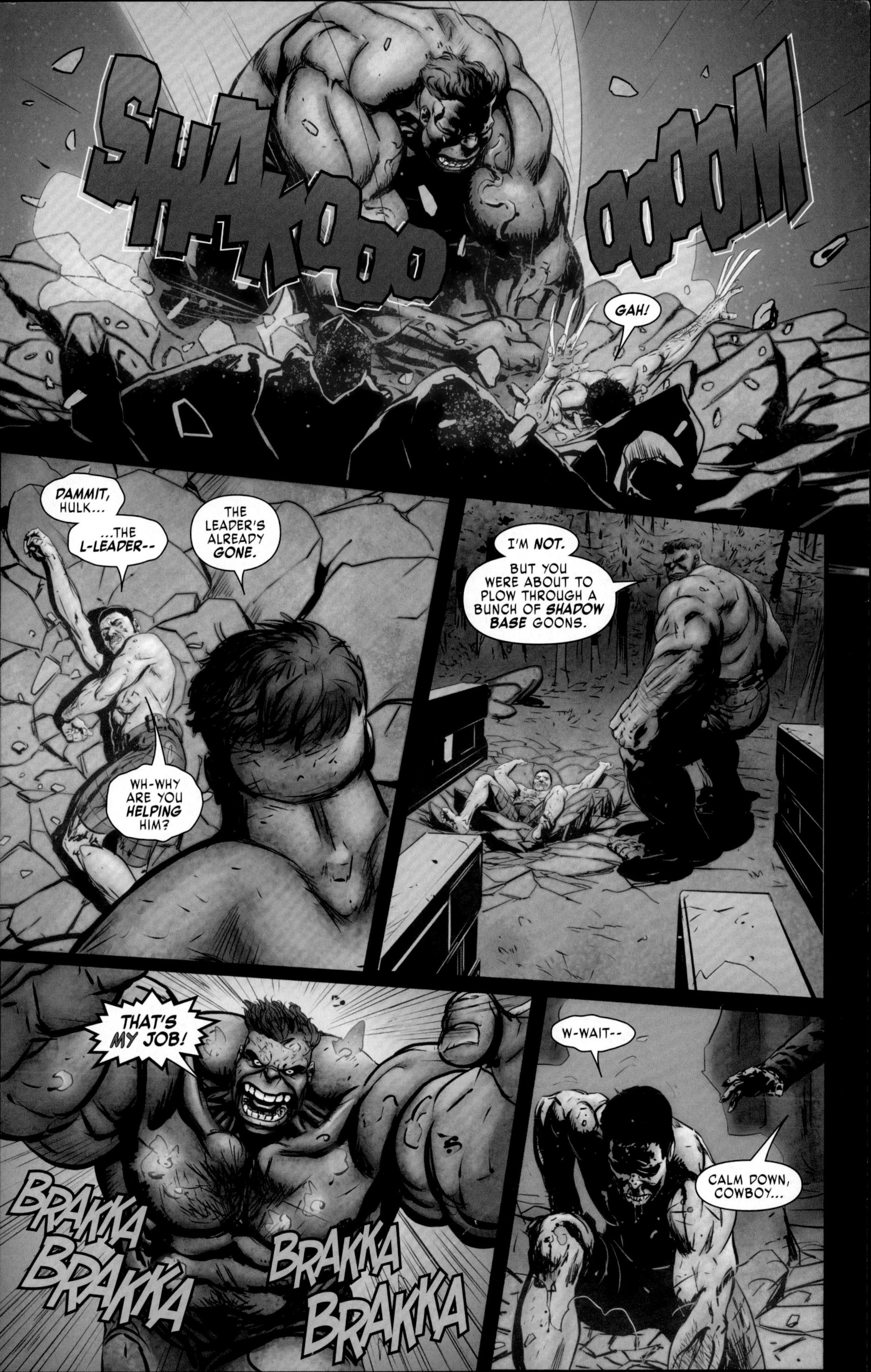

SHAKOOOOOOOOM
GAH!
DAMMIT, HULK...
...THE L-LEADER--
THE LEADER'S ALREADY GONE.
WH-WHY ARE YOU HELPING HIM?
I'M NOT.
BUT YOU WERE ABOUT TO PLOW THROUGH A BUNCH OF SHADOW BASE GOONS.
THAT'S MY JOB!
BRAKKA BRAKKA BRAKKA
BRAKKA BRAKKA BRAKKA
W-WAIT--
CALM DOWN, COWBOY...

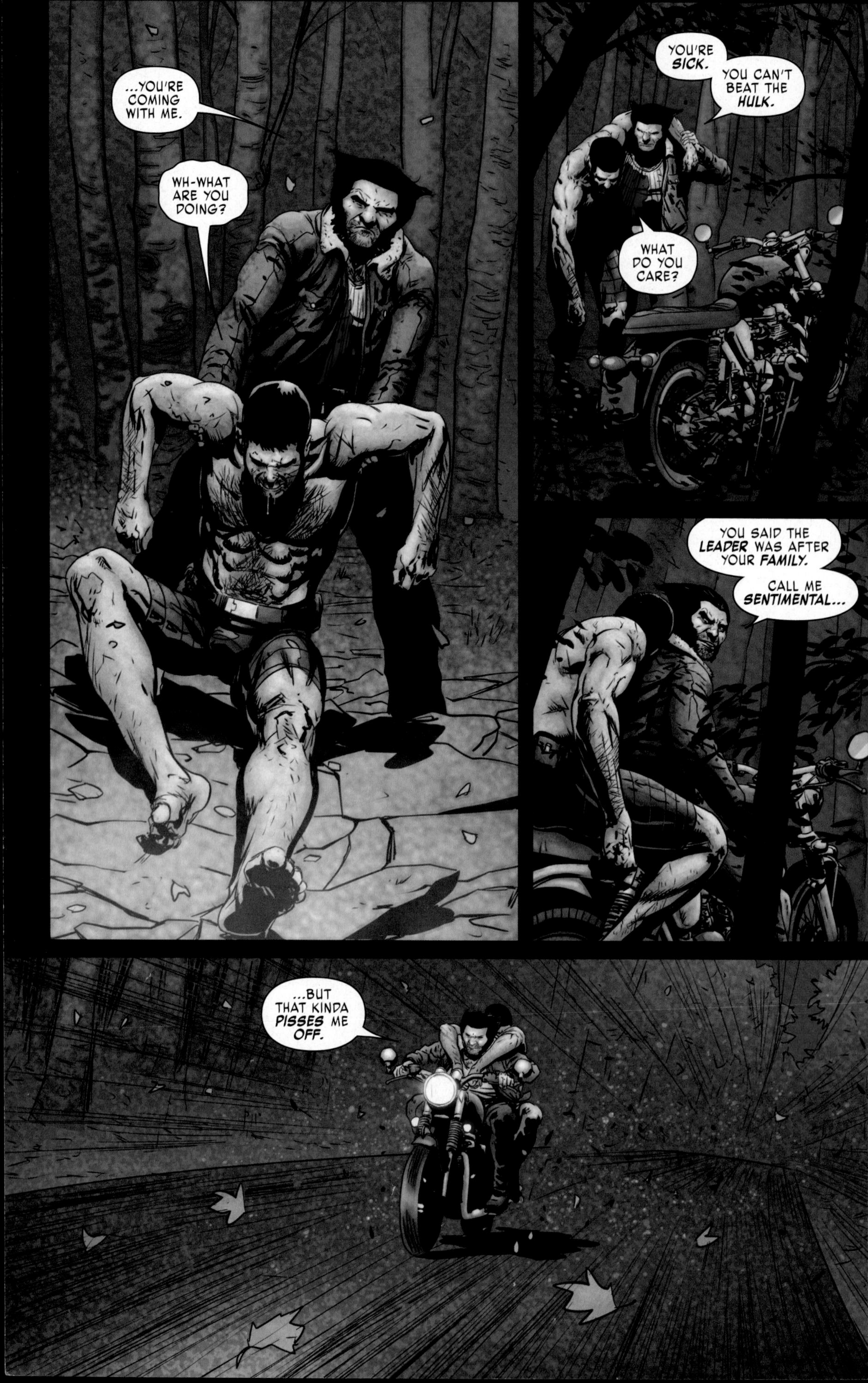

...YOU'RE COMING WITH ME.
WH-WHAT ARE YOU DOING?
YOU'RE SICK.
YOU CAN'T BEAT THE HULK.
WHAT DO YOU CARE?
YOU SAID THE LEADER WAS AFTER YOUR FAMILY.
CALL ME SENTIMENTAL...
...BUT THAT KINDA PISSES ME OFF.

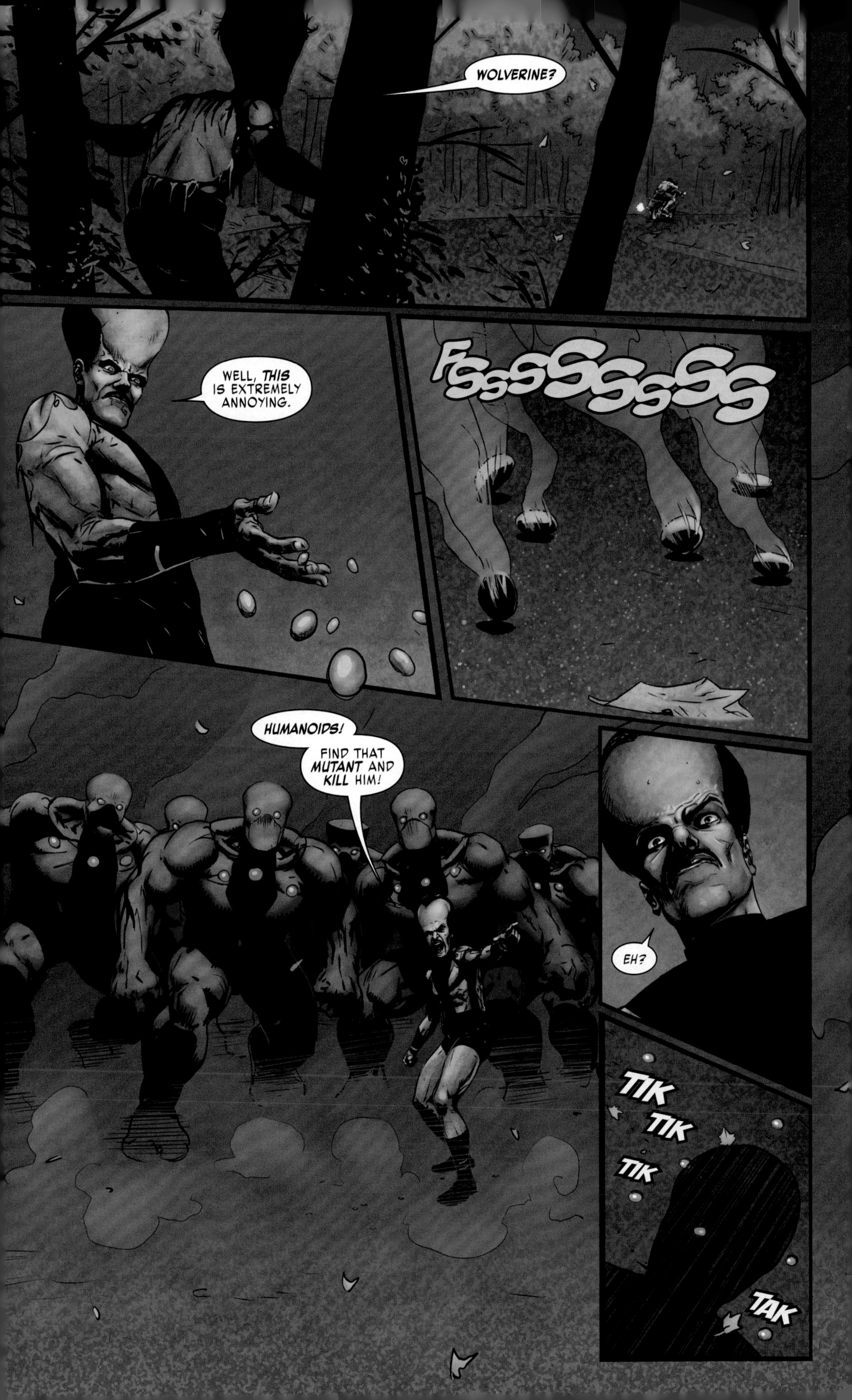
WOLVERINE?
WELL, THIS IS EXTREMELY ANNOYING.
FSSSSSSSSS
HUMANOIDS!
FIND THAT MUTANT AND KILL HIM!
EH?
TIK
TIK
TIK
TAK

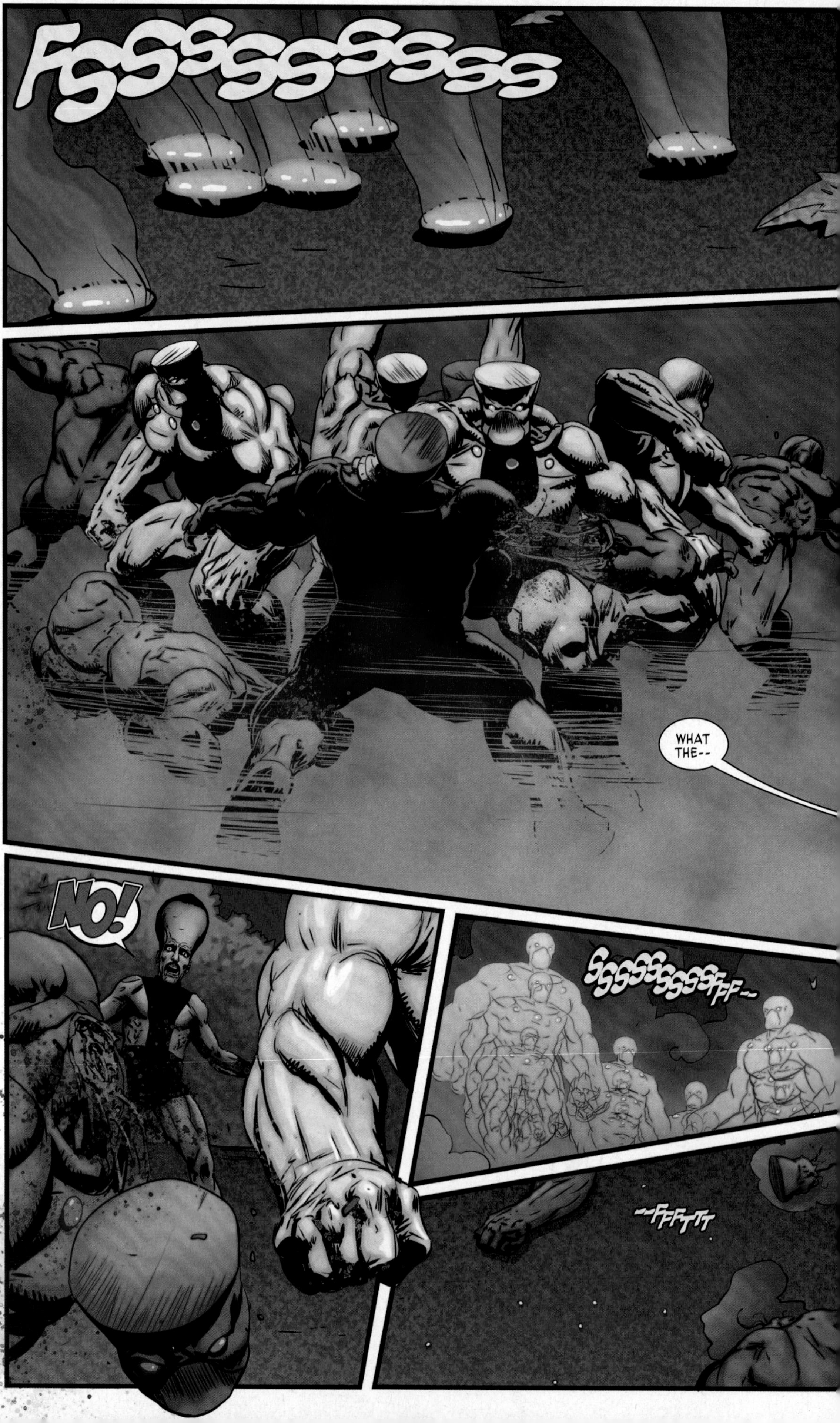
FSSSSSSSSSS
WHAT THE--
NO!
SSSSSSSSSFFF--
--FFFTTT

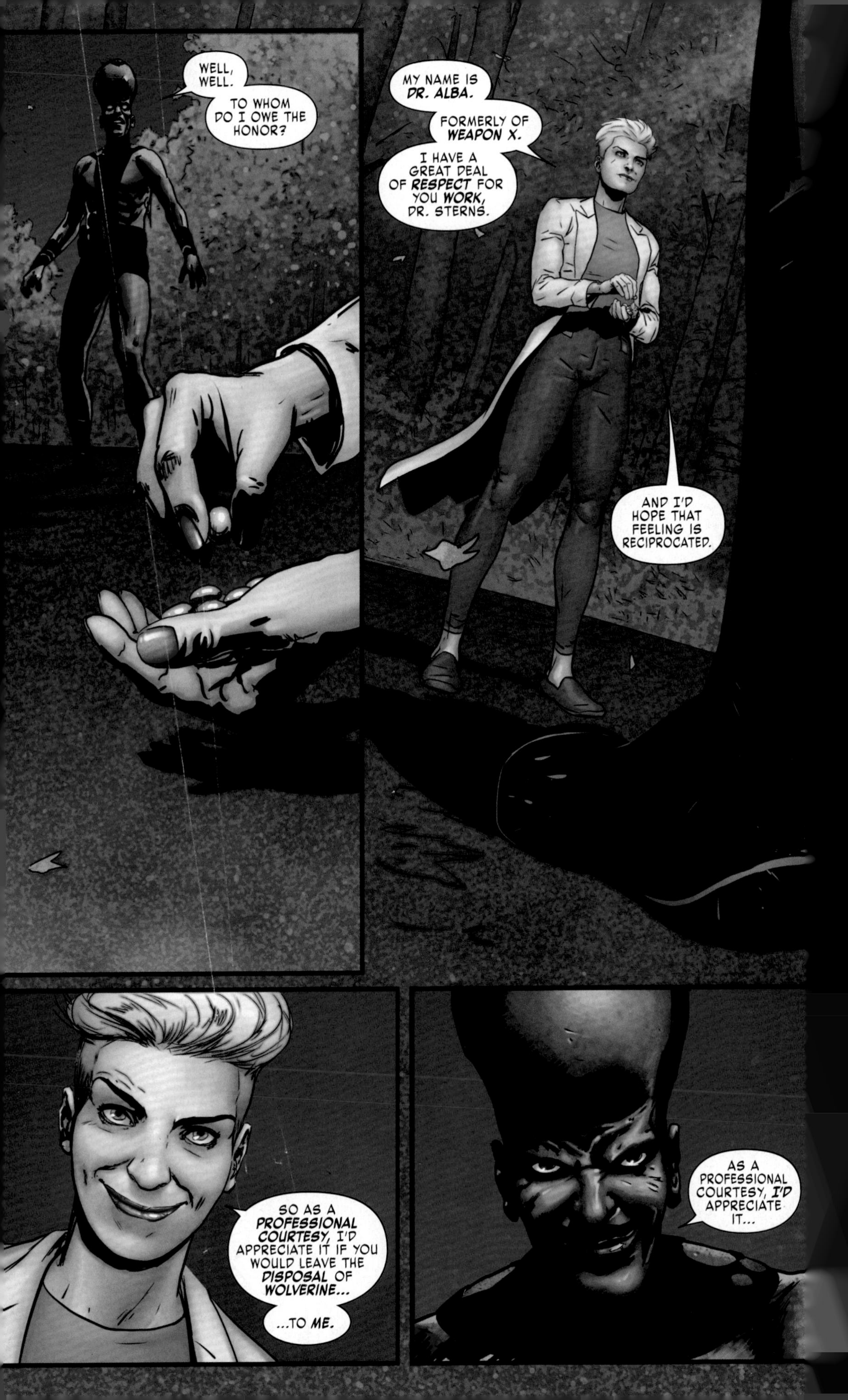
WELL, WELL.
TO WHOM DO I OWE THE HONOR?
MY NAME IS DR. ALBA.
FORMERLY OF WEAPON X.
I HAVE A GREAT DEAL OF RESPECT FOR YOU WORK, DR. STERNS.
AND I'D HOPE THAT FEELING IS RECIPROCATED.
SO AS A PROFESSIONAL COURTESY, I'D APPRECIATE IT IF YOU WOULD LEAVE THE DISPOSAL OF WOLVERINE...
...TO ME.
AS A PROFESSIONAL COURTESY, I'D APPRECIATE IT...

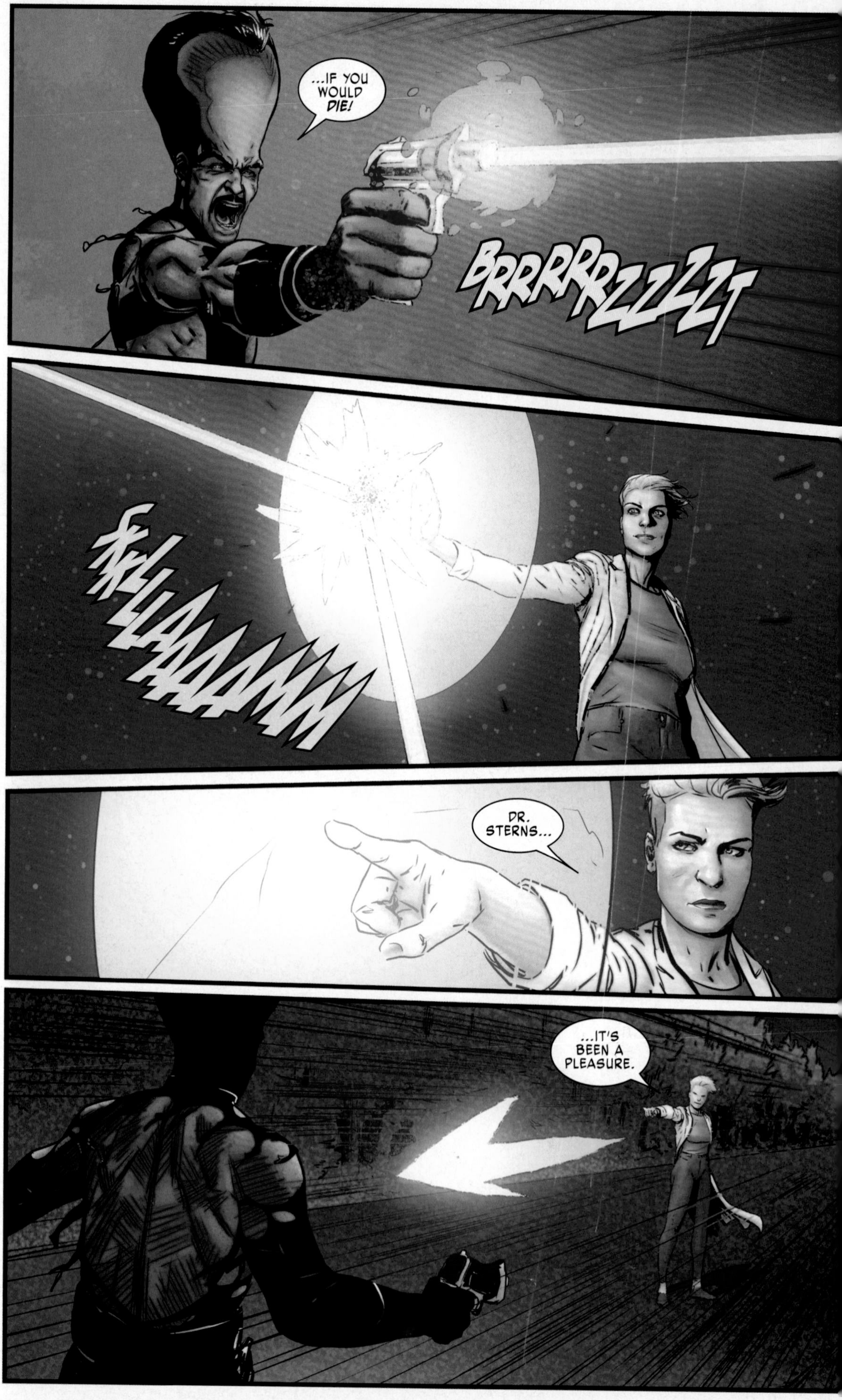

...IF YOU WOULD DIE!
BRRRRRZZZZZT
FKKLLAAAAMM
DR. STERNS...
...IT'S BEEN A PLEASURE.

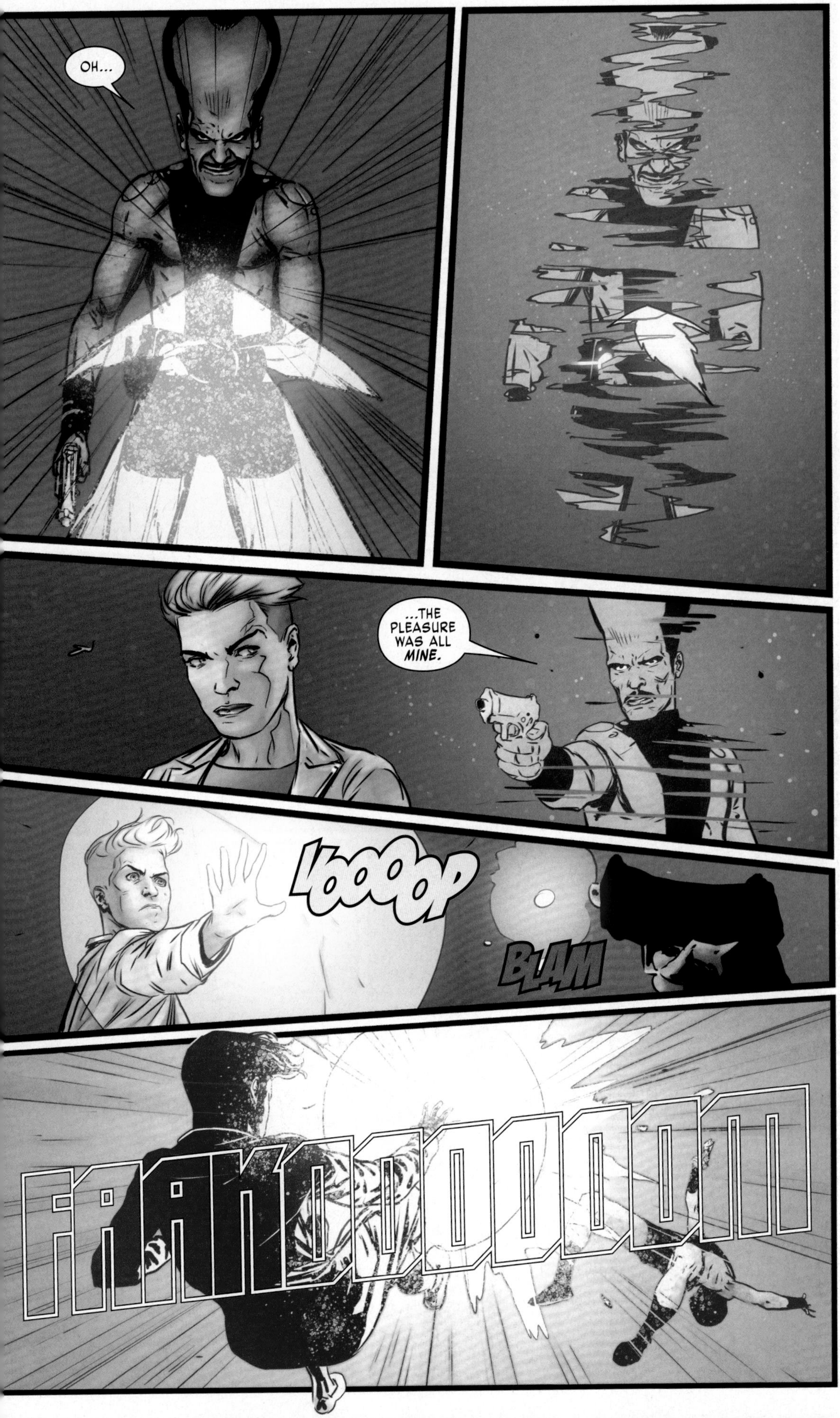
OH...
...THE PLEASURE WAS ALL MINE.
WOOOOP
BLAM
FRAKOOOOOM

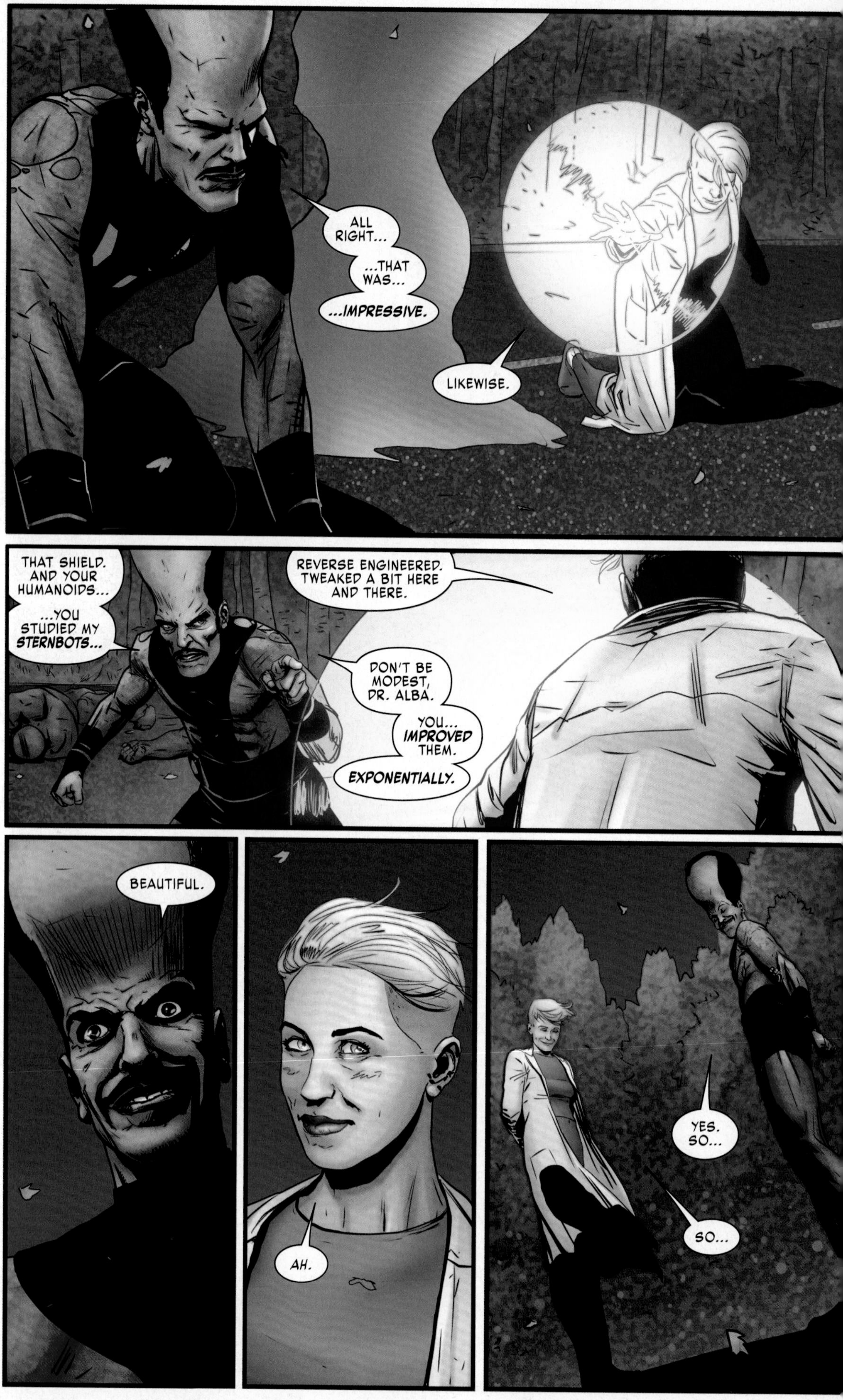
ALL RIGHT...
...THAT WAS...
...IMPRESSIVE.
LIKEWISE.
THAT SHIELD. AND YOUR HUMANOIDS...
...YOU STUDIED MY STERNBOTS...
REVERSE ENGINEERED. TWEAKED A BIT HERE AND THERE.
DON'T BE MODEST, DR. ALBA.
YOU... IMPROVED THEM.
EXPONENTIALLY.
BEAUTIFUL.
AH.
YES. SO...
SO...

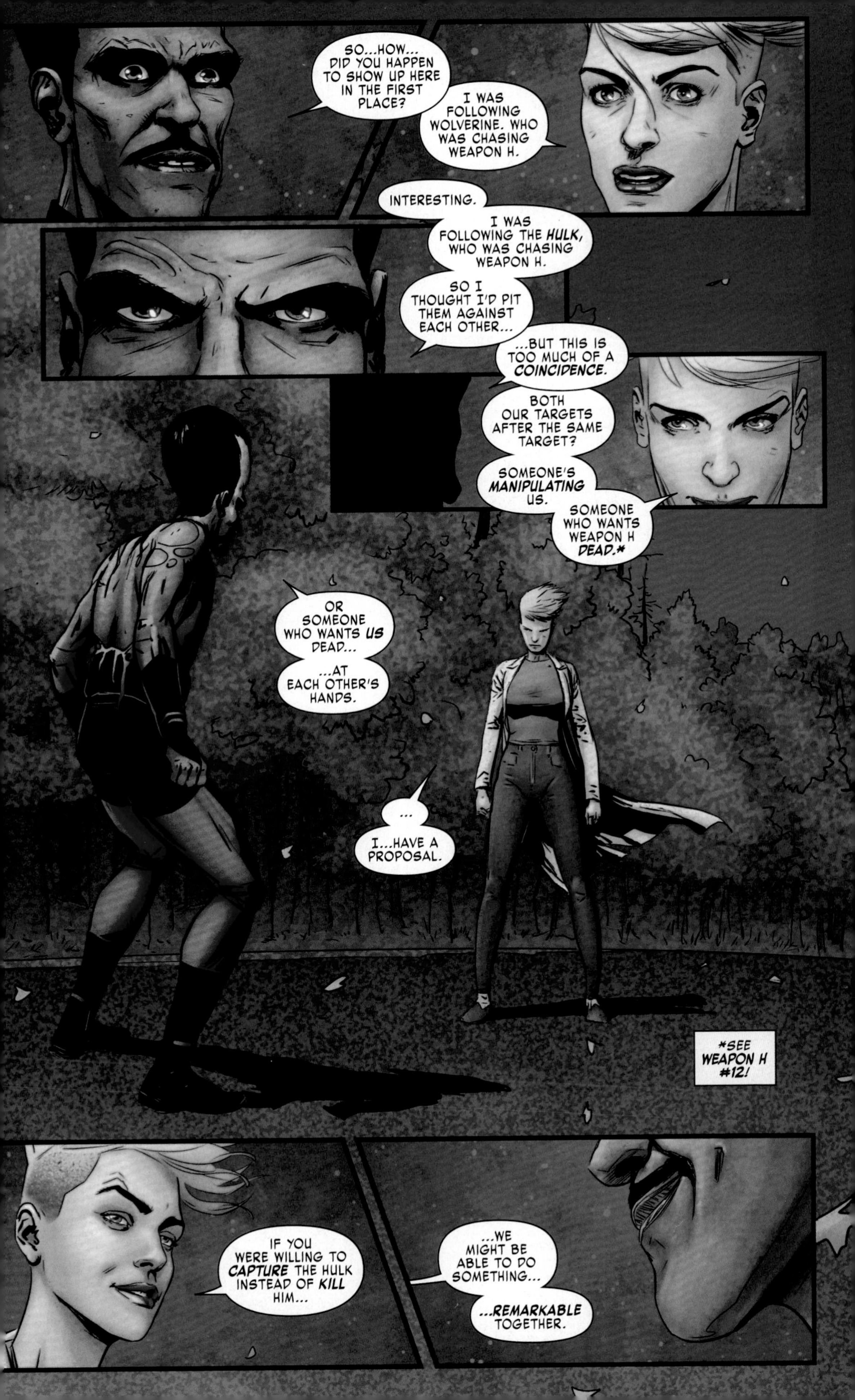
SO...HOW... DID YOU HAPPEN TO SHOW UP HERE IN THE FIRST PLACE?
I WAS FOLLOWING WOLVERINE. WHO WAS CHASING WEAPON H.
INTERESTING.
I WAS FOLLOWING THE HULK, WHO WAS CHASING WEAPON H.
SO I THOUGHT I'D PIT THEM AGAINST EACH OTHER...
...BUT THIS IS TOO MUCH OF A COINCIDENCE.
BOTH OUR TARGETS AFTER THE SAME TARGET?
SOMEONE'S MANIPULATING US.
SOMEONE WHO WANTS WEAPON H DEAD.*
OR SOMEONE WHO WANTS US DEAD...
...AT EACH OTHER'S HANDS.
...
I...HAVE A PROPOSAL.
*SEE WEAPON H #12!
IF YOU WERE WILLING TO CAPTURE THE HULK INSTEAD OF KILL HIM...
...WE MIGHT BE ABLE TO DO SOMETHING...
...REMARKABLE TOGETHER.

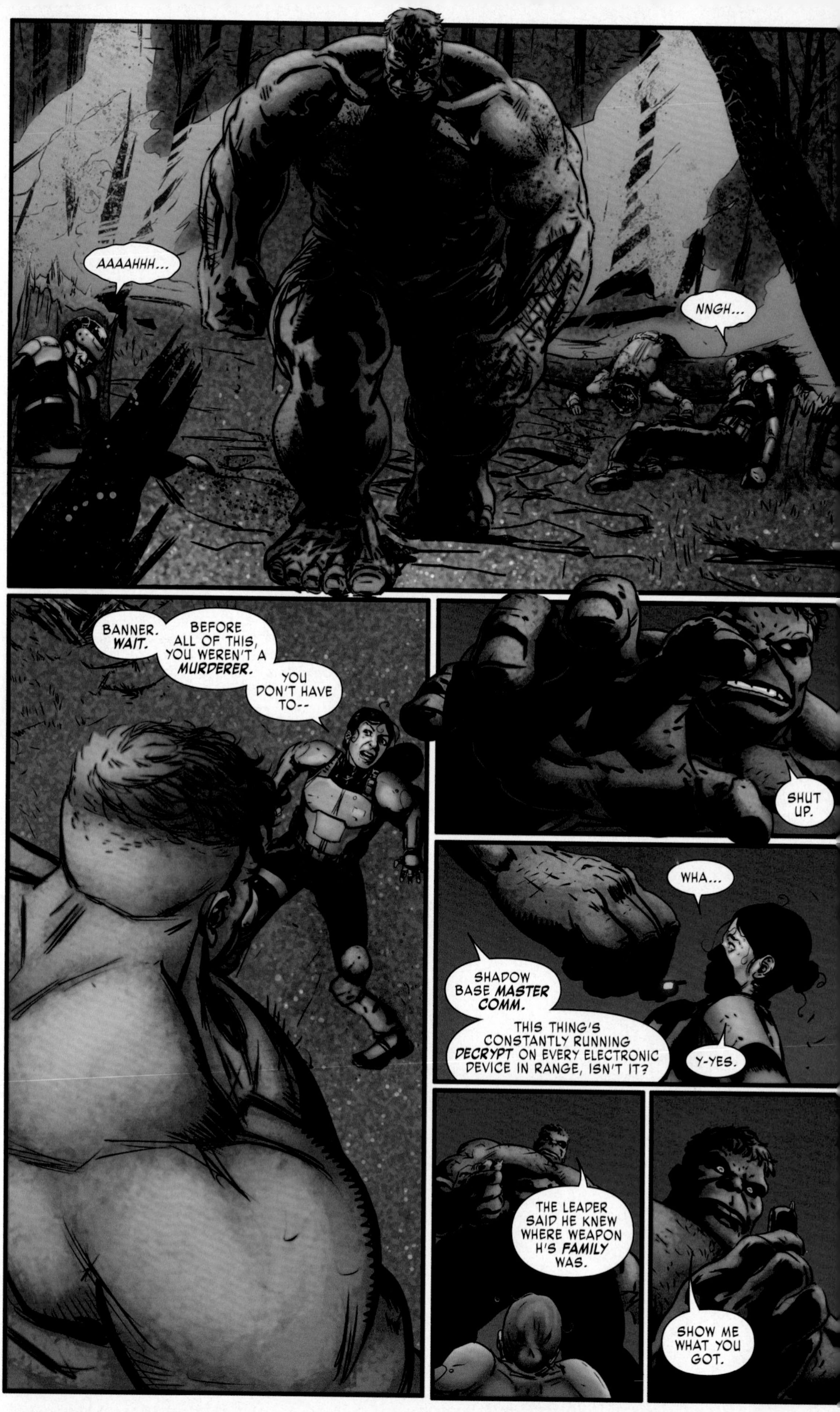
AAAAHHH...
NNGH...
BANNER. WAIT.
BEFORE ALL OF THIS, YOU WEREN'T A MURDERER.
YOU DON'T HAVE TO--
SHUT UP.
WHA...
SHADOW BASE MASTER COMM.
THIS THING'S CONSTANTLY RUNNING DECRYPT ON EVERY ELECTRONIC DEVICE IN RANGE, ISN'T IT?
Y-YES.
THE LEADER SAID HE KNEW WHERE WEAPON H'S FAMILY WAS.
SHOW ME WHAT YOU GOT.

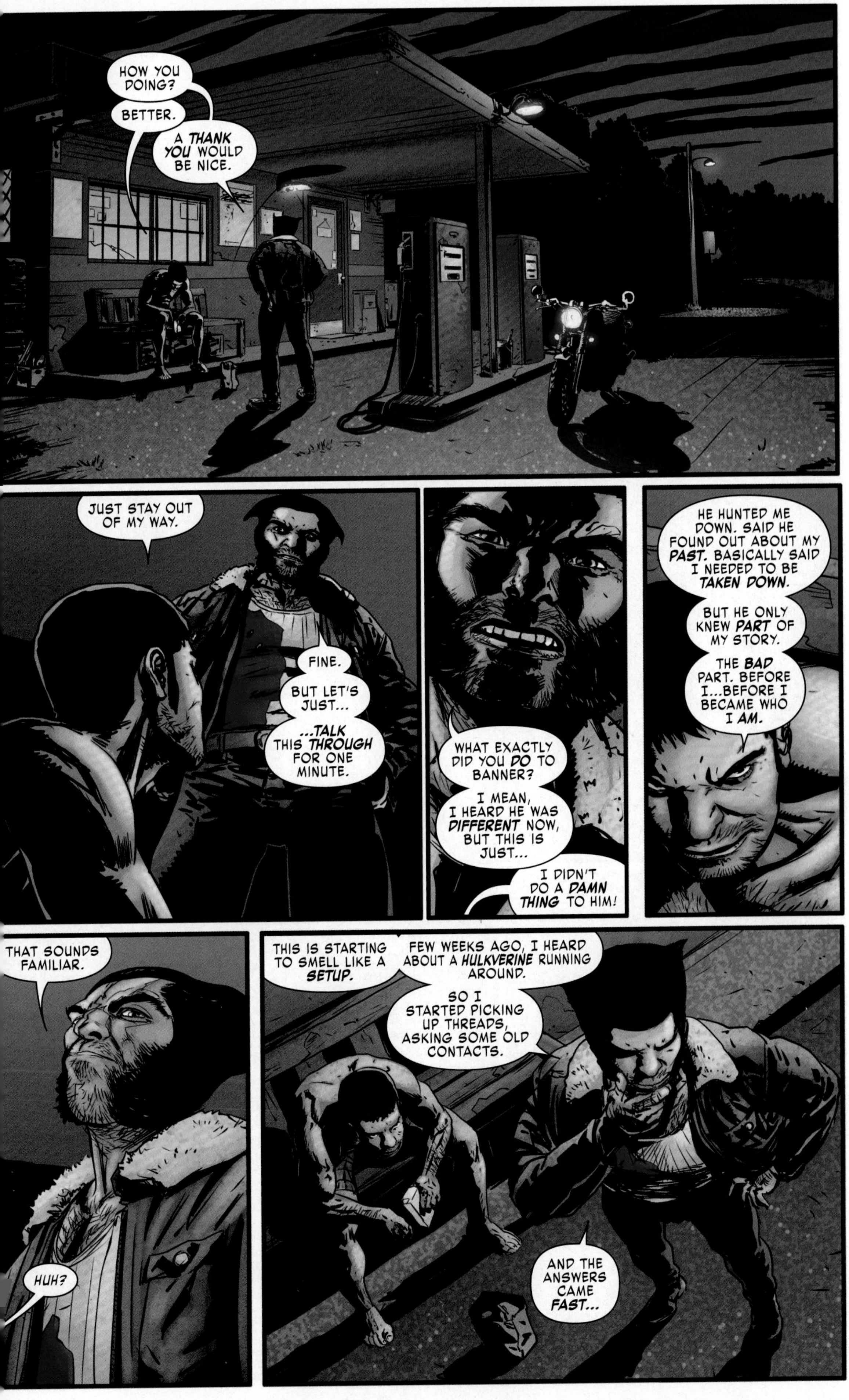
HOW YOU DOING?
BETTER.
A THANK YOU WOULD BE NICE.
JUST STAY OUT OF MY WAY.
FINE.
BUT LET'S JUST...
...TALK THIS THROUGH FOR ONE MINUTE.
WHAT EXACTLY DID YOU DO TO BANNER?
I MEAN, I HEARD HE WAS DIFFERENT NOW, BUT THIS IS JUST...
I DIDN'T DO A DAMN THING TO HIM!
HE HUNTED ME DOWN. SAID HE FOUND OUT ABOUT MY PAST. BASICALLY SAID I NEEDED TO BE TAKEN DOWN.
BUT HE ONLY KNEW PART OF MY STORY.
THE BAD PART. BEFORE I...BEFORE I BECAME WHO I AM.
THAT SOUNDS FAMILIAR.
HUH?
THIS IS STARTING TO SMELL LIKE A SETUP.
FEW WEEKS AGO, I HEARD ABOUT A HULKVERINE RUNNING AROUND.
SO I STARTED PICKING UP THREADS, ASKING SOME OLD CONTACTS.
AND THE ANSWERS CAME FAST...

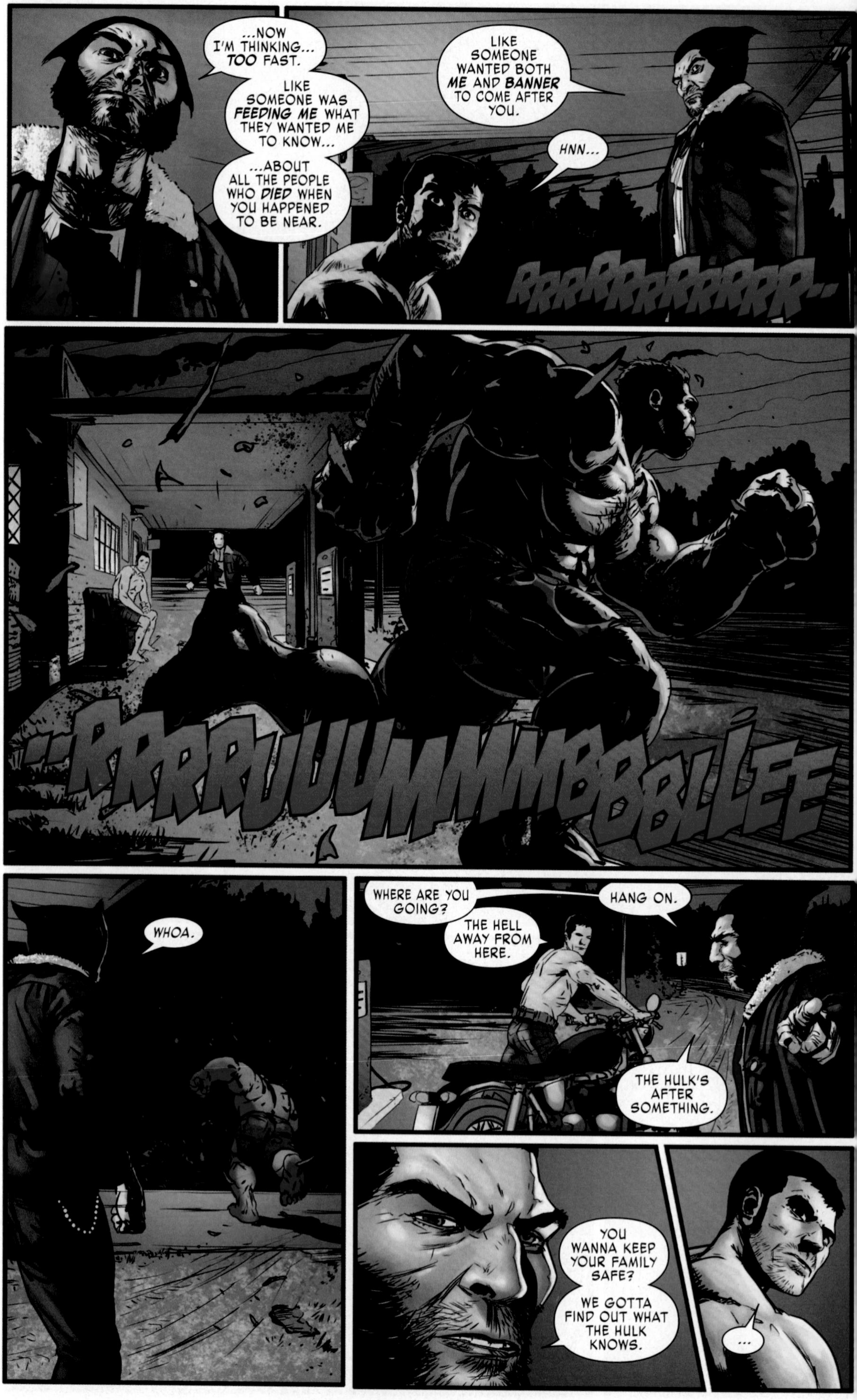
...NOW I'M THINKING... TOO FAST.
LIKE SOMEONE WAS FEEDING ME WHAT THEY WANTED ME TO KNOW...
...ABOUT ALL THE PEOPLE WHO DIED WHEN YOU HAPPENED TO BE NEAR.
LIKE SOMEONE WANTED BOTH ME AND BANNER TO COME AFTER YOU.
HNN...
RRRRRRRRRRRR..
..RRRRUUUMMMBBLEE
WHOA.
WHERE ARE YOU GOING?
HANG ON.
THE HELL AWAY FROM HERE.
THE HULK'S AFTER SOMETHING.
YOU WANNA KEEP YOUR FAMILY SAFE?
WE GOTTA FIND OUT WHAT THE HULK KNOWS.
...

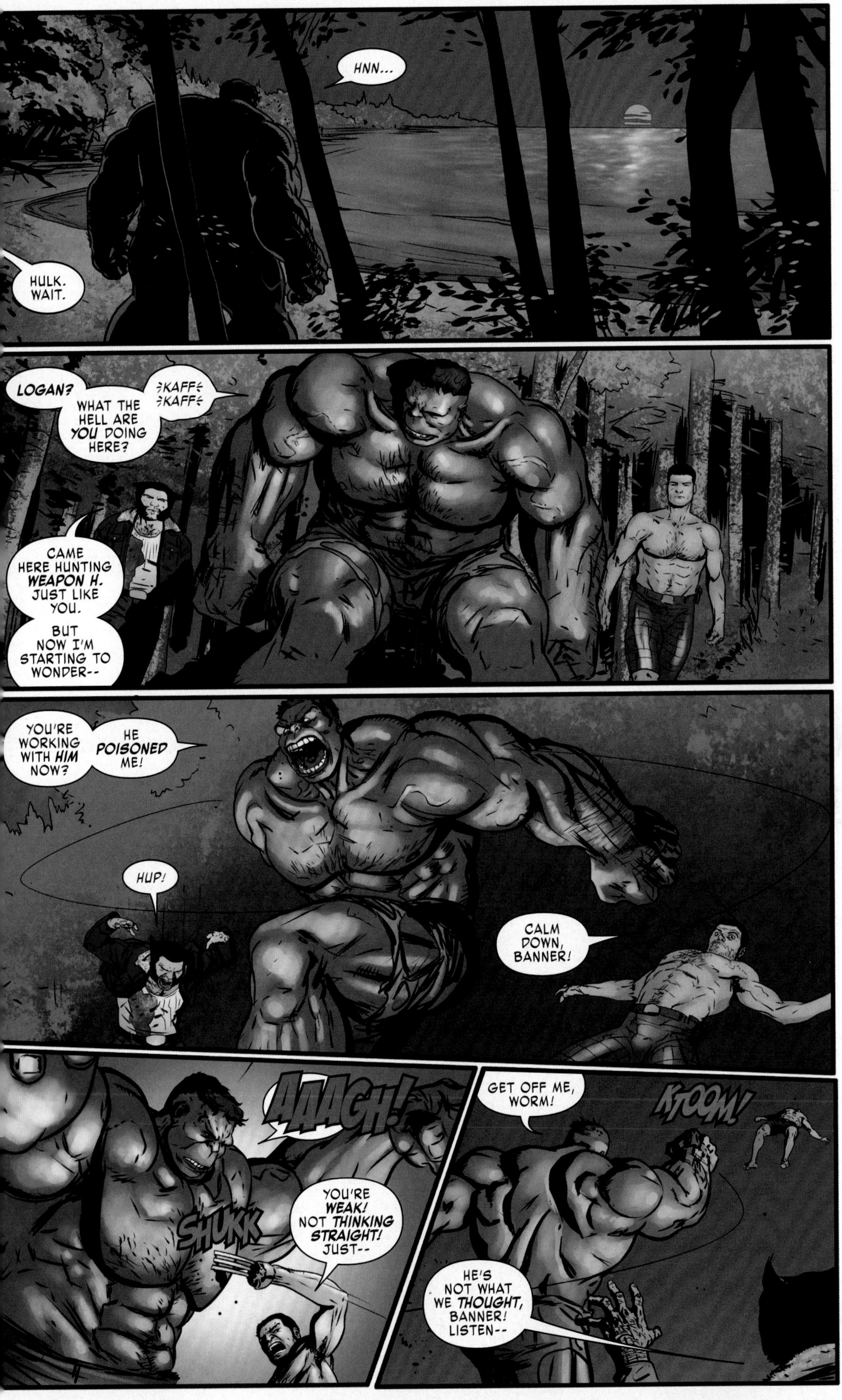
HNN...
HULK. WAIT.
LOGAN? WHAT THE HELL ARE YOU DOING HERE?
≠KAFF≠ ≠KAFF≠
CAME HERE HUNTING WEAPON H. JUST LIKE YOU.
BUT NOW I'M STARTING TO WONDER--
YOU'RE WORKING WITH HIM NOW?
HE POISONED ME!
HUP!
CALM DOWN, BANNER!
AAAGH!
SHUKK
YOU'RE WEAK! NOT THINKING STRAIGHT! JUST--
GET OFF ME, WORM!
KTOOM!
HE'S NOT WHAT WE THOUGHT, BANNER! LISTEN--

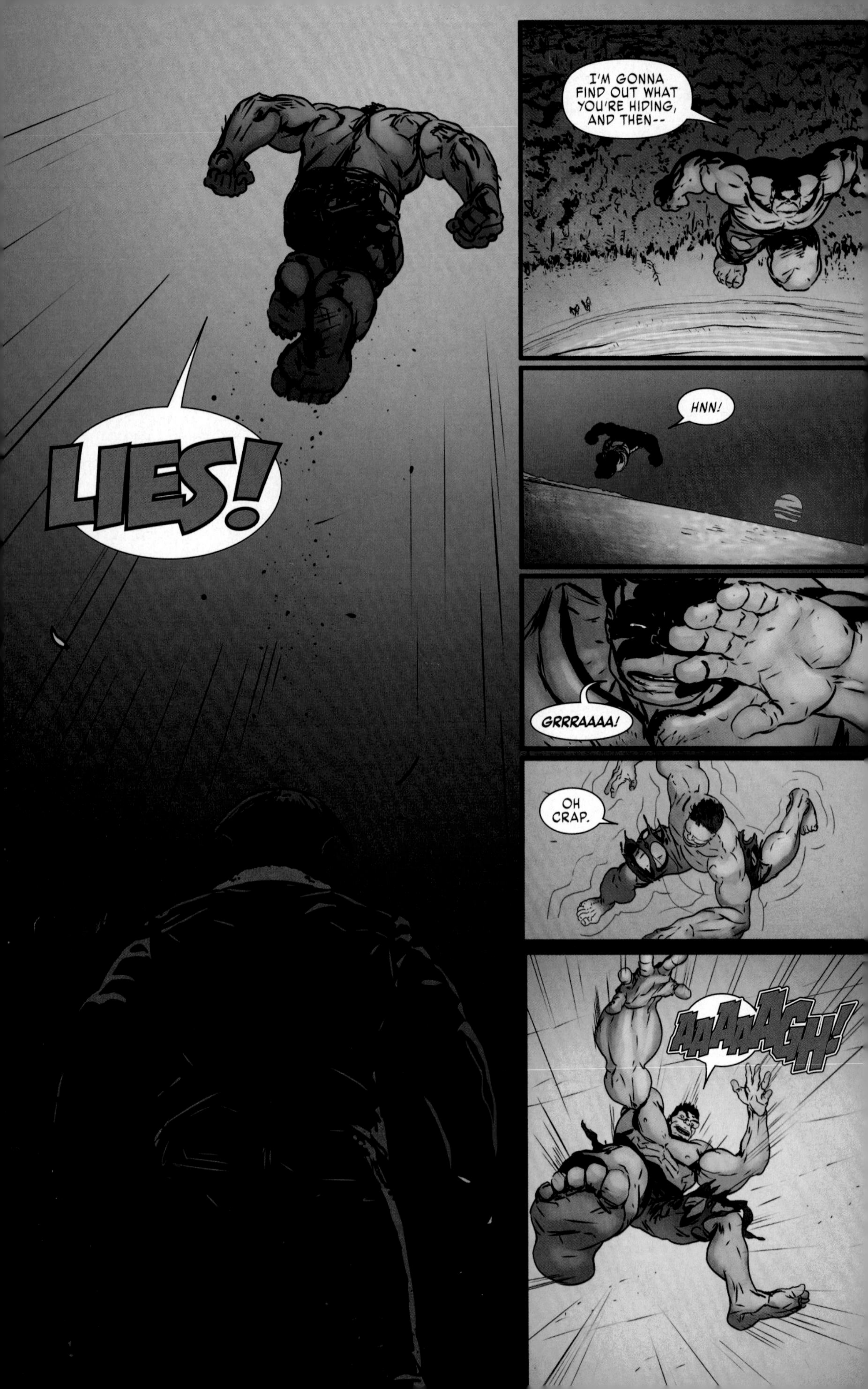
LIES!
I'M GONNA FIND OUT WHAT YOU'RE HIDING, AND THEN--
HNN!
GRRRAAAA!
OH CRAP.
AAAAAAGH!

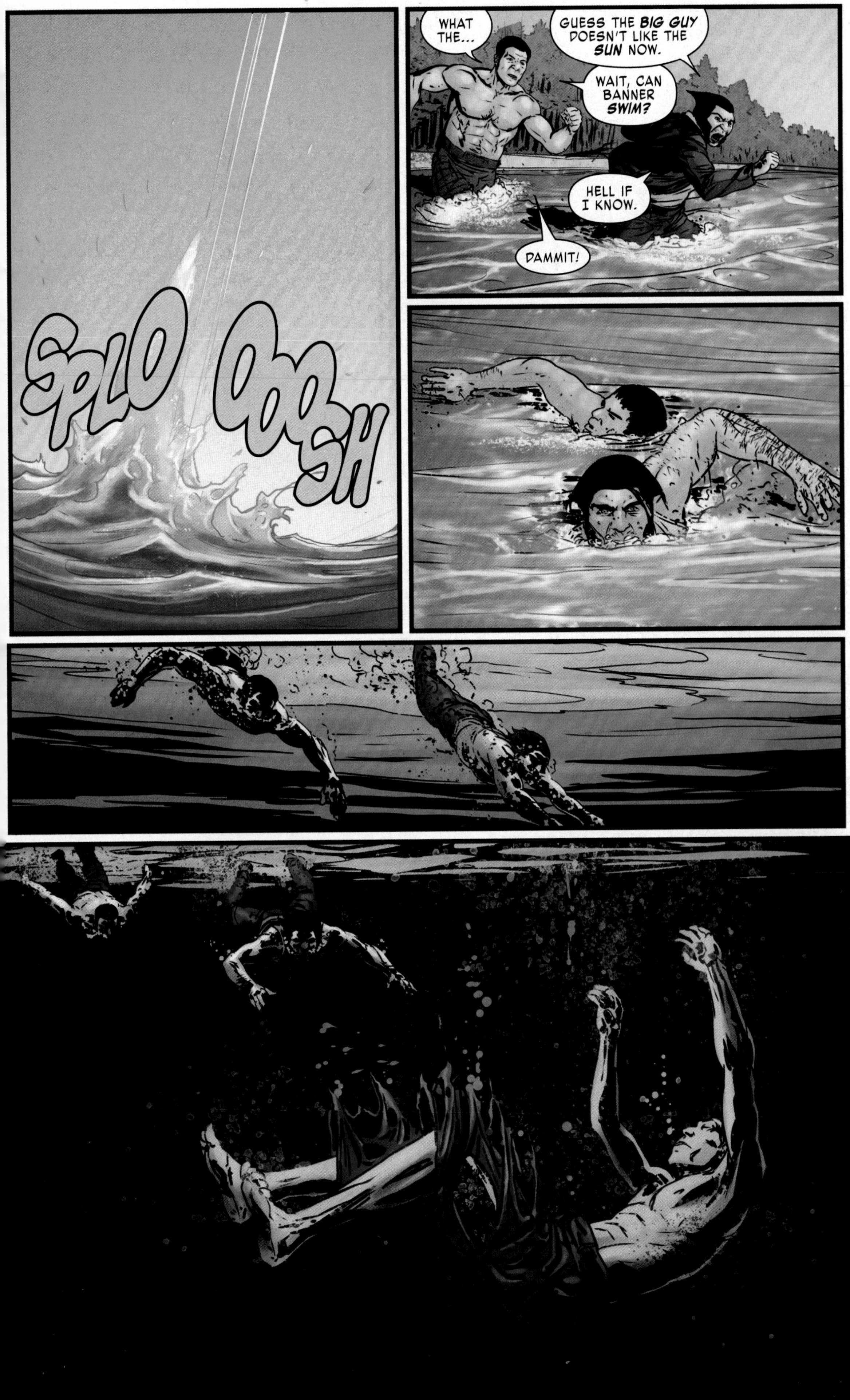
SPLOOOOSH
WHAT THE...
GUESS THE BIG GUY DOESN'T LIKE THE SUN NOW.
WAIT, CAN BANNER SWIM?
HELL IF I KNOW.
DAMMIT!

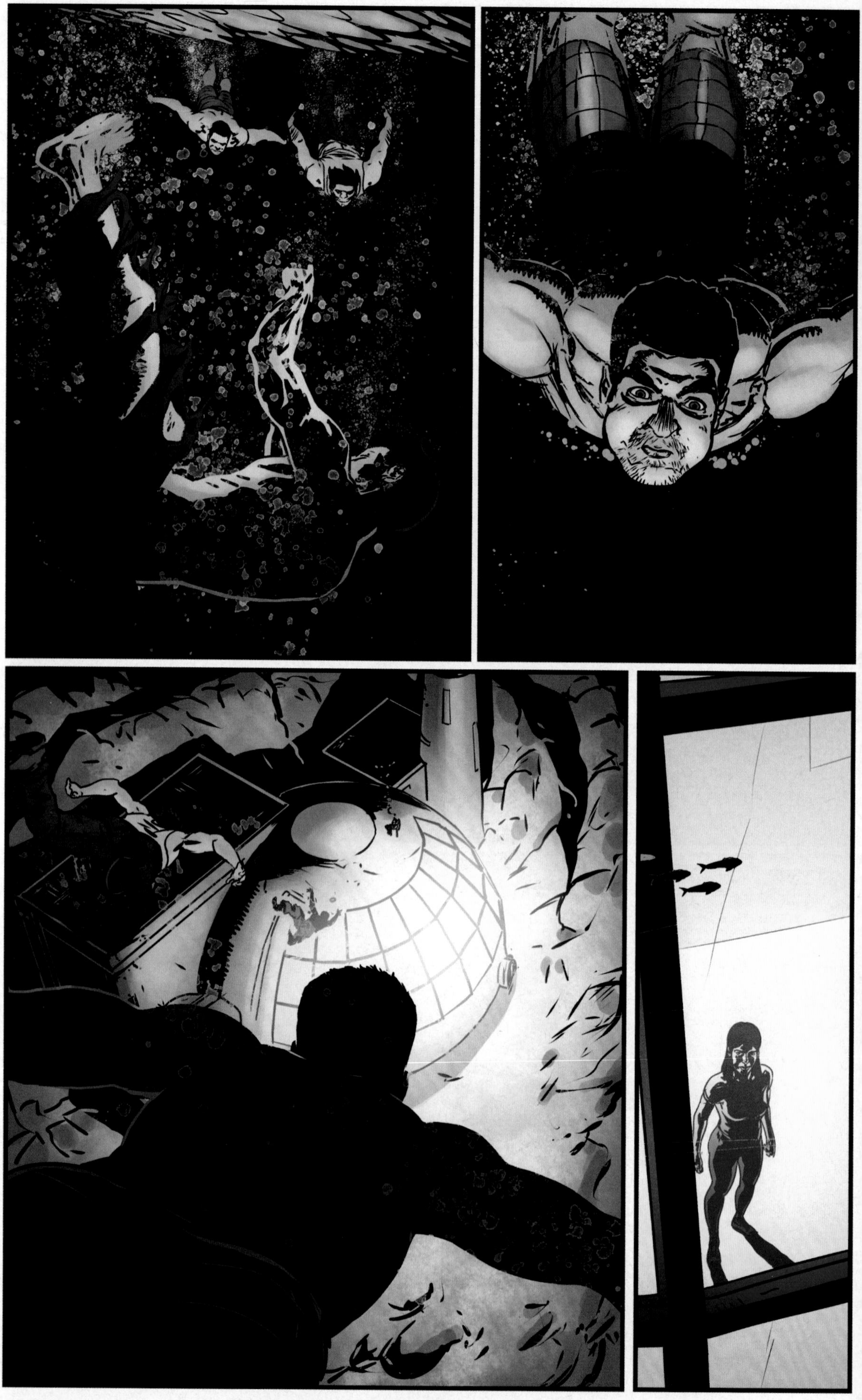

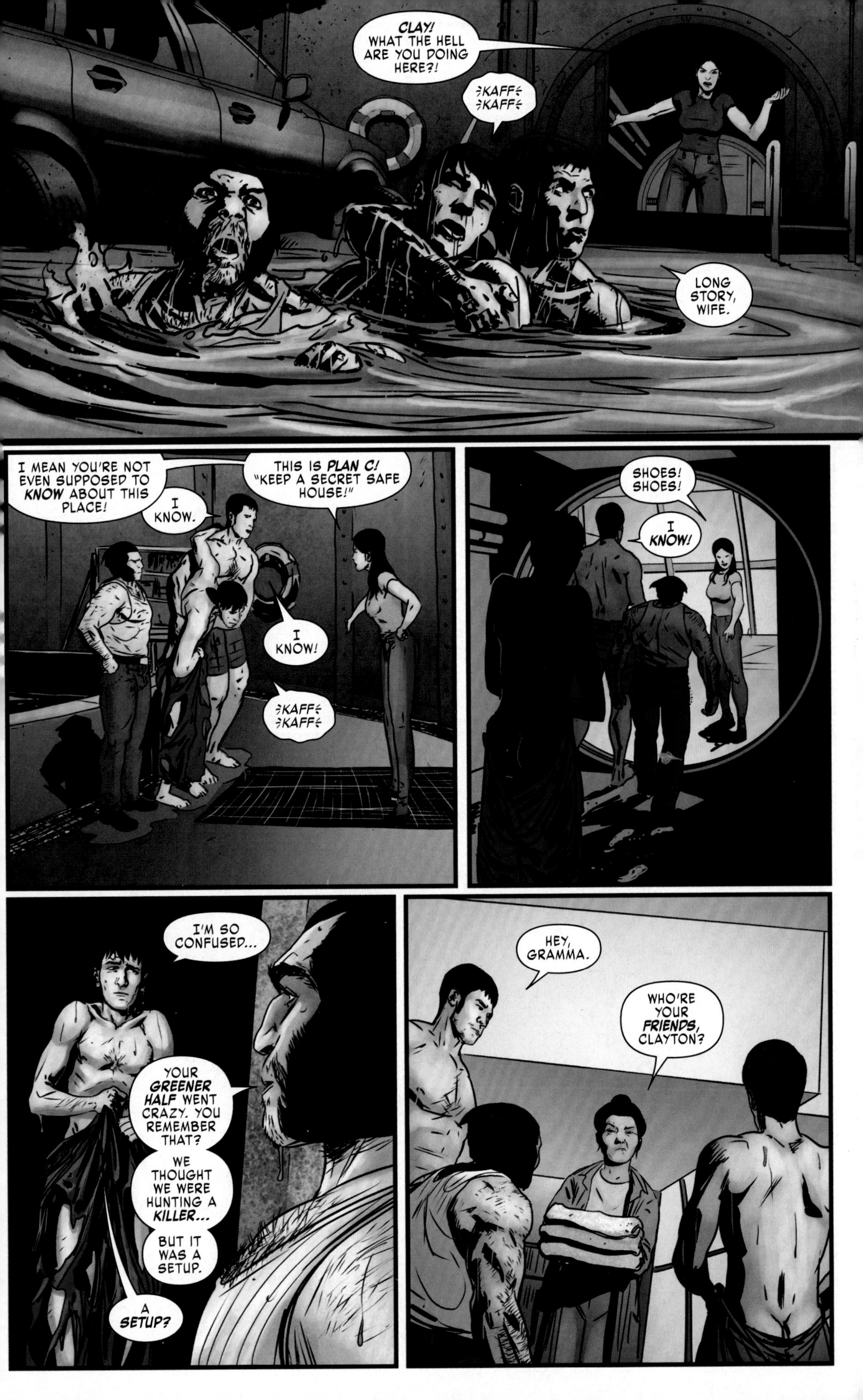
CLAY! WHAT THE HELL ARE YOU DOING HERE?!
KAFF KAFF
LONG STORY, WIFE.
I MEAN YOU'RE NOT EVEN SUPPOSED TO KNOW ABOUT THIS PLACE!
I KNOW.
THIS IS PLAN C! "KEEP A SECRET SAFE HOUSE!"
I KNOW!
KAFF KAFF
SHOES! SHOES!
I KNOW!
I'M SO CONFUSED...
YOUR GREENER HALF WENT CRAZY. YOU REMEMBER THAT?
WE THOUGHT WE WERE HUNTING A KILLER...
BUT IT WAS A SETUP.
A SETUP?
HEY, GRAMMA.
WHO'RE YOUR FRIENDS, CLAYTON?

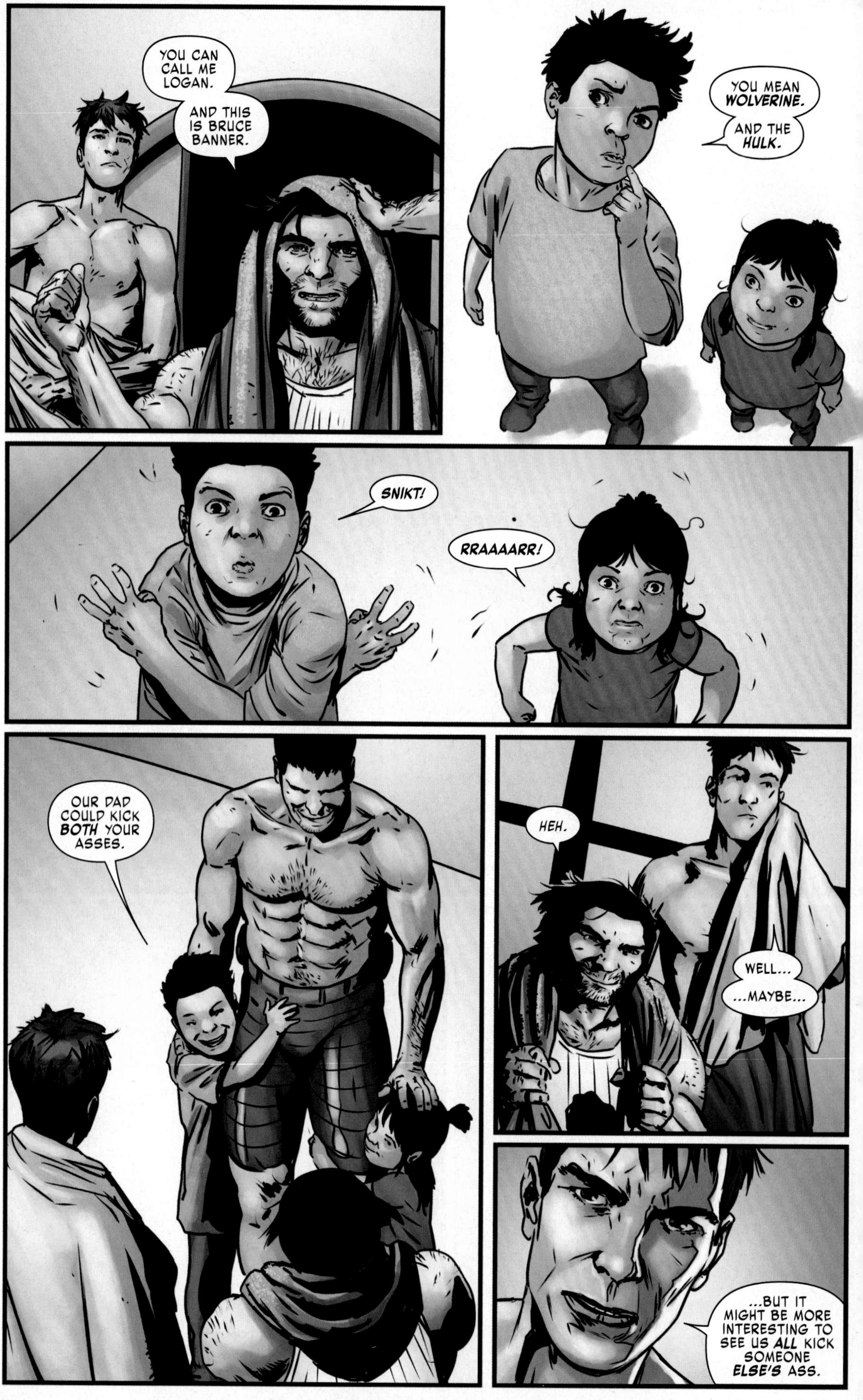
YOU CAN CALL ME LOGAN.
AND THIS IS BRUCE BANNER.
YOU MEAN *WOLVERINE.*
AND THE *HULK.*
SNIKT!
RRAAAARR!
OUR DAD COULD KICK *BOTH* YOUR ASSES.
HEH.
WELL...
...MAYBE...
...BUT IT MIGHT BE MORE INTERESTING TO SEE US *ALL* KICK SOMEONE *ELSE'S* ASS.

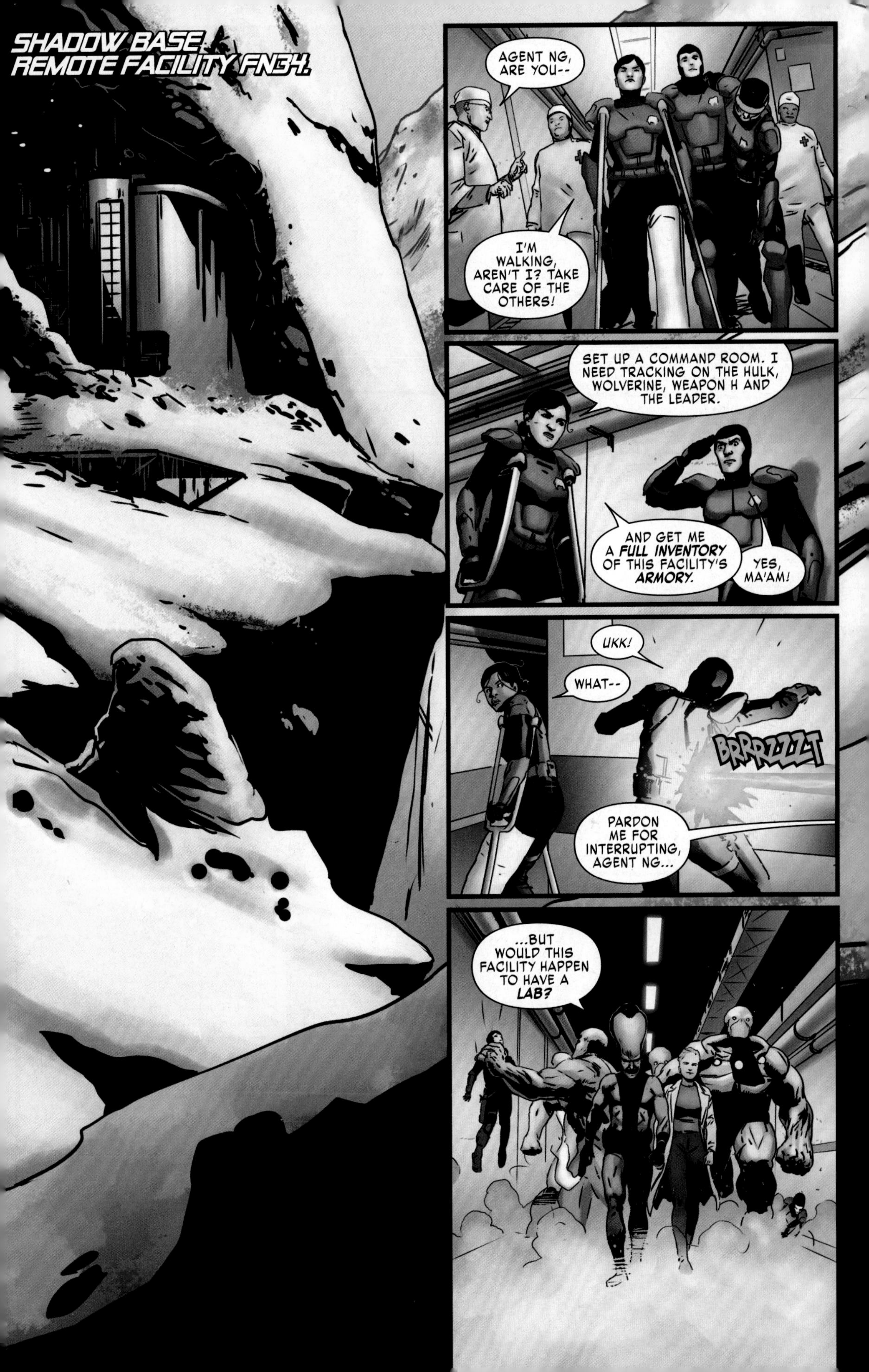
SHADOW BASE REMOTE FACILITY FN34.
AGENT NG, ARE YOU--
I'M WALKING, AREN'T I? TAKE CARE OF THE OTHERS!
SET UP A COMMAND ROOM. I NEED TRACKING ON THE HULK, WOLVERINE, WEAPON H AND THE LEADER.
AND GET ME A FULL INVENTORY OF THIS FACILITY'S ARMORY.
YES, MA'AM!
UKK!
WHAT--
BRRRZZZT
PARDON ME FOR INTERRUPTING, AGENT NG...
...BUT WOULD THIS FACILITY HAPPEN TO HAVE A LAB?

JUST LOVELY. DON'T YOU THINK, DR. ALBA?

PERFECT.

NOW LOOK...

I CHOSE *CLAYTON CORTEZ* FOR THE WEAPON H PROGRAM BECAUSE OF HIS *DISCIPLINE.*

HE'S *MILITARY.* THE "BEST OF THE BEST," AS THEY SAY.

HE COULD CONTROL HIS EMOTIONS UNDER THE MOST TRYING CIRCUMSTANCES...

...SOMETHING THE *ORIGINAL* HULK AND WOLVERINE SEEM TO BE ABSOLUTELY *INCAPABLE* OF.

WHICH MEANT *CORTEZ* COULD *CONTROL* THE HULK'S AND WOLVERINE'S *POWER...*

...AND BECOME THE *GREATEST LIVING WEAPON* EVER CREATED.

BUT THAT ALSO MEANT HE *COULD...*

...AND *DID...*

...ESCAPE *MY* CONTROL.

SO ANNOYING.

IT WAS.

BUT NOW...

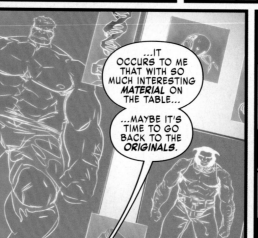

...IT OCCURS TO ME THAT WITH SO MUCH INTERESTING *MATERIAL* ON THE TABLE...

...MAYBE IT'S TIME TO GO BACK TO THE *ORIGINALS.*

WAIT! YOU JUST SAID THE HULK AND WOLVERINE ARE COMPLETELY *UNCONTROLLABLE!*

IF YOU...IF YOU DO WHAT I THINK YOU'RE PLANNING TO DO--

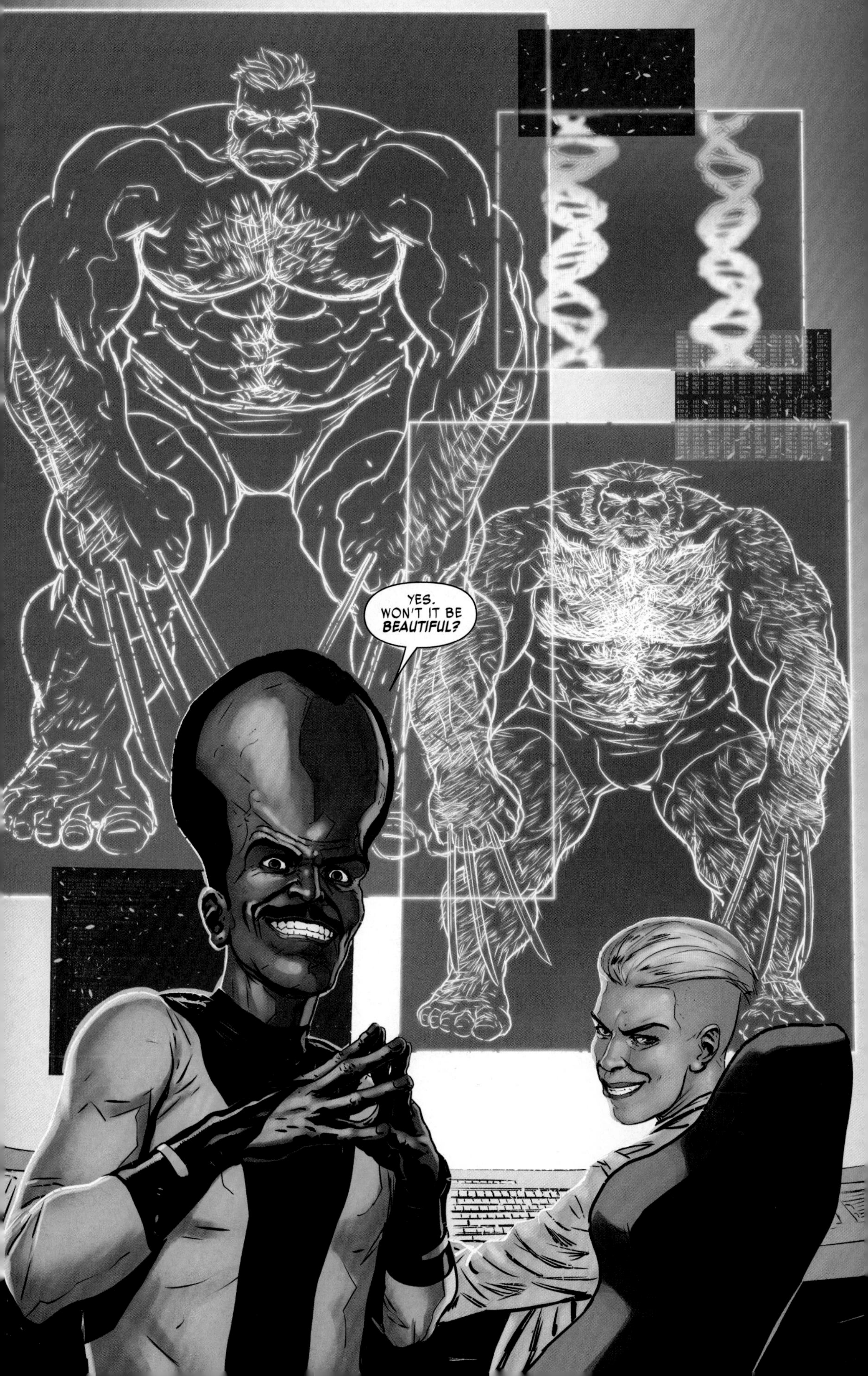
YES. WON'T IT BE BEAUTIFUL?

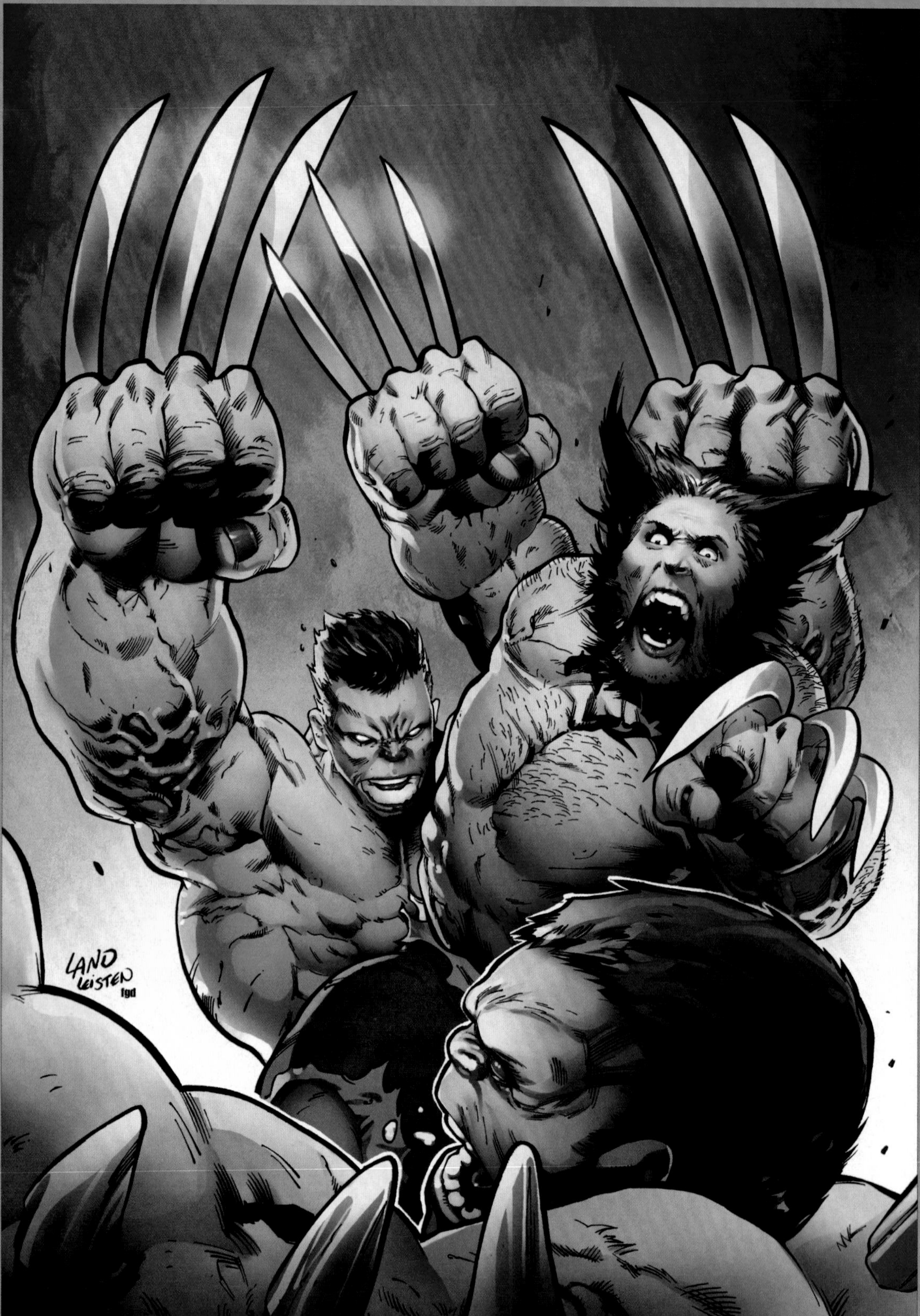
LANO
LEISTEN
fgd

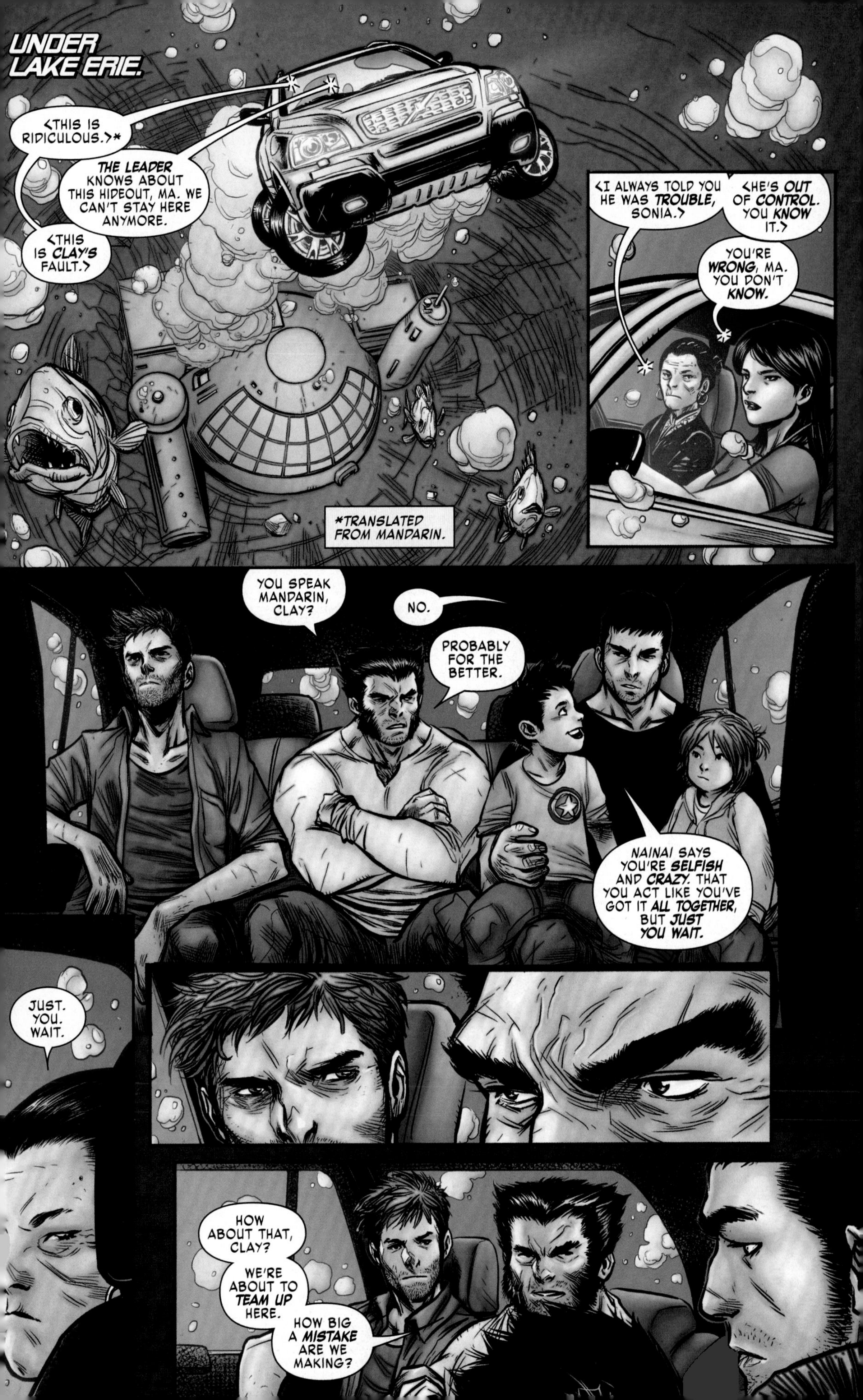
UNDER LAKE ERIE.
<THIS IS RIDICULOUS.>*
THE LEADER KNOWS ABOUT THIS HIDEOUT, MA. WE CAN'T STAY HERE ANYMORE.
<THIS IS CLAY'S FAULT.>
*TRANSLATED FROM MANDARIN.
<I ALWAYS TOLD YOU HE WAS TROUBLE, SONIA.>
<HE'S OUT OF CONTROL. YOU KNOW IT.>
YOU'RE WRONG, MA. YOU DON'T KNOW.
YOU SPEAK MANDARIN, CLAY?
NO.
PROBABLY FOR THE BETTER.
NAINAI SAYS YOU'RE SELFISH AND CRAZY. THAT YOU ACT LIKE YOU'VE GOT IT ALL TOGETHER, BUT JUST YOU WAIT.
JUST. YOU. WAIT.
HOW ABOUT THAT, CLAY?
WE'RE ABOUT TO TEAM UP HERE.
HOW BIG A MISTAKE ARE WE MAKING?

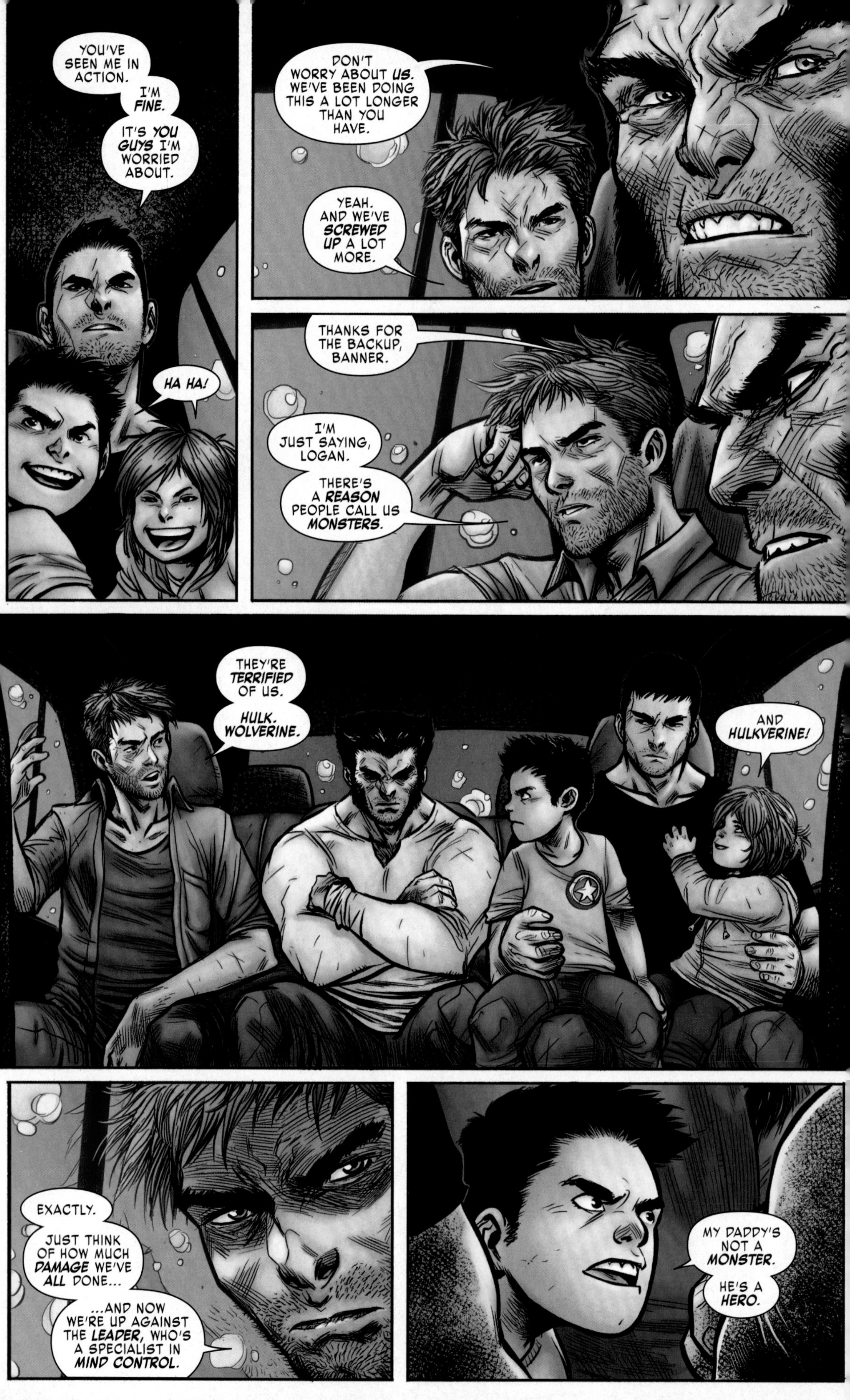
YOU'VE SEEN ME IN ACTION.
I'M FINE.
IT'S YOU GUYS I'M WORRIED ABOUT.
HA HA!
DON'T WORRY ABOUT US. WE'VE BEEN DOING THIS A LOT LONGER THAN YOU HAVE.
YEAH. AND WE'VE SCREWED UP A LOT MORE.
THANKS FOR THE BACKUP, BANNER.
I'M JUST SAYING, LOGAN.
THERE'S A REASON PEOPLE CALL US MONSTERS.
THEY'RE TERRIFIED OF US.
HULK. WOLVERINE.
AND HULKVERINE!
EXACTLY.
JUST THINK OF HOW MUCH DAMAGE WE'VE ALL DONE...
...AND NOW WE'RE UP AGAINST THE LEADER, WHO'S A SPECIALIST IN MIND CONTROL.
MY DADDY'S NOT A MONSTER.
HE'S A HERO.

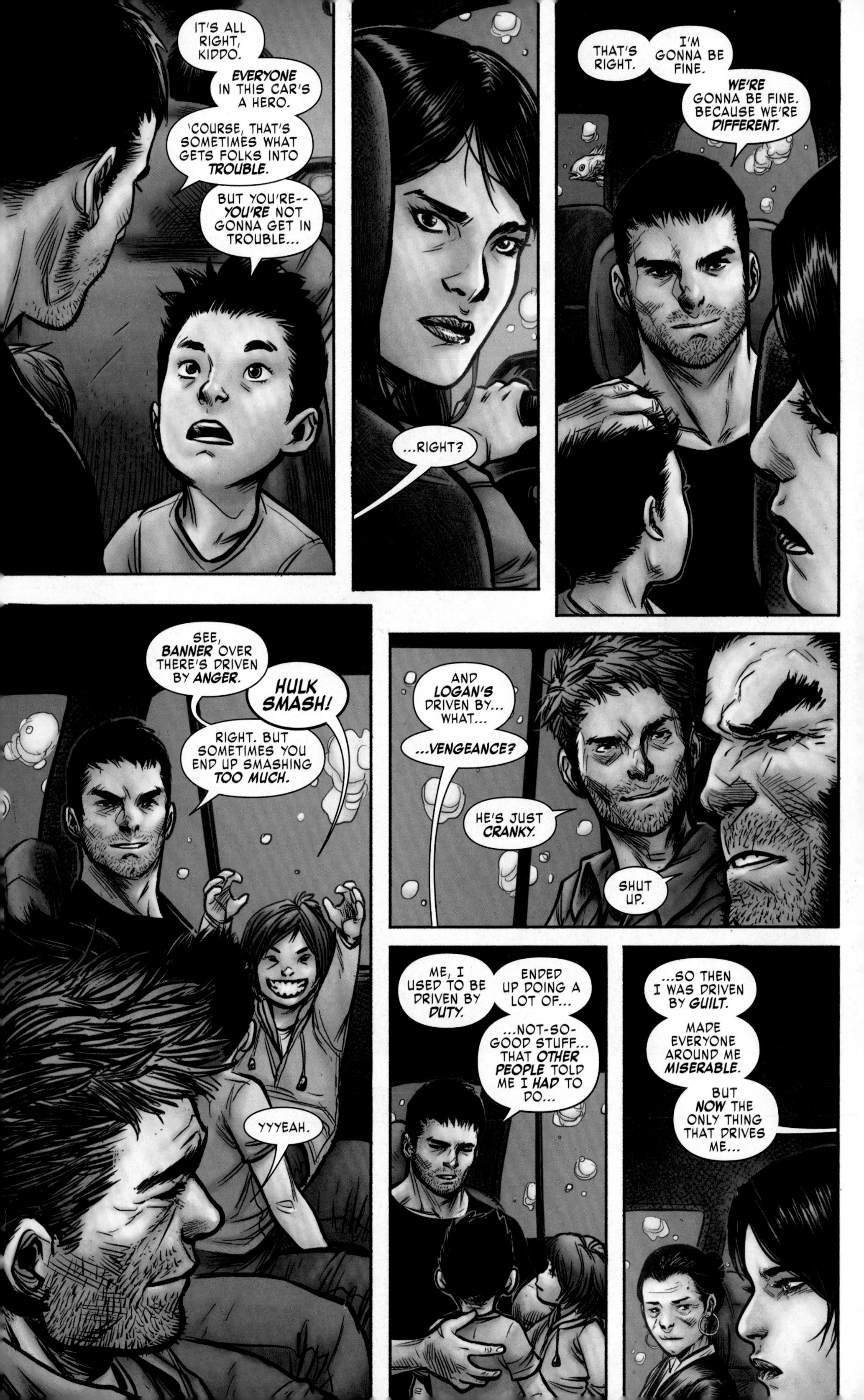

IT'S ALL RIGHT, KIDDO.
EVERYONE IN THIS CAR'S A HERO.
'COURSE, THAT'S SOMETIMES WHAT GETS FOLKS INTO TROUBLE.
BUT YOU'RE-- YOU'RE NOT GONNA GET IN TROUBLE...
...RIGHT?
THAT'S RIGHT.
I'M GONNA BE FINE.
WE'RE GONNA BE FINE. BECAUSE WE'RE DIFFERENT.
SEE, BANNER OVER THERE'S DRIVEN BY ANGER.
HULK SMASH!
RIGHT. BUT SOMETIMES YOU END UP SMASHING TOO MUCH.
YYYEAH.
AND LOGAN'S DRIVEN BY... WHAT...
...VENGEANCE?
HE'S JUST CRANKY.
SHUT UP.
ME, I USED TO BE DRIVEN BY DUTY.
ENDED UP DOING A LOT OF...
...NOT-SO-GOOD STUFF... THAT OTHER PEOPLE TOLD ME I HAD TO DO...
...SO THEN I WAS DRIVEN BY GUILT.
MADE EVERYONE AROUND ME MISERABLE.
BUT NOW THE ONLY THING THAT DRIVES ME...

...IS
LOVE.

DADDY.

HMPH.

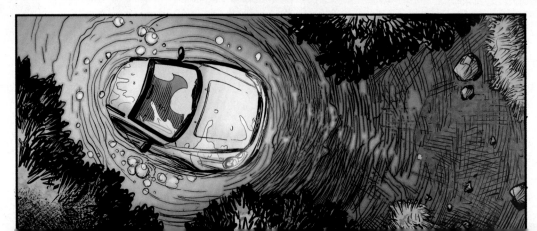

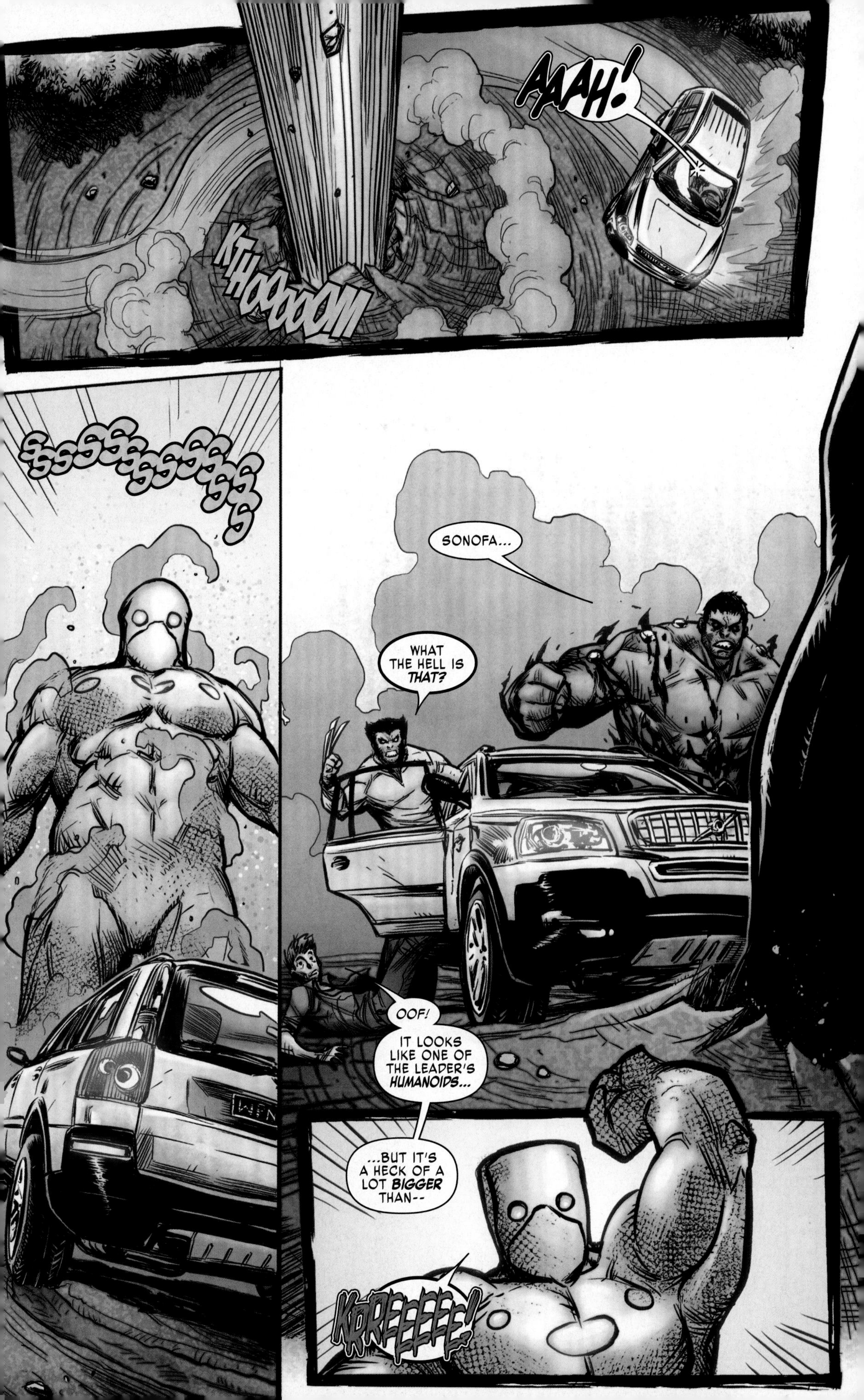
KTHOOOOOOM
AAAH!
SSSSSSSSSSSS
SONOFA...
WHAT THE HELL IS *THAT?*
OOF!
IT LOOKS LIKE ONE OF THE LEADER'S *HUMANOIDS*...
...BUT IT'S A HECK OF A LOT *BIGGER* THAN--
KRREEEEEE!

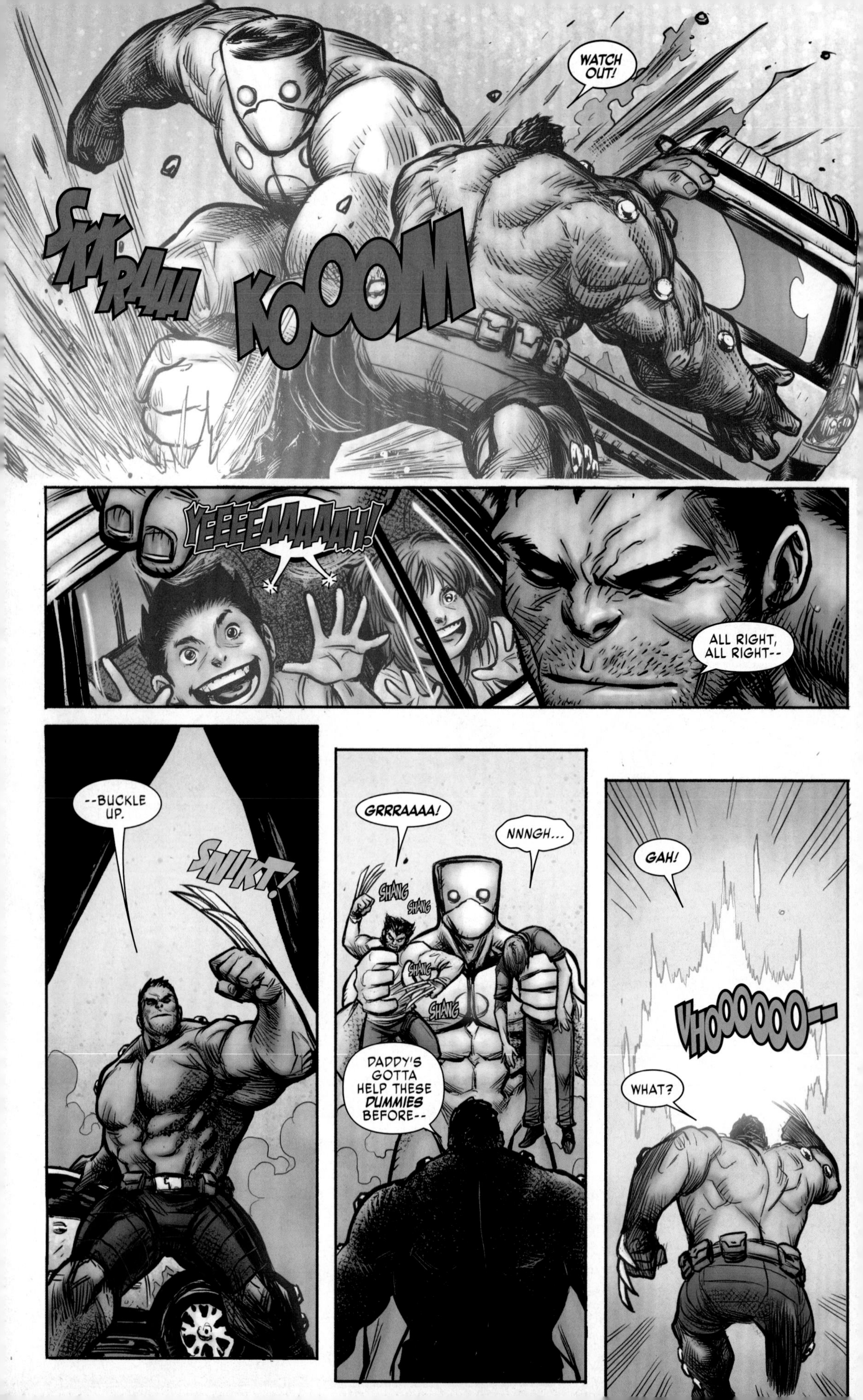
WATCH OUT!
SKKRAAAA
KOOOOM
YEEEEAAAAAAH!
ALL RIGHT, ALL RIGHT--
--BUCKLE UP.
SNIKT!
GRRRAAAA!
NNNGH...
SHANG
SHANG
SHANG
SHANG
DADDY'S GOTTA HELP THESE DUMMIES BEFORE--
GAH!
VHOOOOOO--
WHAT?

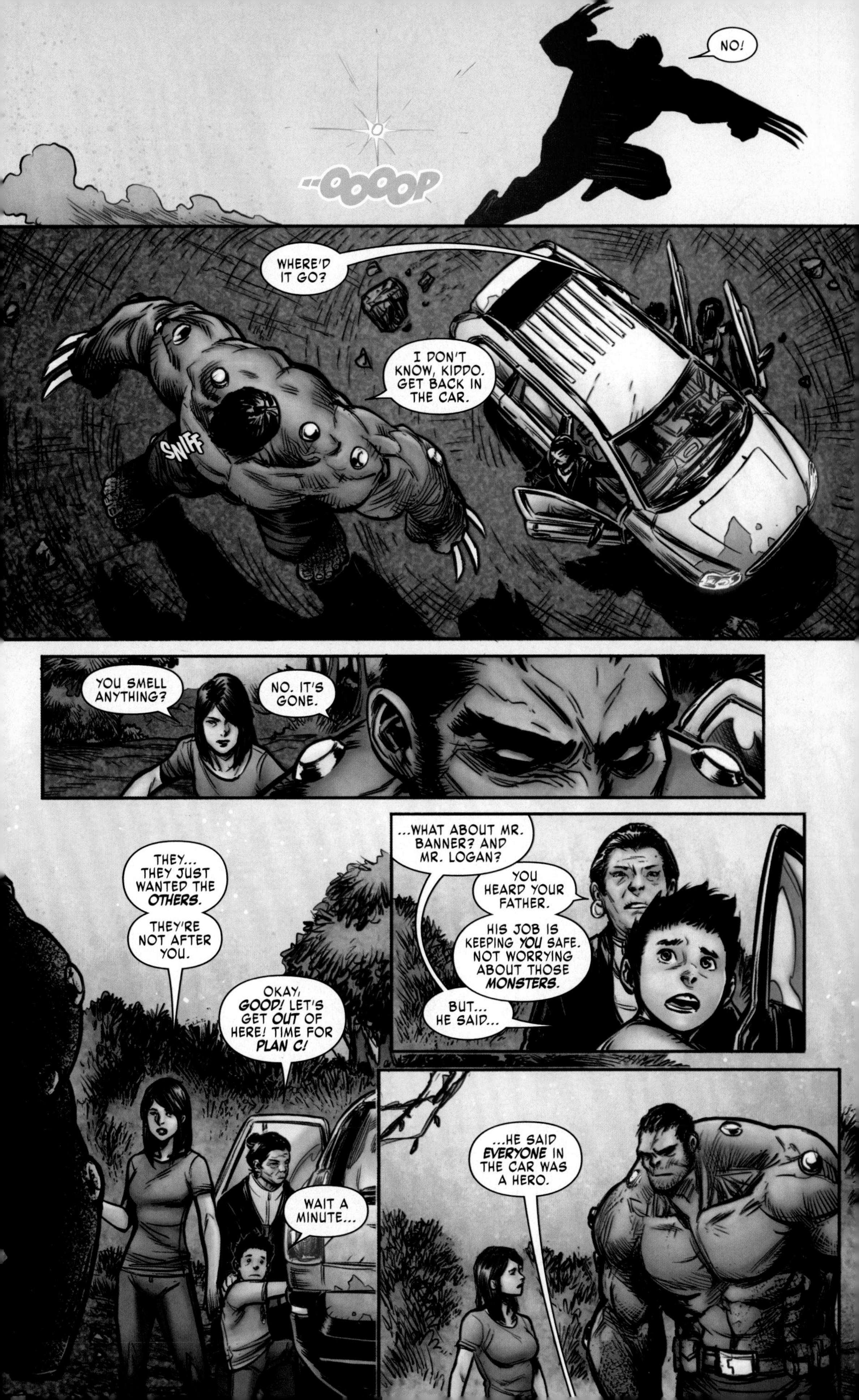
NO!
-OOOOP
WHERE'D IT GO?
I DON'T KNOW, KIDDO. GET BACK IN THE CAR.
SNIFF
YOU SMELL ANYTHING?
NO. IT'S GONE.
THEY... THEY JUST WANTED THE OTHERS.
THEY'RE NOT AFTER YOU.
OKAY, GOOD! LET'S GET OUT OF HERE! TIME FOR PLAN C!
...WHAT ABOUT MR. BANNER? AND MR. LOGAN?
YOU HEARD YOUR FATHER.
HIS JOB IS KEEPING YOU SAFE. NOT WORRYING ABOUT THOSE MONSTERS.
BUT... HE SAID...
WAIT A MINUTE...
...HE SAID EVERYONE IN THE CAR WAS A HERO.

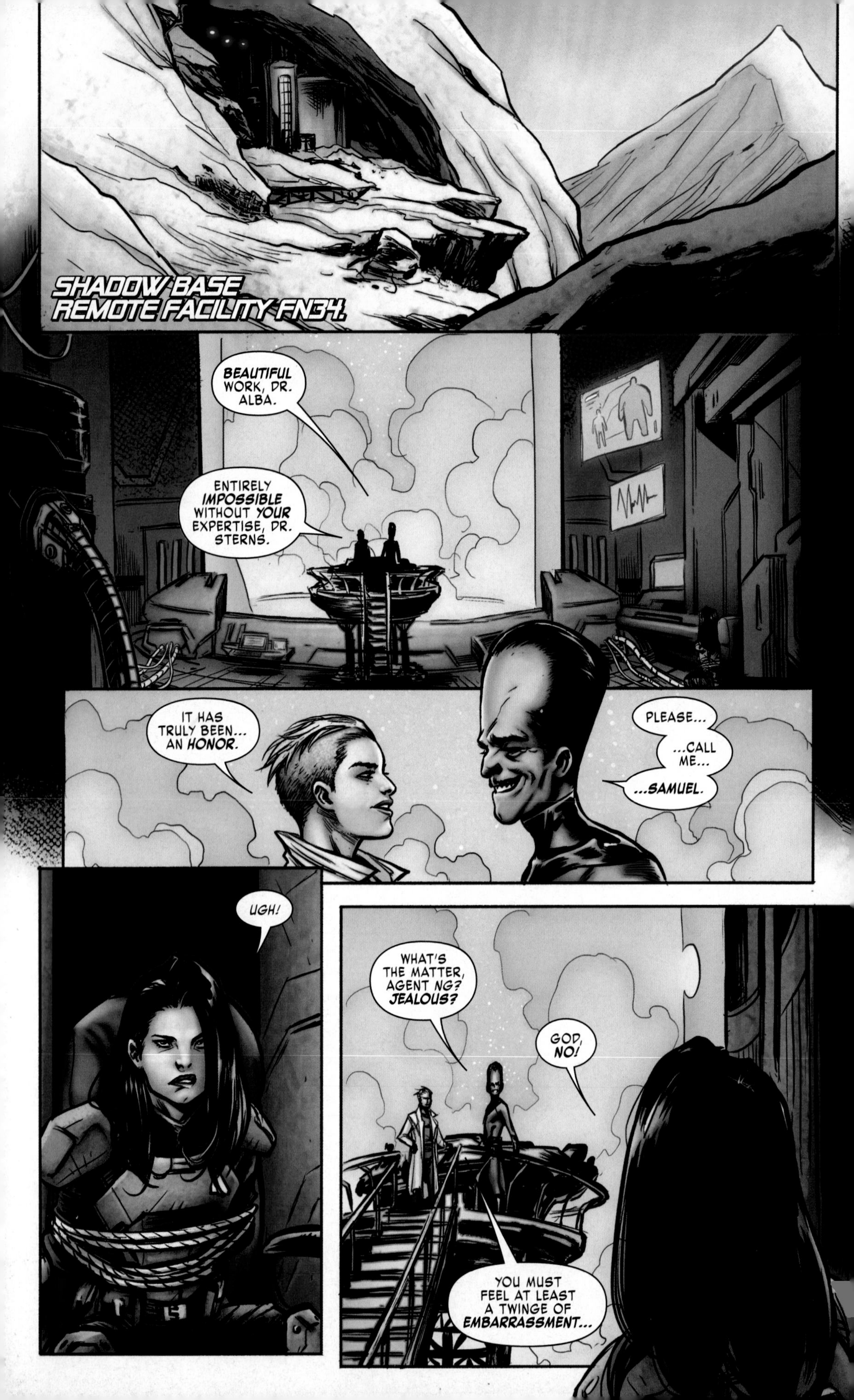
SHADOW BASE
REMOTE FACILITY FN34.
BEAUTIFUL WORK, DR. ALBA.
ENTIRELY IMPOSSIBLE WITHOUT YOUR EXPERTISE, DR. STERNS.
IT HAS TRULY BEEN... AN HONOR.
PLEASE...
...CALL ME...
...SAMUEL.
UGH!
WHAT'S THE MATTER, AGENT NG? JEALOUS?
GOD, NO!
YOU MUST FEEL AT LEAST A TWINGE OF EMBARRASSMENT...

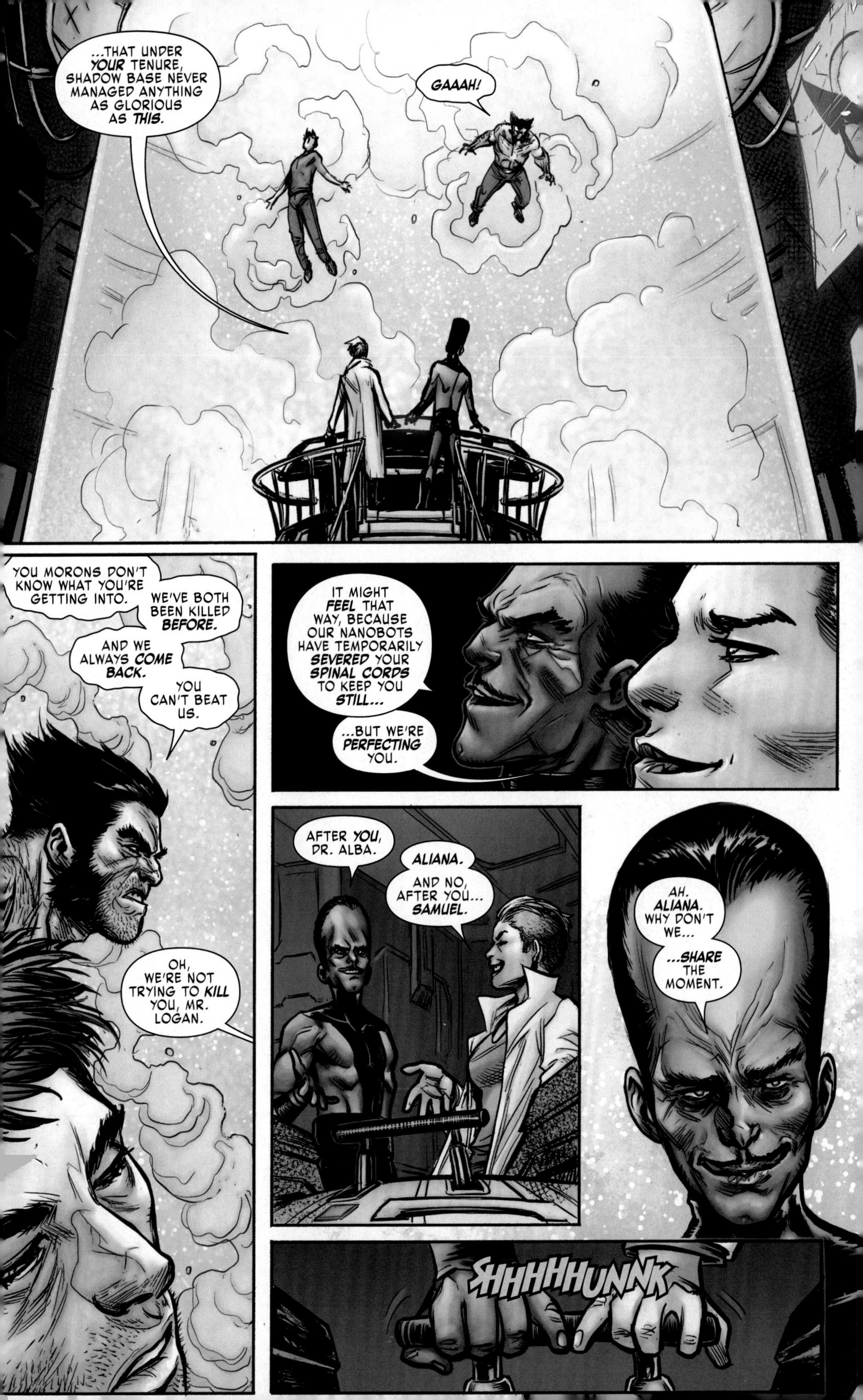
...THAT UNDER YOUR TENURE, SHADOW BASE NEVER MANAGED ANYTHING AS GLORIOUS AS THIS.
GAAAH!
YOU MORONS DON'T KNOW WHAT YOU'RE GETTING INTO.
WE'VE BOTH BEEN KILLED BEFORE.
AND WE ALWAYS COME BACK.
YOU CAN'T BEAT US.
OH, WE'RE NOT TRYING TO KILL YOU, MR. LOGAN.
IT MIGHT FEEL THAT WAY, BECAUSE OUR NANOBOTS HAVE TEMPORARILY SEVERED YOUR SPINAL CORDS TO KEEP YOU STILL...
...BUT WE'RE PERFECTING YOU.
AFTER YOU, DR. ALBA.
ALIANA.
AND NO, AFTER YOU... SAMUEL.
AH. ALIANA. WHY DON'T WE...
...SHARE THE MOMENT.
SHHHHHUNNK

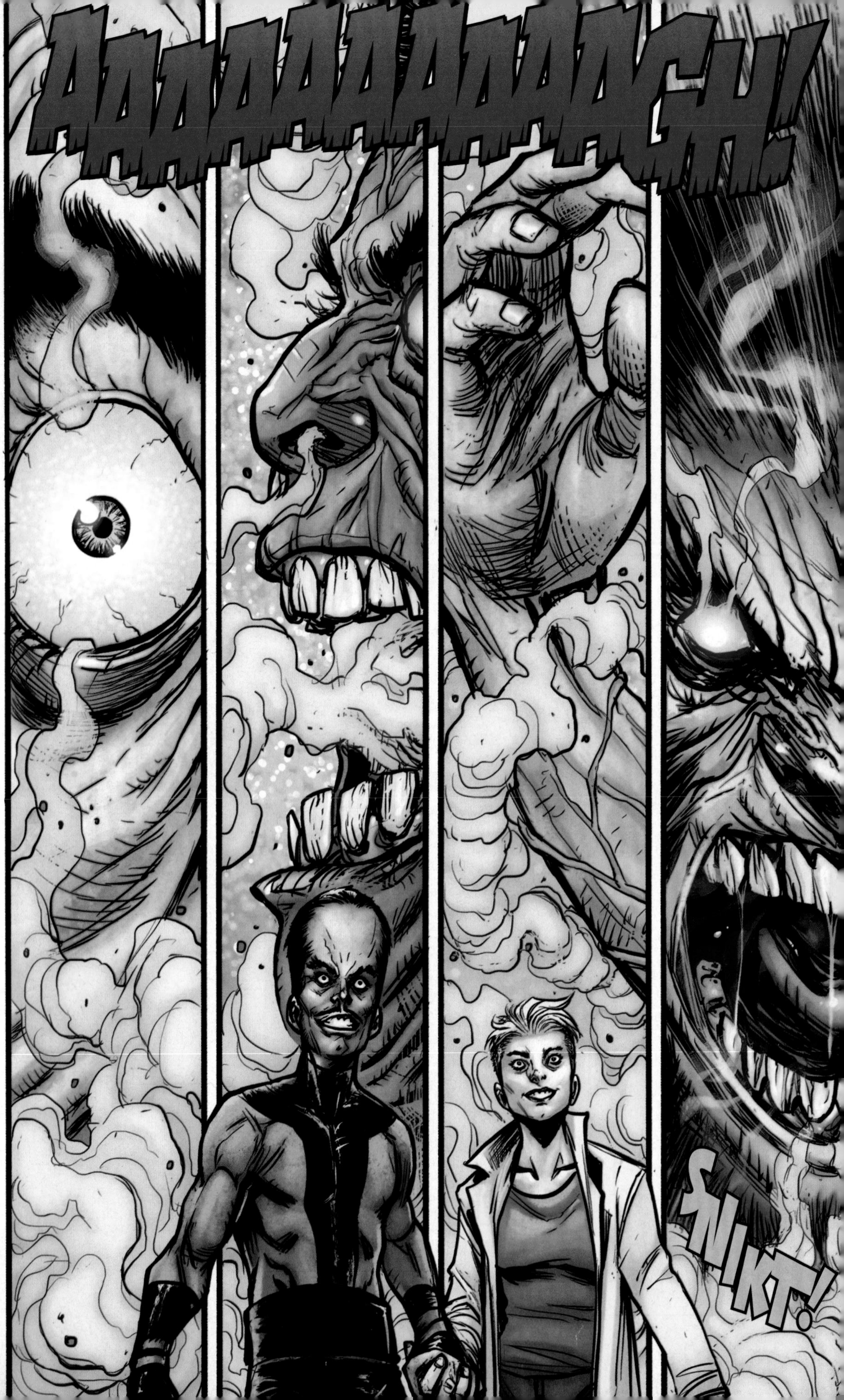
AAAAAAAAAAAGH!
SNIKT!

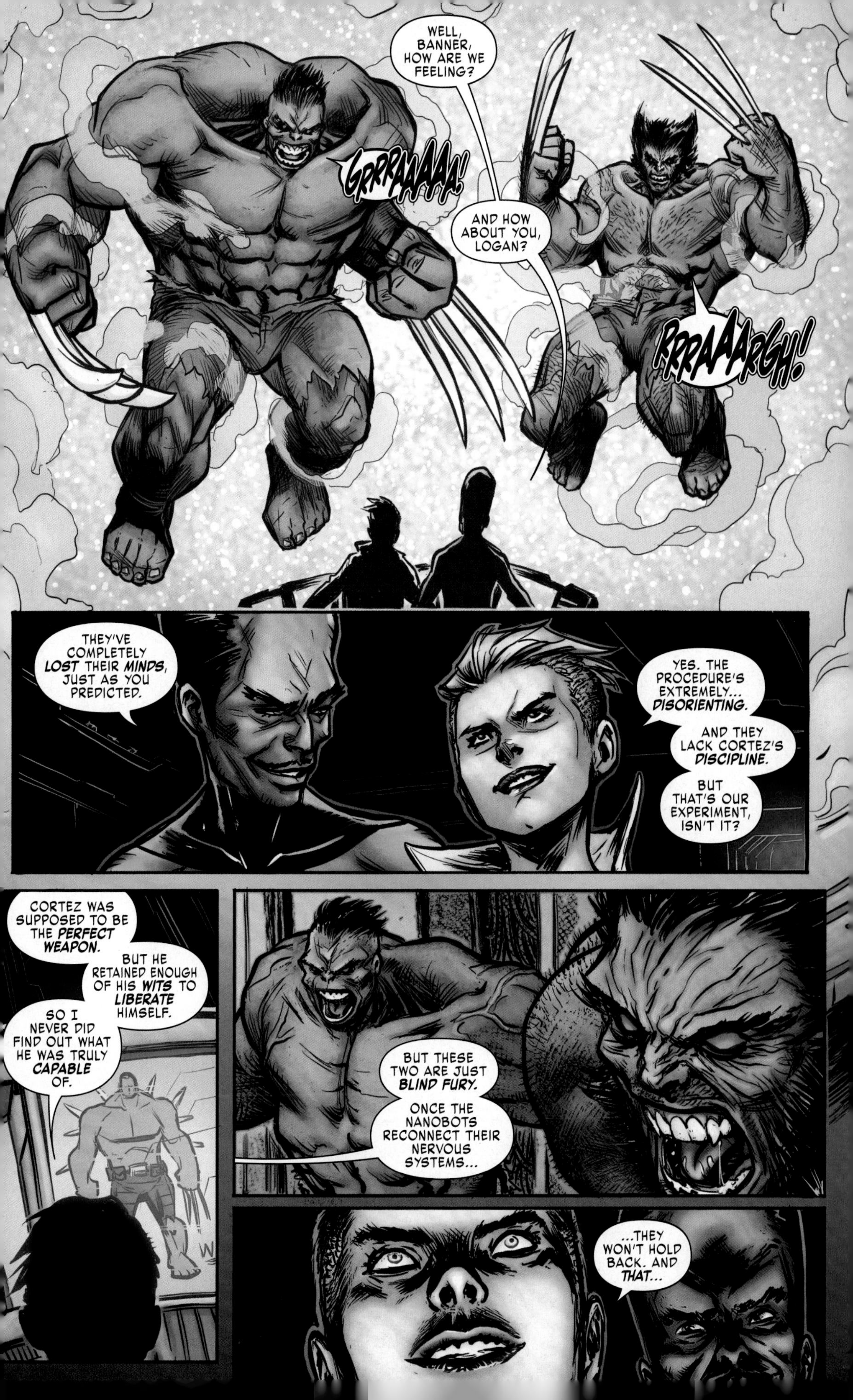
WELL, BANNER, HOW ARE WE FEELING?
GRRRAAAAA!
AND HOW ABOUT YOU, LOGAN?
RRRAAARGH!
THEY'VE COMPLETELY LOST THEIR MINDS, JUST AS YOU PREDICTED.
YES. THE PROCEDURE'S EXTREMELY... DISORIENTING.
AND THEY LACK CORTEZ'S DISCIPLINE.
BUT THAT'S OUR EXPERIMENT, ISN'T IT?
CORTEZ WAS SUPPOSED TO BE THE PERFECT WEAPON.
BUT HE RETAINED ENOUGH OF HIS WITS TO LIBERATE HIMSELF.
SO I NEVER DID FIND OUT WHAT HE WAS TRULY CAPABLE OF.
BUT THESE TWO ARE JUST BLIND FURY.
ONCE THE NANOBOTS RECONNECT THEIR NERVOUS SYSTEMS...
...THEY WON'T HOLD BACK. AND THAT...

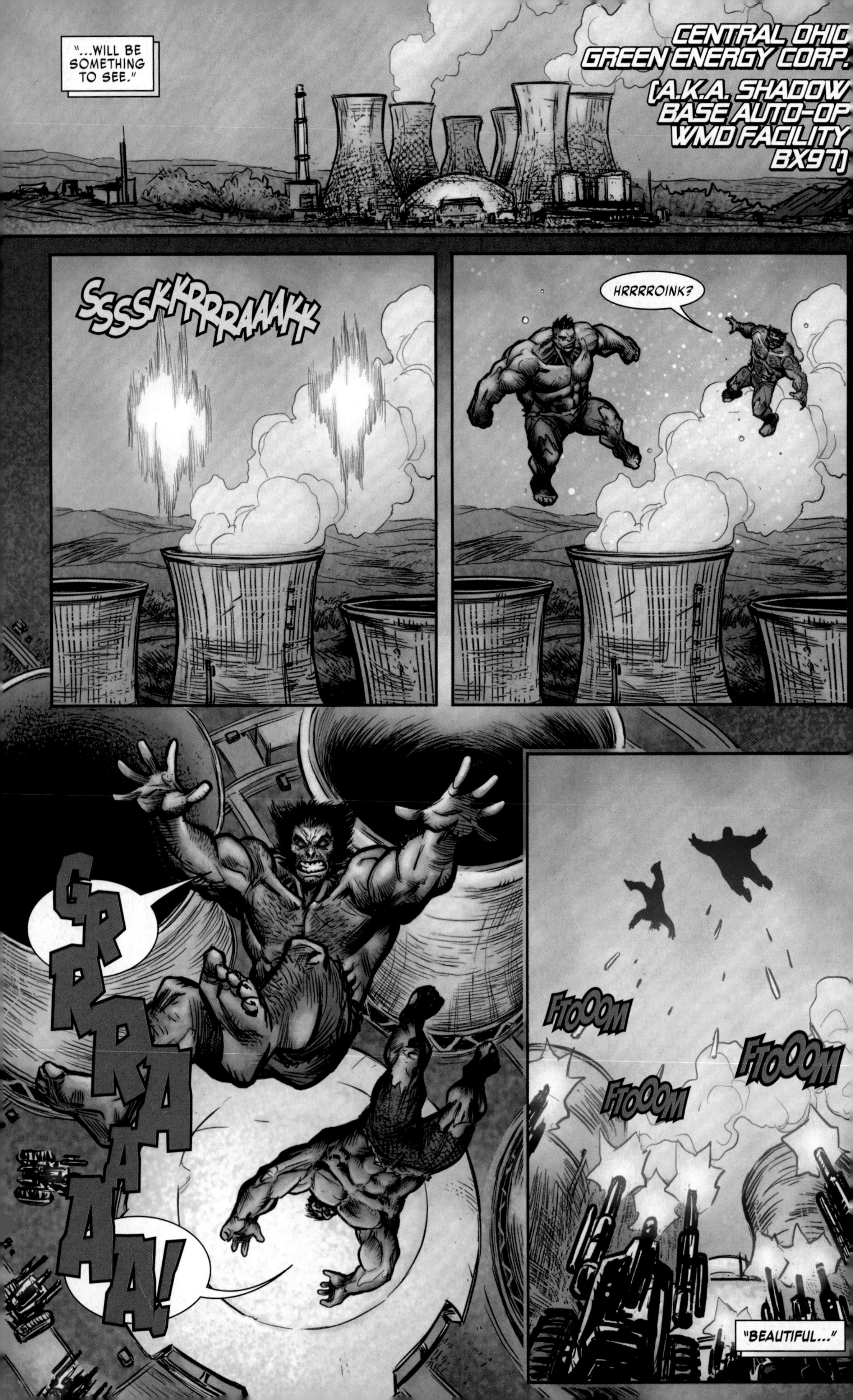
"...WILL BE SOMETHING TO SEE."
CENTRAL OHIO GREEN ENERGY CORP.
(A.K.A. SHADOW BASE AUTO-OP WMD FACILITY BX97)
SSSSKKRRRRAAAKK
HRRRROINK?
GRRRRAAAAA!
FTOOOM
FTOOOM
FTOOOM
"BEAUTIFUL..."

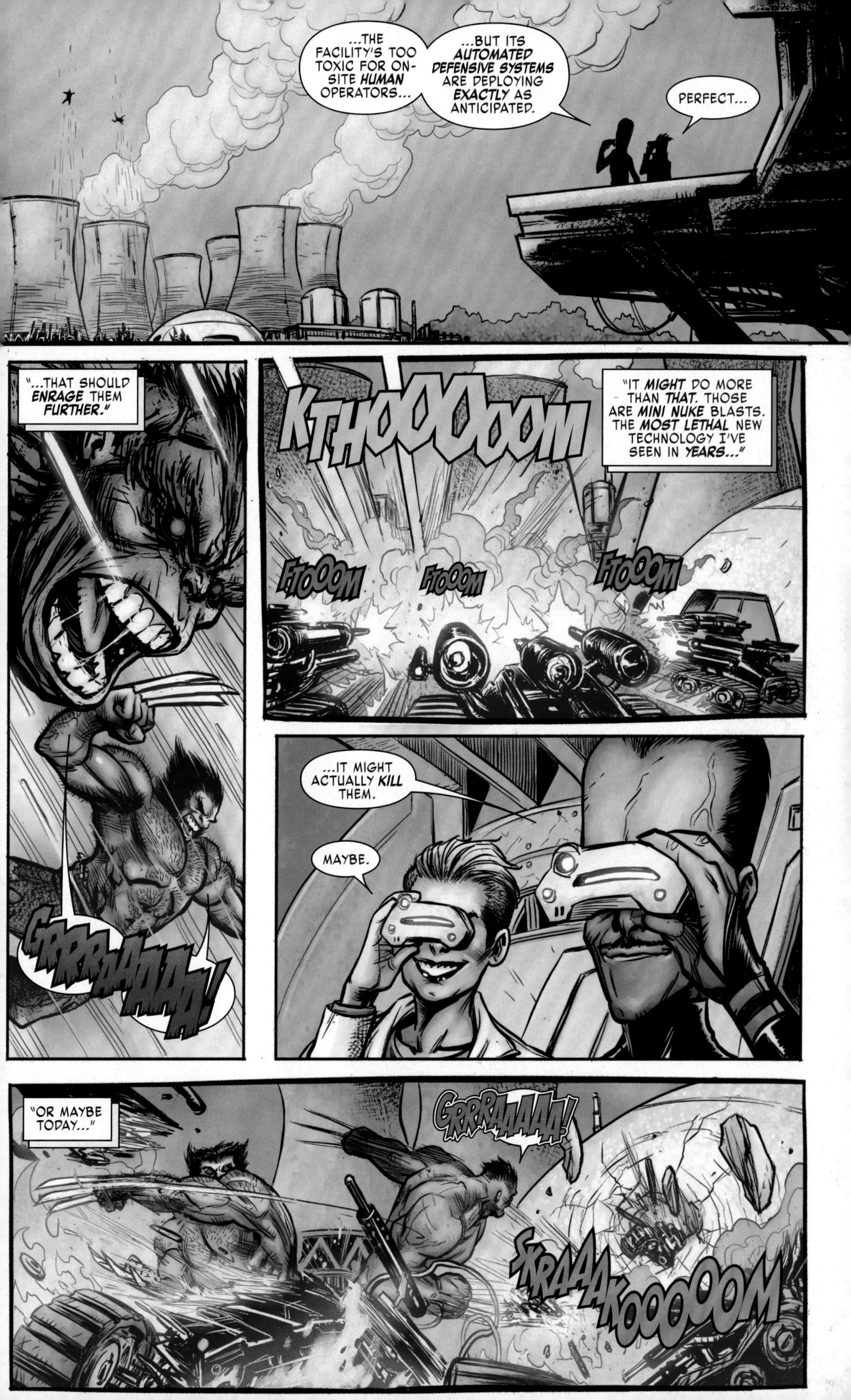
...THE FACILITY'S TOO TOXIC FOR ON-SITE HUMAN OPERATORS...
...BUT ITS AUTOMATED DEFENSIVE SYSTEMS ARE DEPLOYING EXACTLY AS ANTICIPATED.
PERFECT...
"...THAT SHOULD ENRAGE THEM FURTHER."
GRRRAAAAAAA!
KTHOOOOOOM
"IT MIGHT DO MORE THAN THAT. THOSE ARE MINI NUKE BLASTS. THE MOST LETHAL NEW TECHNOLOGY I'VE SEEN IN YEARS..."
FTOOOM
FTOOOM
FTOOOM
...IT MIGHT ACTUALLY KILL THEM.
MAYBE.
"OR MAYBE TODAY..."
GRRRAAAAAA!
SKRAAAKOOOOOM

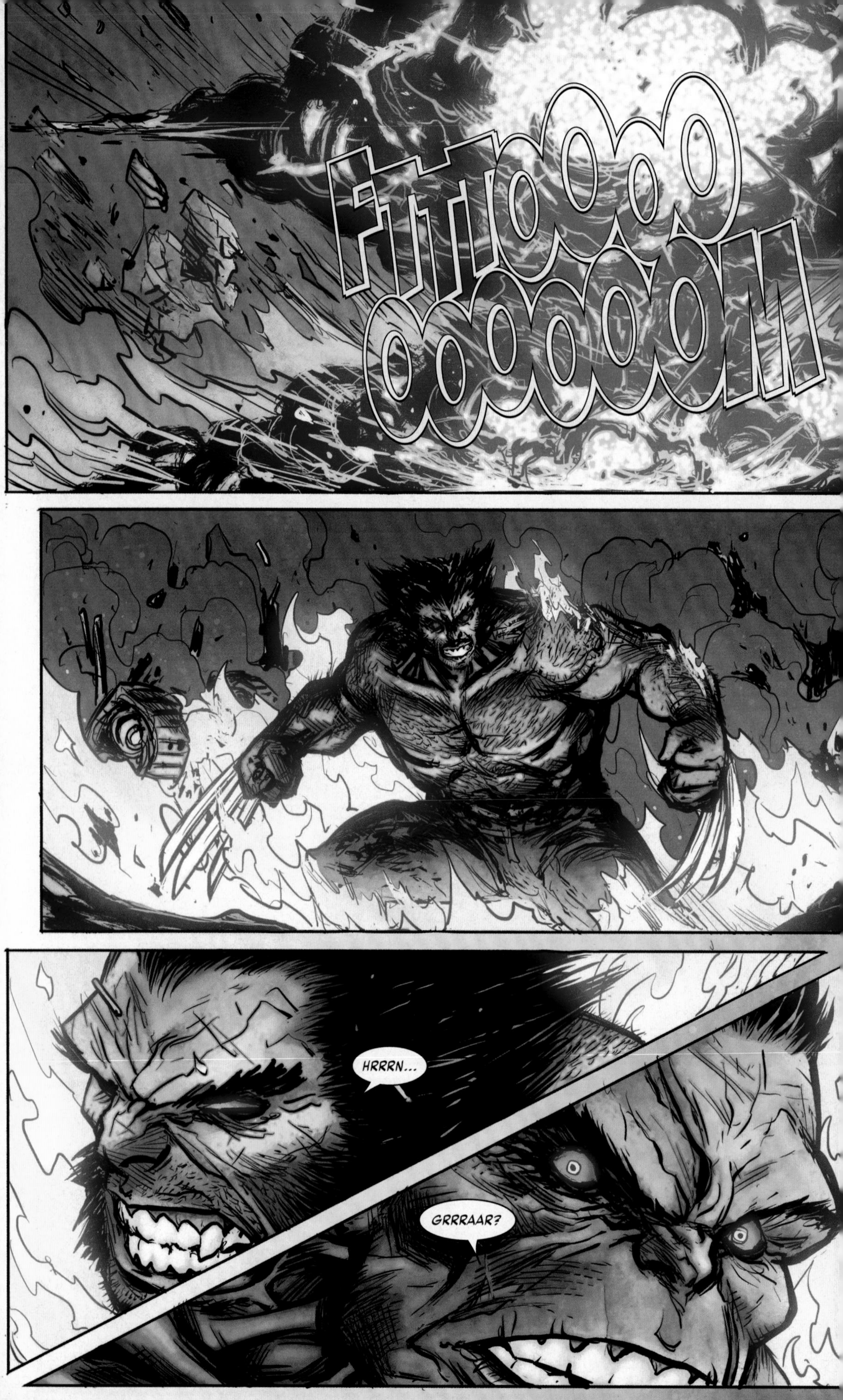
FTTTOOOOOOOOOOOOM
HRRRN...
GRRRAAR?

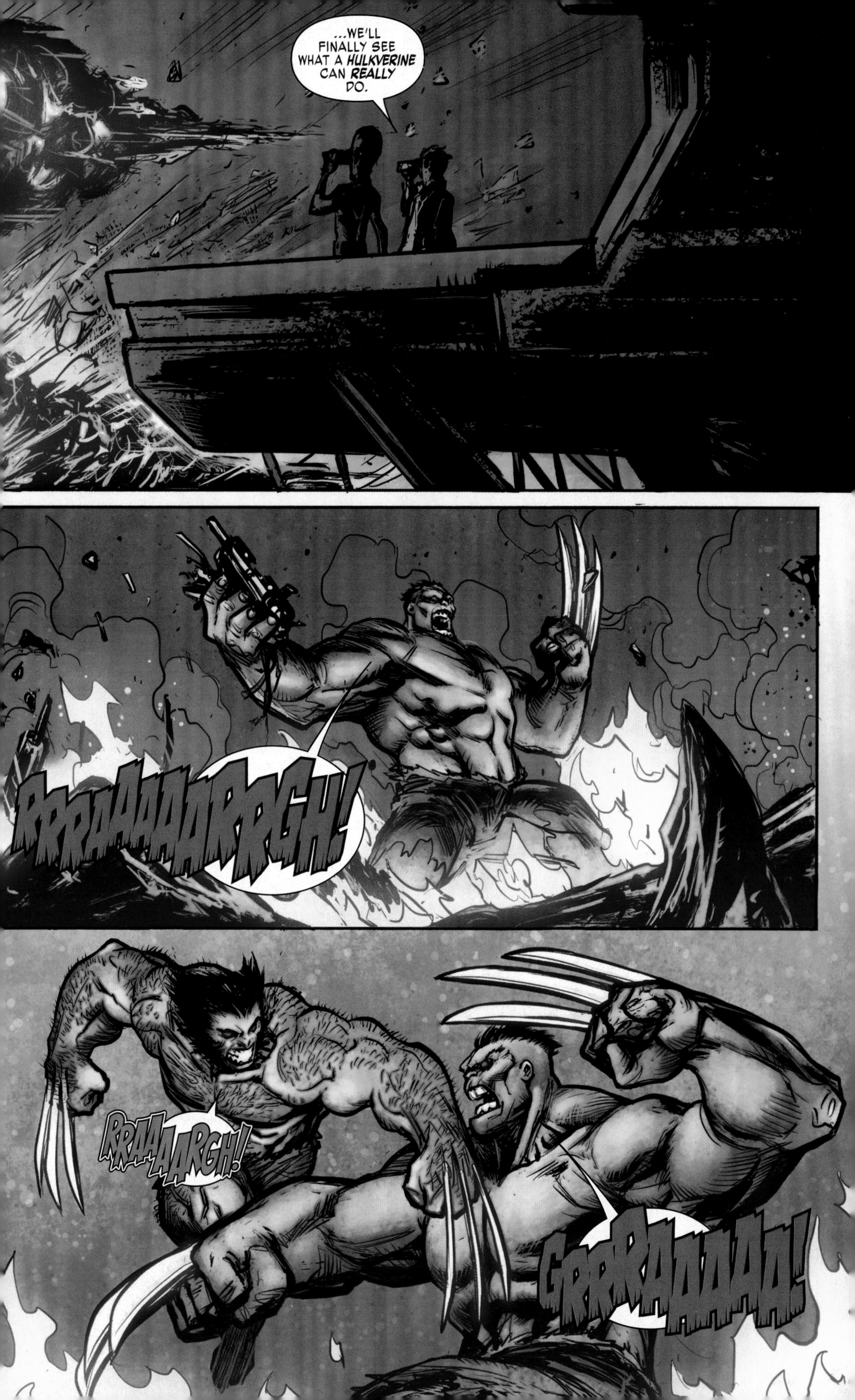
...WE'LL FINALLY SEE WHAT A HULKVERINE CAN REALLY DO.
RRRAAAARRGH!
RRAAAARGH!
GRRRAAAAA!

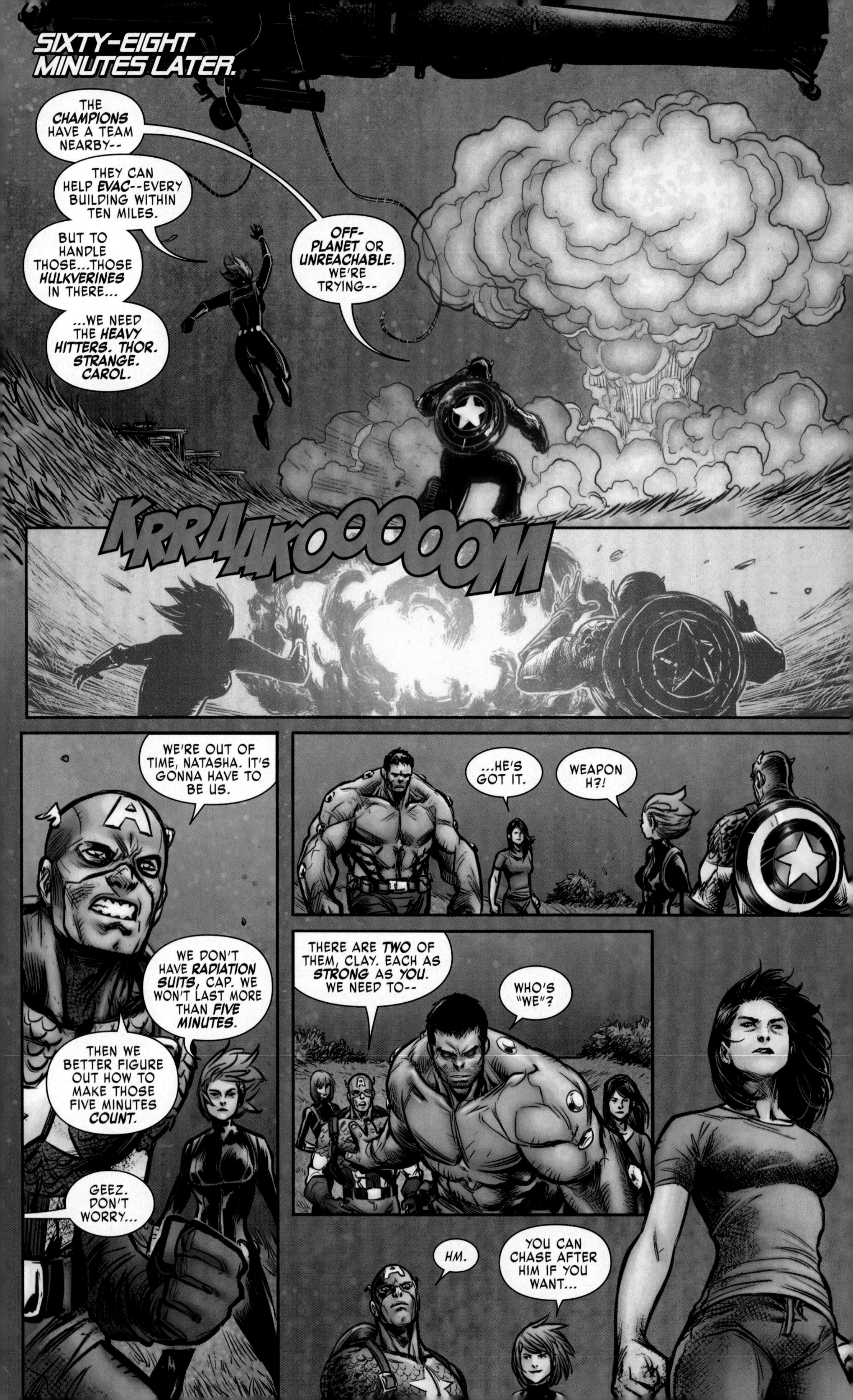
SIXTY-EIGHT MINUTES LATER.
THE CHAMPIONS HAVE A TEAM NEARBY--
THEY CAN HELP EVAC--EVERY BUILDING WITHIN TEN MILES.
BUT TO HANDLE THOSE...THOSE HULKVERINES IN THERE...
...WE NEED THE HEAVY HITTERS. THOR. STRANGE. CAROL.
OFF-PLANET OR UNREACHABLE. WE'RE TRYING--
KRRAAKOOOOOOM
WE'RE OUT OF TIME, NATASHA. IT'S GONNA HAVE TO BE US.
WE DON'T HAVE RADIATION SUITS, CAP. WE WON'T LAST MORE THAN FIVE MINUTES.
THEN WE BETTER FIGURE OUT HOW TO MAKE THOSE FIVE MINUTES COUNT.
GEEZ. DON'T WORRY...
...HE'S GOT IT.
WEAPON H?!
THERE ARE TWO OF THEM, CLAY. EACH AS STRONG AS YOU. WE NEED TO--
WHO'S "WE"?
HM.
YOU CAN CHASE AFTER HIM IF YOU WANT...

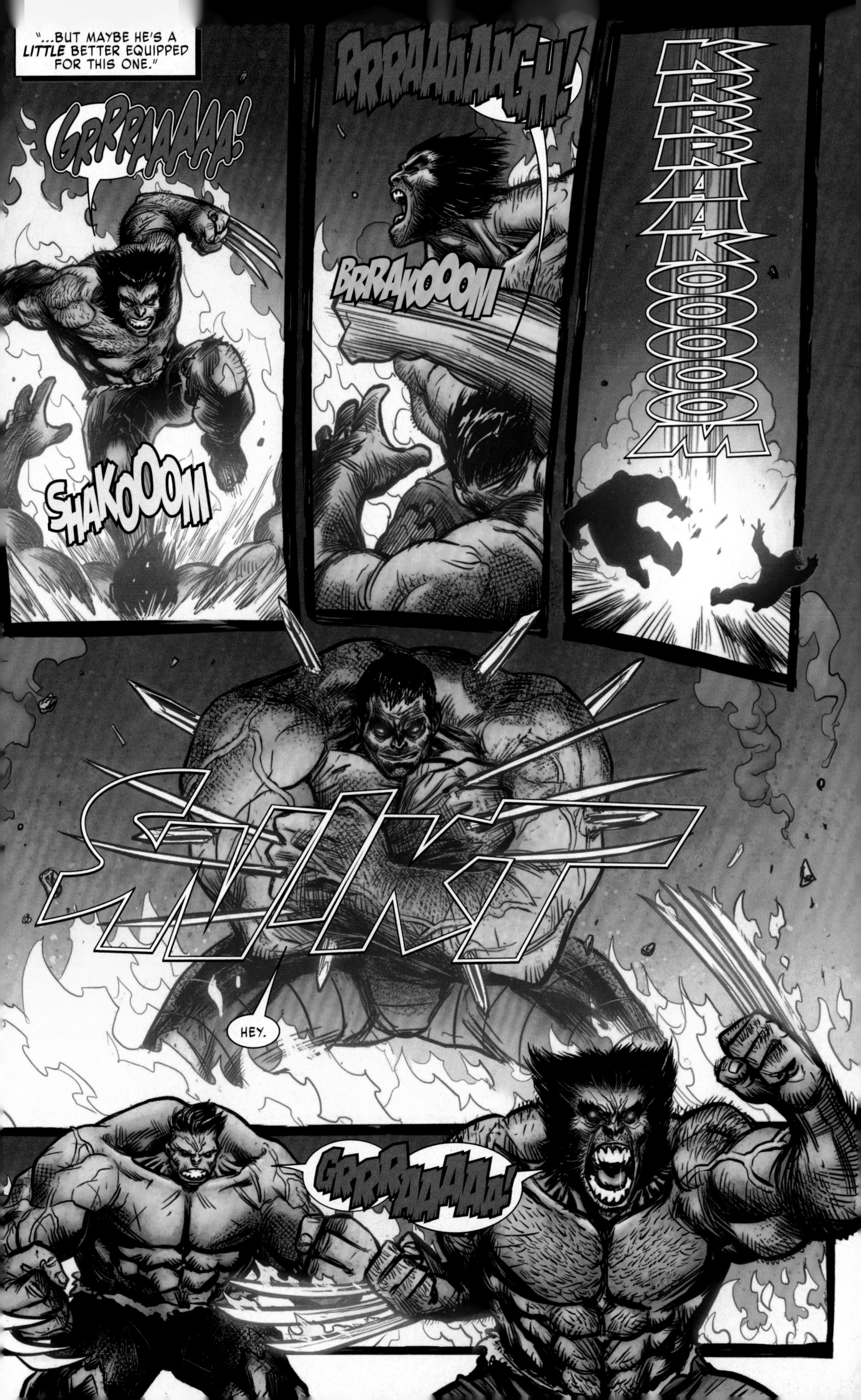
"...BUT MAYBE HE'S A *LITTLE* BETTER EQUIPPED FOR THIS ONE."
GRRRAAAAA!
SHAKOOOM
RRRAAAAAGH!
BRRRAKOOOM
KRRRAKOOOOOOM
SNIKT
HEY.
GRRRAAAAA!

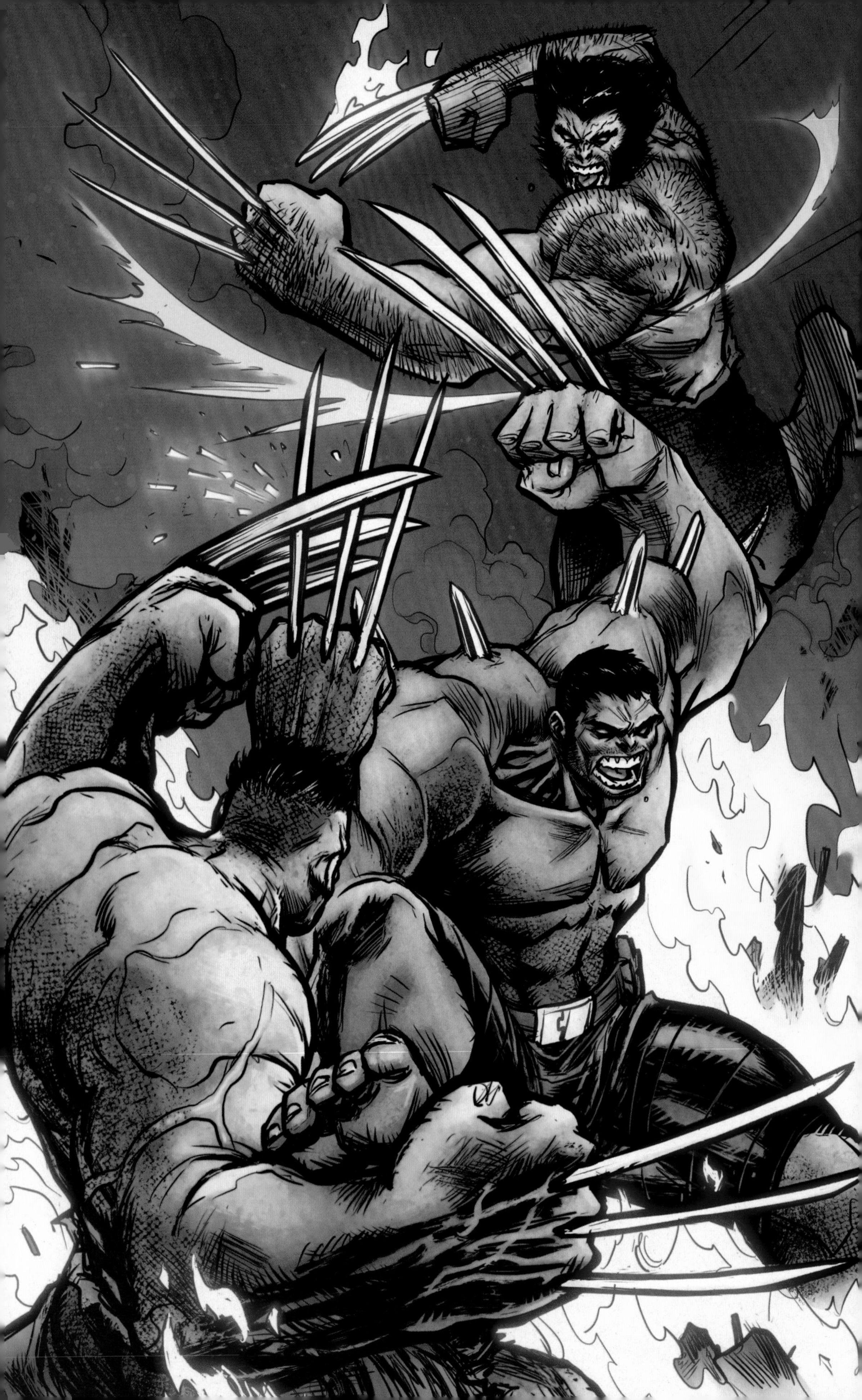

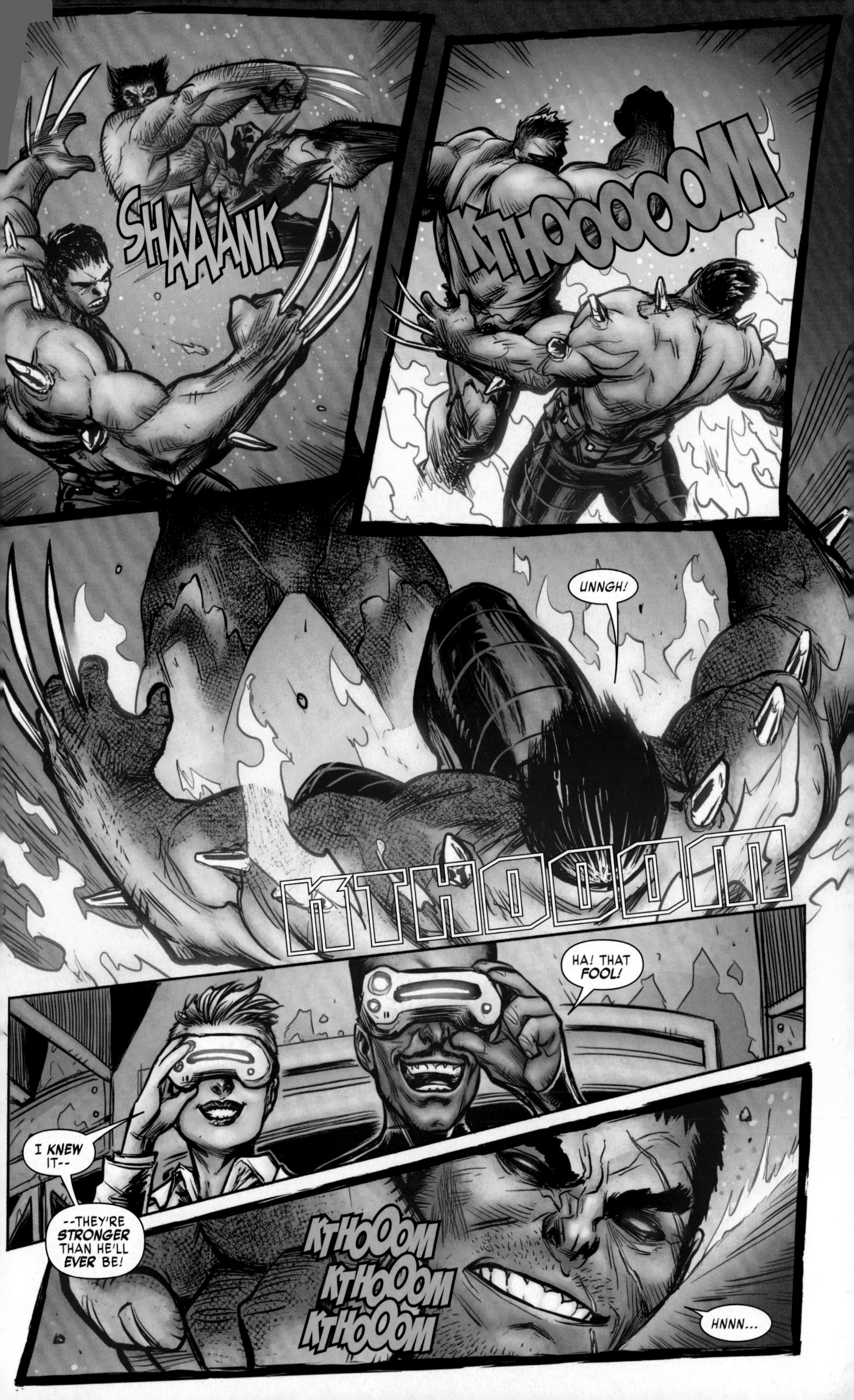
SHAAANK
KTHOOOOOM
UNNGH!
KTHOOOM
HA! THAT FOOL!
I KNEW IT--
--THEY'RE STRONGER THAN HE'LL EVER BE!
KTHOOOM
KTHOOOM
KTHOOOM
HNNN...

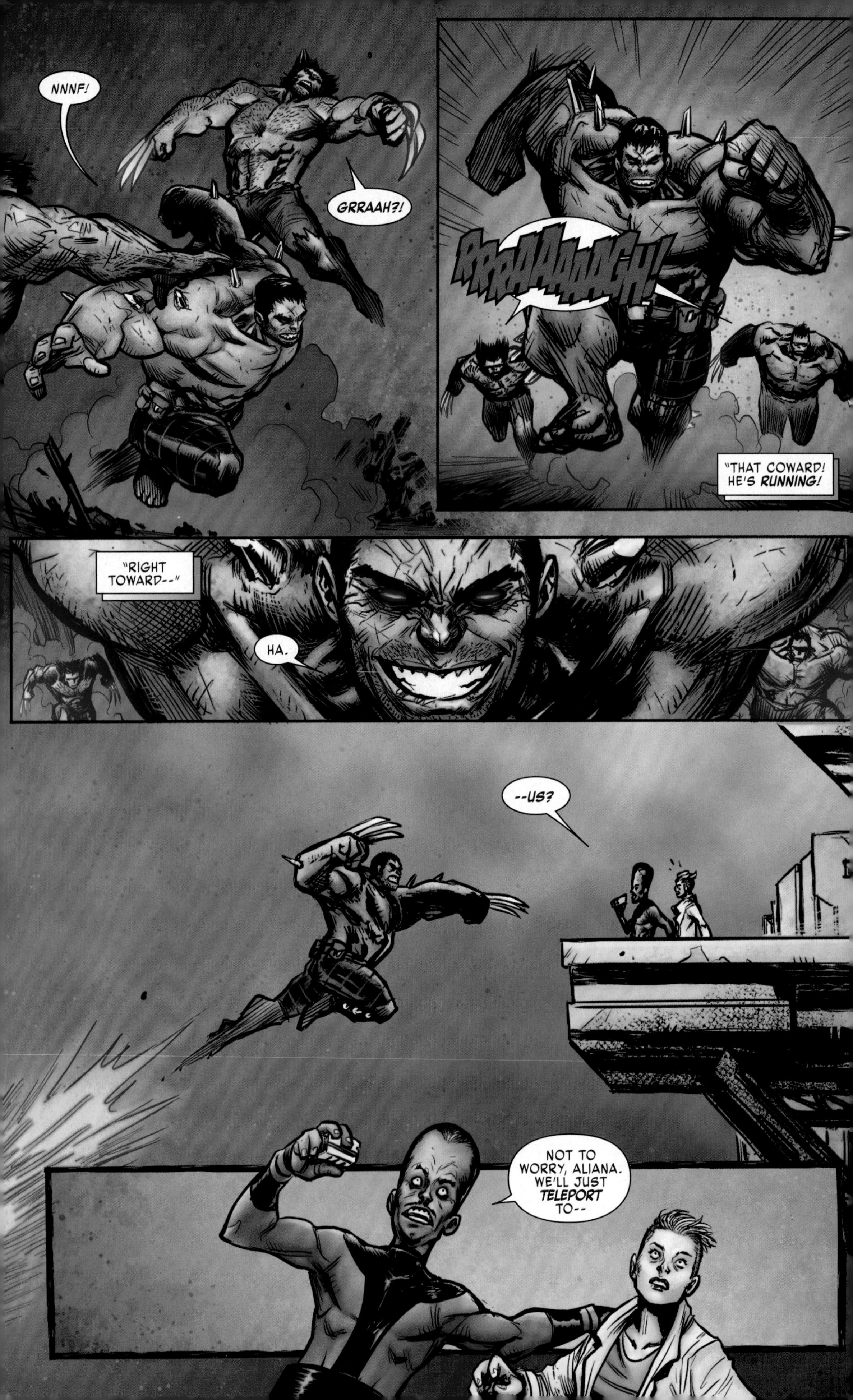

NNNF!
GRRAAH?!
RRRAAAAAAGH!
"THAT COWARD! HE'S RUNNING!
"RIGHT TOWARD--"
HA.
--US?
NOT TO WORRY, ALIANA. WE'LL JUST TELEPORT TO--

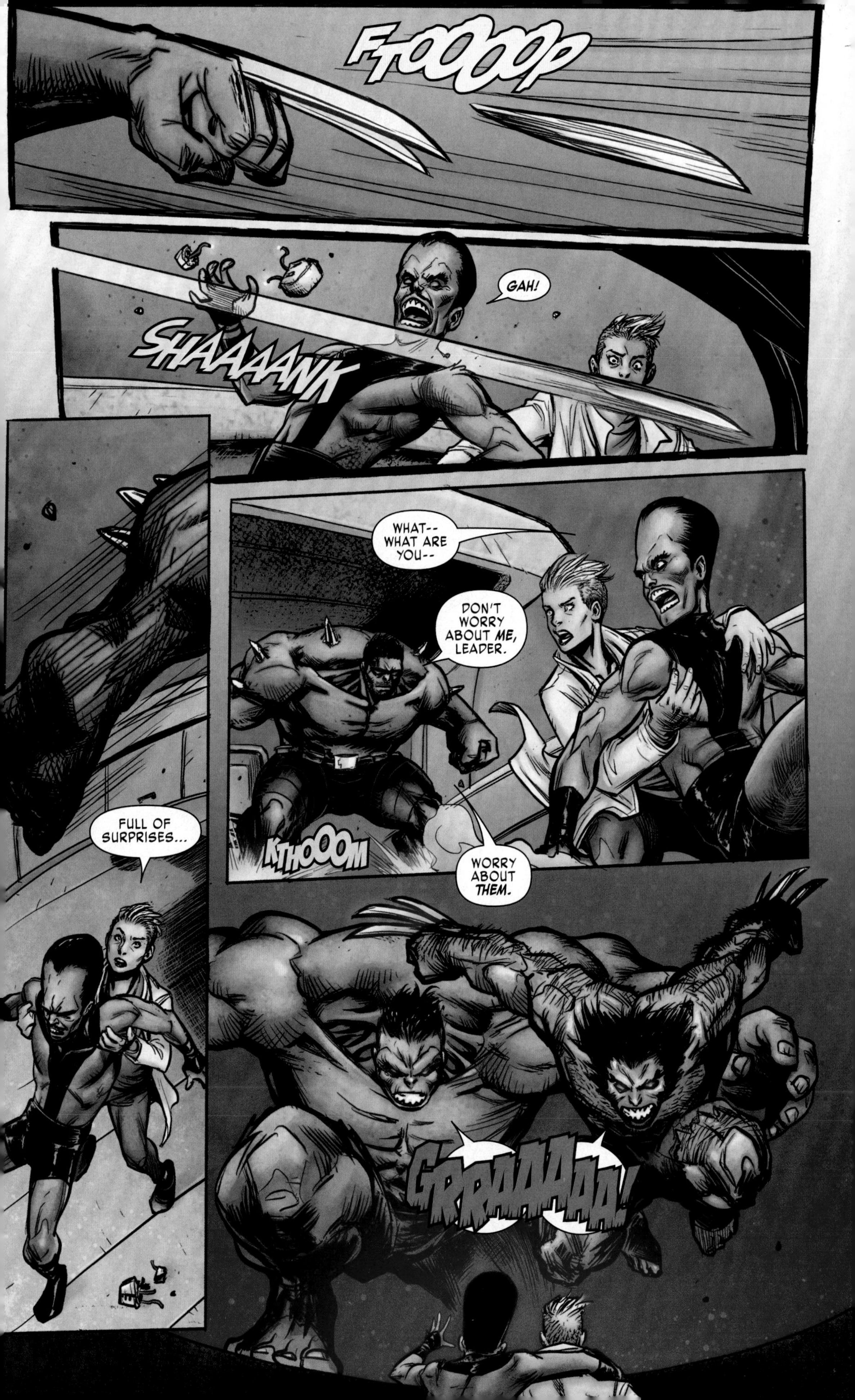
FTOOOOP
GAH!
SHAAAANK
WHAT--
WHAT ARE
YOU--
DON'T
WORRY
ABOUT ME,
LEADER.
KTHOOOM
WORRY
ABOUT
THEM.
FULL OF
SURPRISES...
GRRAAAAA!

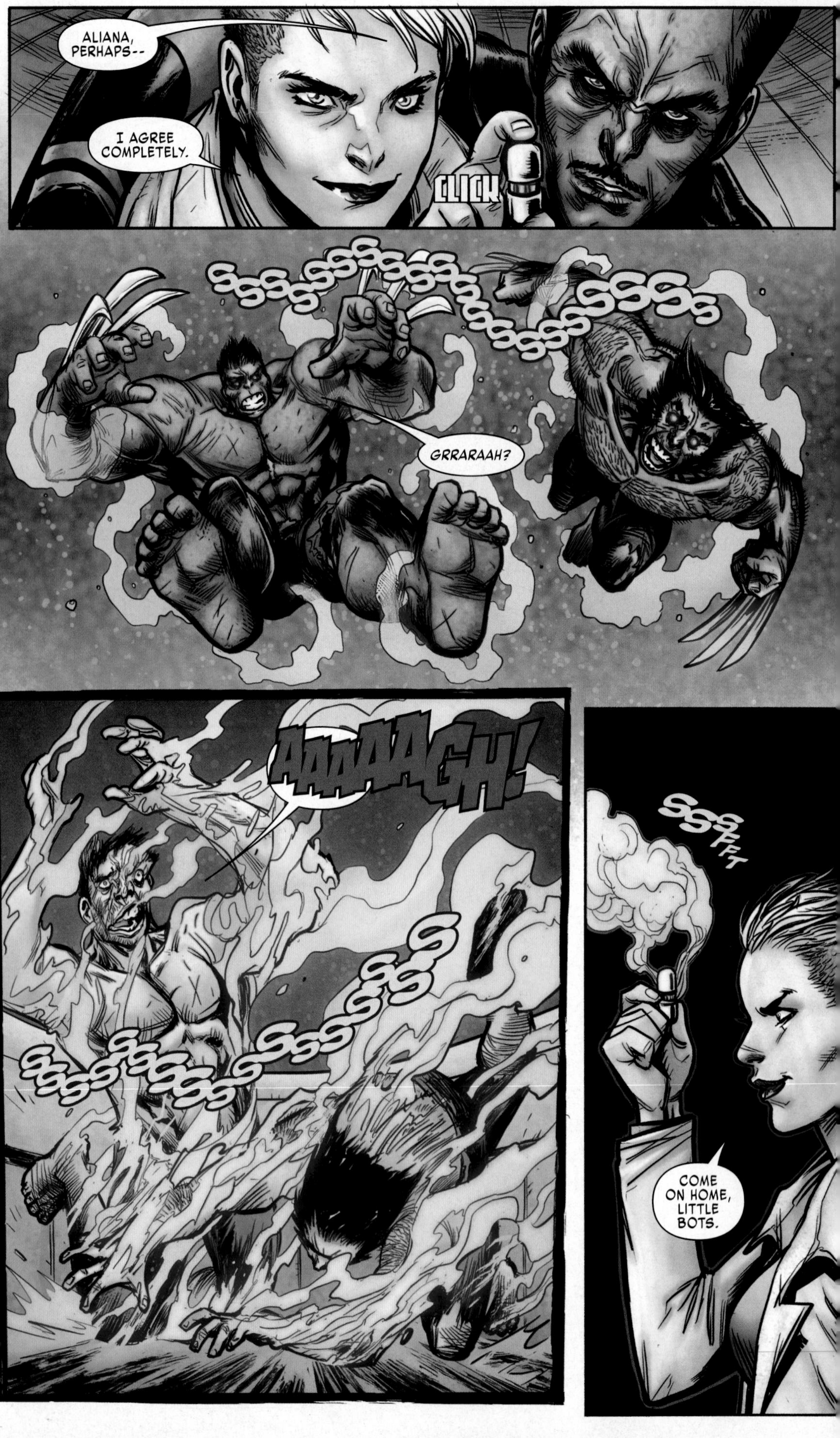
ALIANA, PERHAPS--
I AGREE COMPLETELY.
CLICK
SSSSSSSSSSSSSSSSSSSSSS
GRRARAAH?
AAAAAAGH!
SSSSSSSSSSSSSSSSS
SSSFFT
COME ON HOME, LITTLE BOTS.

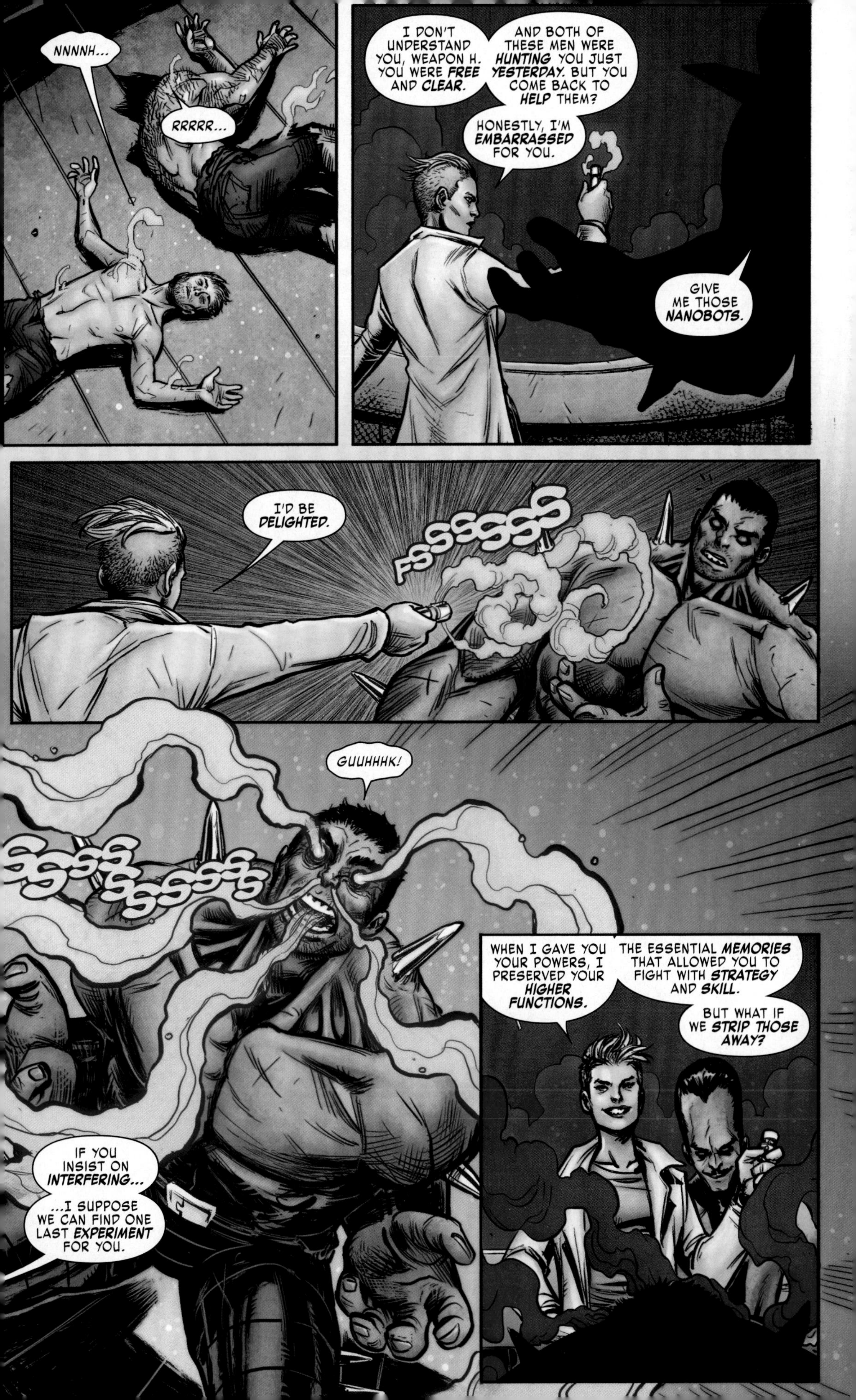

NNNNH...
RRRRR...
I DON'T UNDERSTAND YOU, WEAPON H. YOU WERE FREE AND CLEAR.
AND BOTH OF THESE MEN WERE HUNTING YOU JUST YESTERDAY. BUT YOU COME BACK TO HELP THEM?
HONESTLY, I'M EMBARRASSED FOR YOU.
GIVE ME THOSE NANOBOTS.
I'D BE DELIGHTED.
FSSSSSSS
GUUHHHK!
SSSSSSSSSSS
IF YOU INSIST ON INTERFERING...
...I SUPPOSE WE CAN FIND ONE LAST EXPERIMENT FOR YOU.
WHEN I GAVE YOU YOUR POWERS, I PRESERVED YOUR HIGHER FUNCTIONS.
THE ESSENTIAL MEMORIES THAT ALLOWED YOU TO FIGHT WITH STRATEGY AND SKILL.
BUT WHAT IF WE STRIP THOSE AWAY?

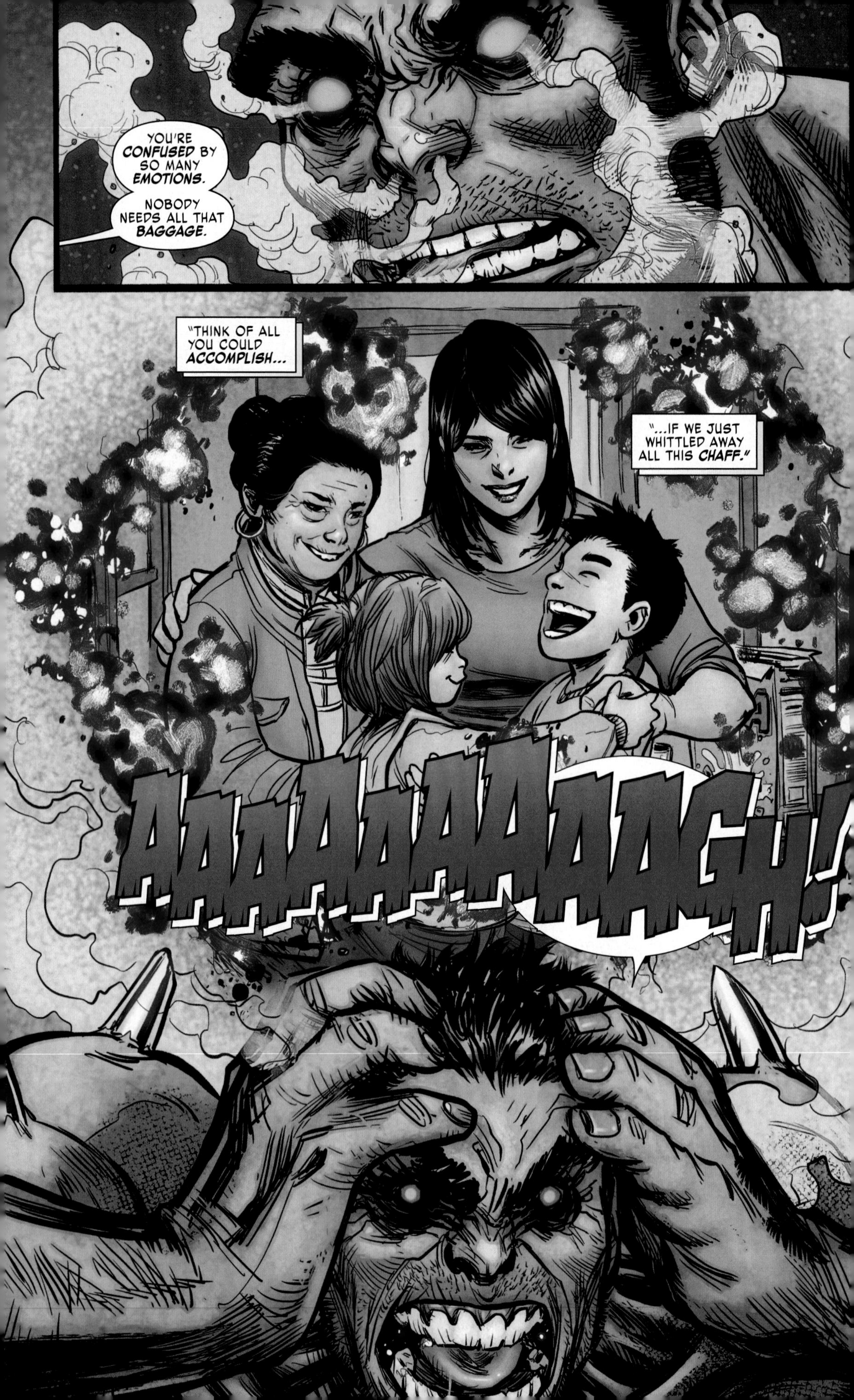
YOU'RE CONFUSED BY SO MANY EMOTIONS.
NOBODY NEEDS ALL THAT BAGGAGE.
"THINK OF ALL YOU COULD ACCOMPLISH...
"...IF WE JUST WHITTLED AWAY ALL THIS CHAFF."
AAAAAAAAAGH!

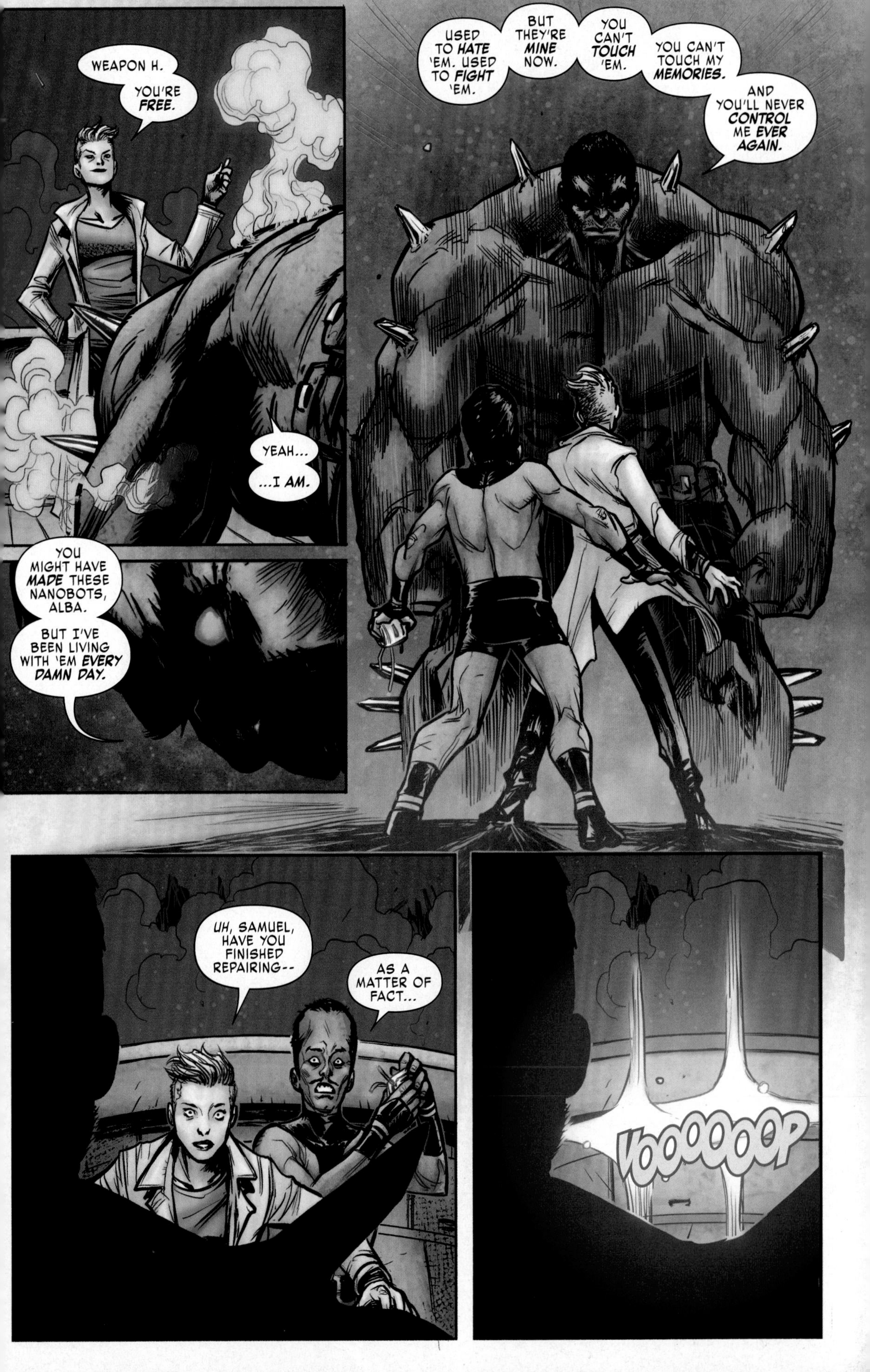
WEAPON H.
YOU'RE FREE.
YEAH...
...I AM.
YOU MIGHT HAVE MADE THESE NANOBOTS, ALBA.
BUT I'VE BEEN LIVING WITH 'EM EVERY DAMN DAY.
USED TO HATE 'EM. USED TO FIGHT 'EM.
BUT THEY'RE MINE NOW.
YOU CAN'T TOUCH 'EM.
YOU CAN'T TOUCH MY MEMORIES.
AND YOU'LL NEVER CONTROL ME EVER AGAIN.
UH, SAMUEL, HAVE YOU FINISHED REPAIRING--
AS A MATTER OF FACT...
VOOOOOOP

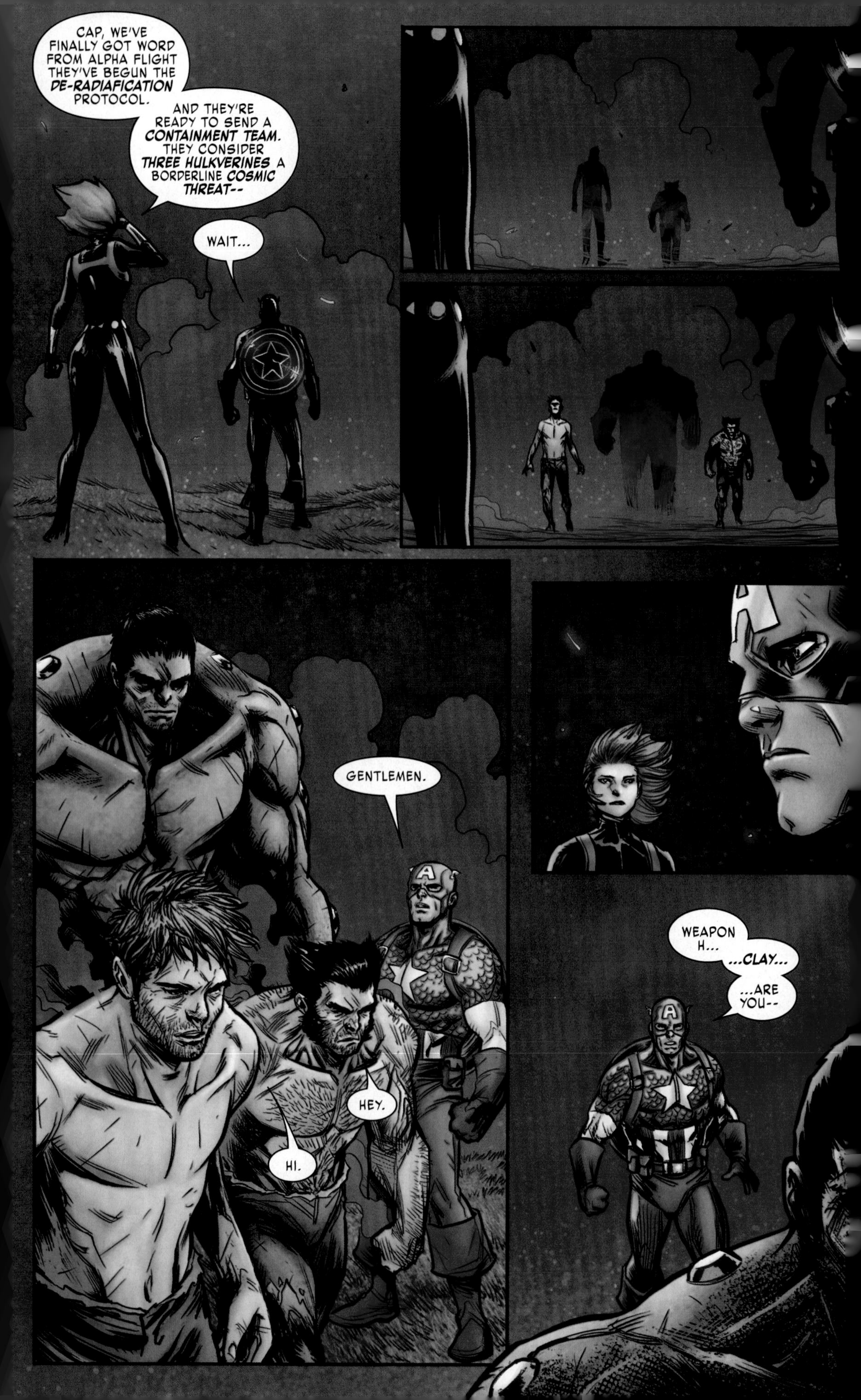
CAP, WE'VE FINALLY GOT WORD FROM ALPHA FLIGHT THEY'VE BEGUN THE DE-RADIAFICATION PROTOCOL.
AND THEY'RE READY TO SEND A CONTAINMENT TEAM. THEY CONSIDER THREE HULKVERINES A BORDERLINE COSMIC THREAT--
WAIT...
GENTLEMEN.
HEY.
HI.
WEAPON H...
...CLAY...
...ARE YOU--

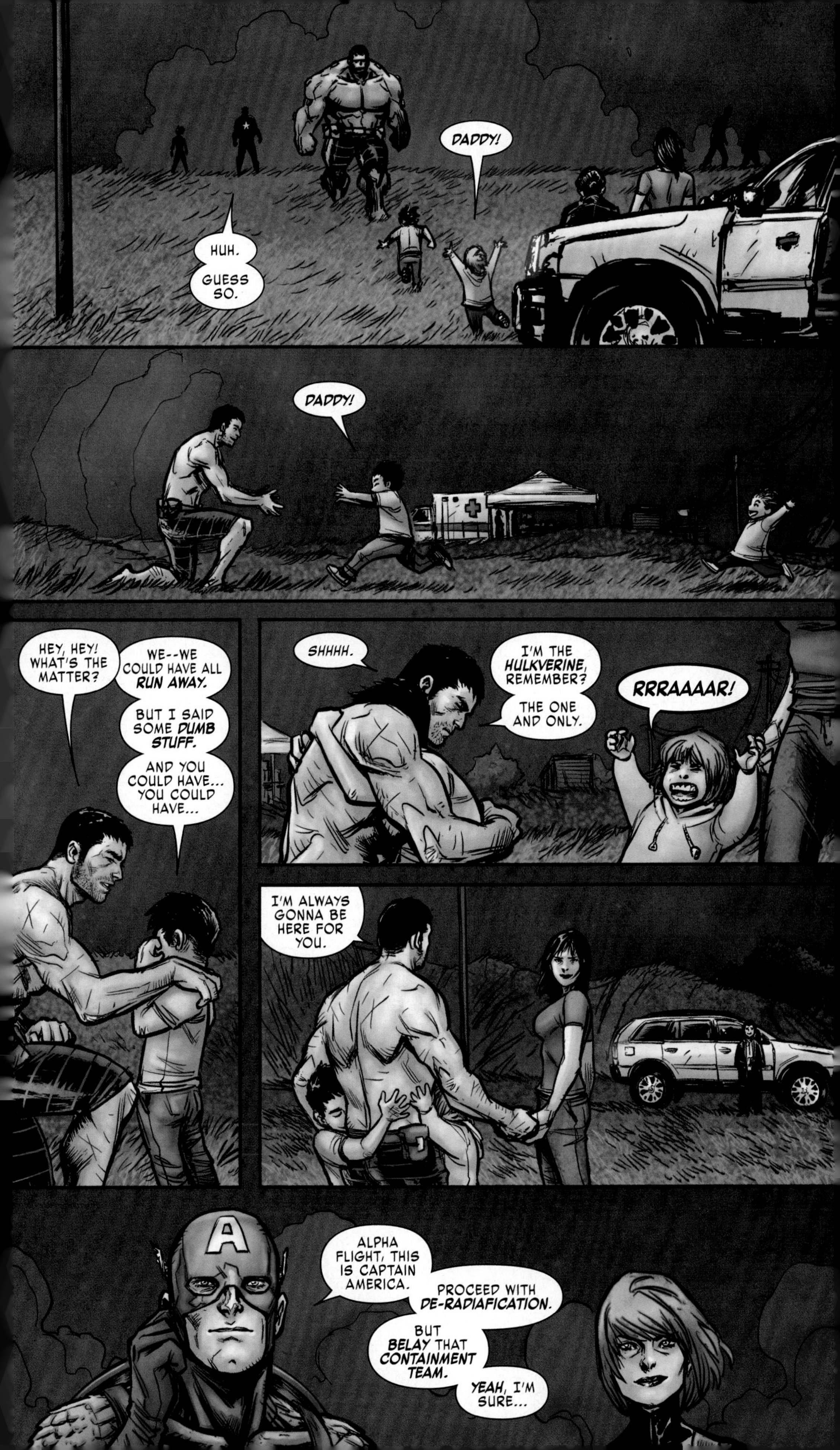
DADDY!
HUH.
GUESS SO.
DADDY!
HEY, HEY! WHAT'S THE MATTER?
WE--WE COULD HAVE ALL RUN AWAY.
BUT I SAID SOME DUMB STUFF.
AND YOU COULD HAVE... YOU COULD HAVE...
SHHHH.
I'M THE HULKVERINE, REMEMBER?
THE ONE AND ONLY.
RRRAAAAR!
I'M ALWAYS GONNA BE HERE FOR YOU.
ALPHA FLIGHT, THIS IS CAPTAIN AMERICA.
PROCEED WITH DE-RADIAFICATION.
BUT BELAY THAT CONTAINMENT TEAM.
YEAH, I'M SURE...

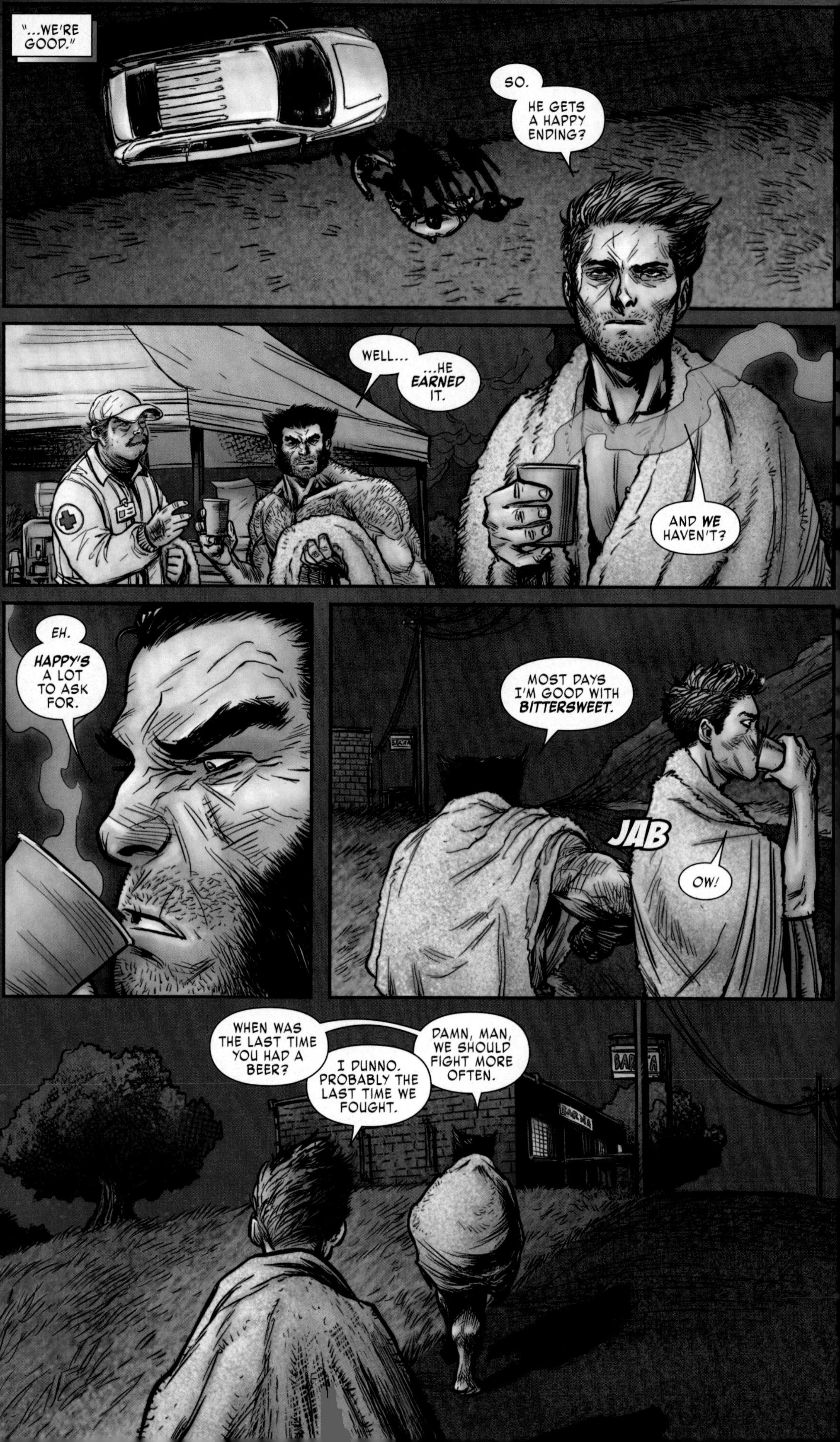
"...WE'RE GOOD."
SO.
HE GETS A HAPPY ENDING?
WELL...
...HE EARNED IT.
AND WE HAVEN'T?
EH.
HAPPY'S A LOT TO ASK FOR.
MOST DAYS I'M GOOD WITH BITTERSWEET.
JAB
OW!
WHEN WAS THE LAST TIME YOU HAD A BEER?
I DUNNO. PROBABLY THE LAST TIME WE FOUGHT.
DAMN, MAN, WE SHOULD FIGHT MORE OFTEN.

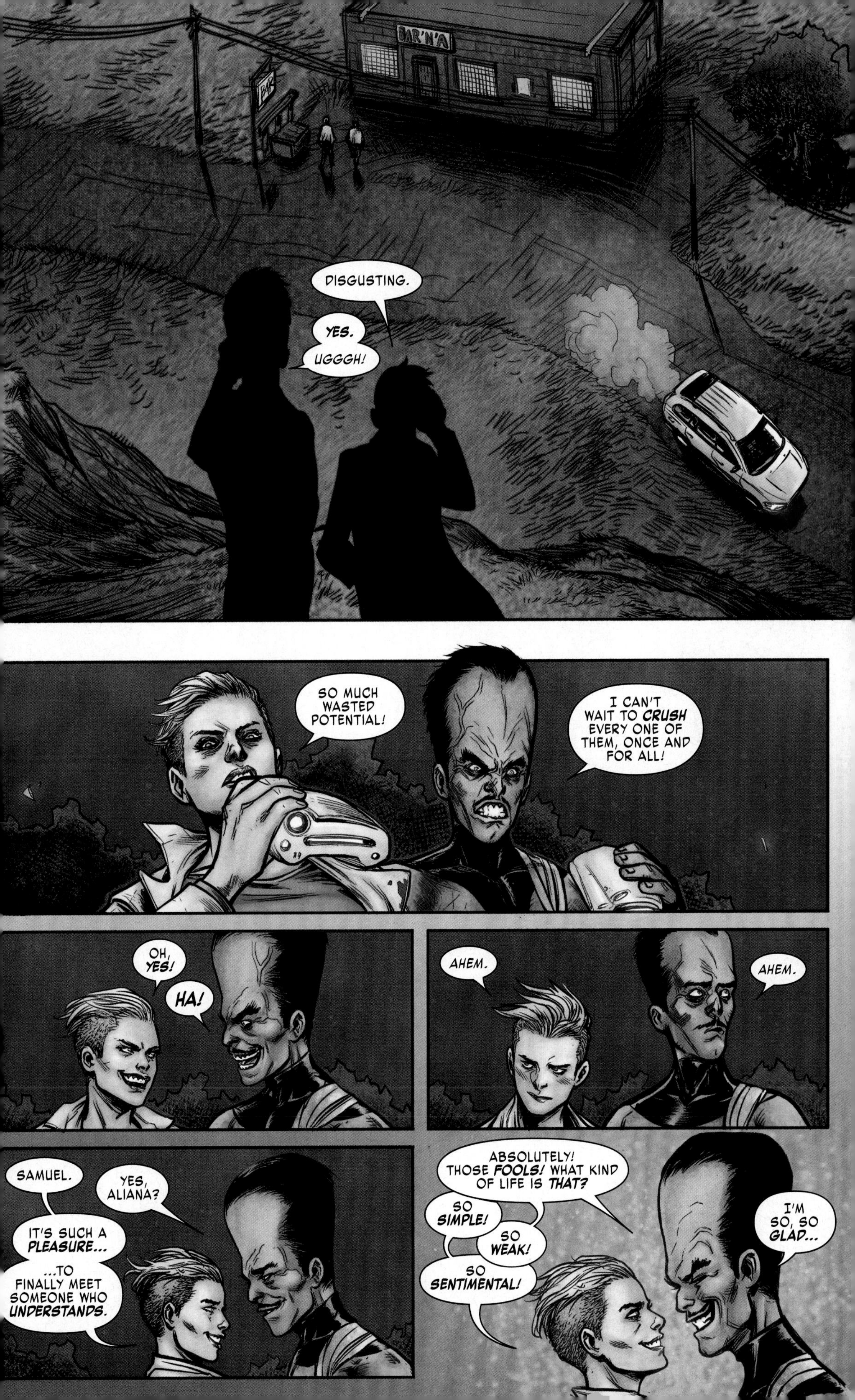
BAR'N'A
BAR
DISGUSTING.
YES.
UGGGH!
SO MUCH WASTED POTENTIAL!
I CAN'T WAIT TO CRUSH EVERY ONE OF THEM, ONCE AND FOR ALL!
OH, YES!
HA!
AHEM.
AHEM.
SAMUEL.
YES, ALIANA?
IT'S SUCH A PLEASURE...
...TO FINALLY MEET SOMEONE WHO UNDERSTANDS.
ABSOLUTELY! THOSE FOOLS! WHAT KIND OF LIFE IS THAT?
SO SIMPLE!
SO WEAK!
SO SENTIMENTAL!
I'M SO, SO GLAD...

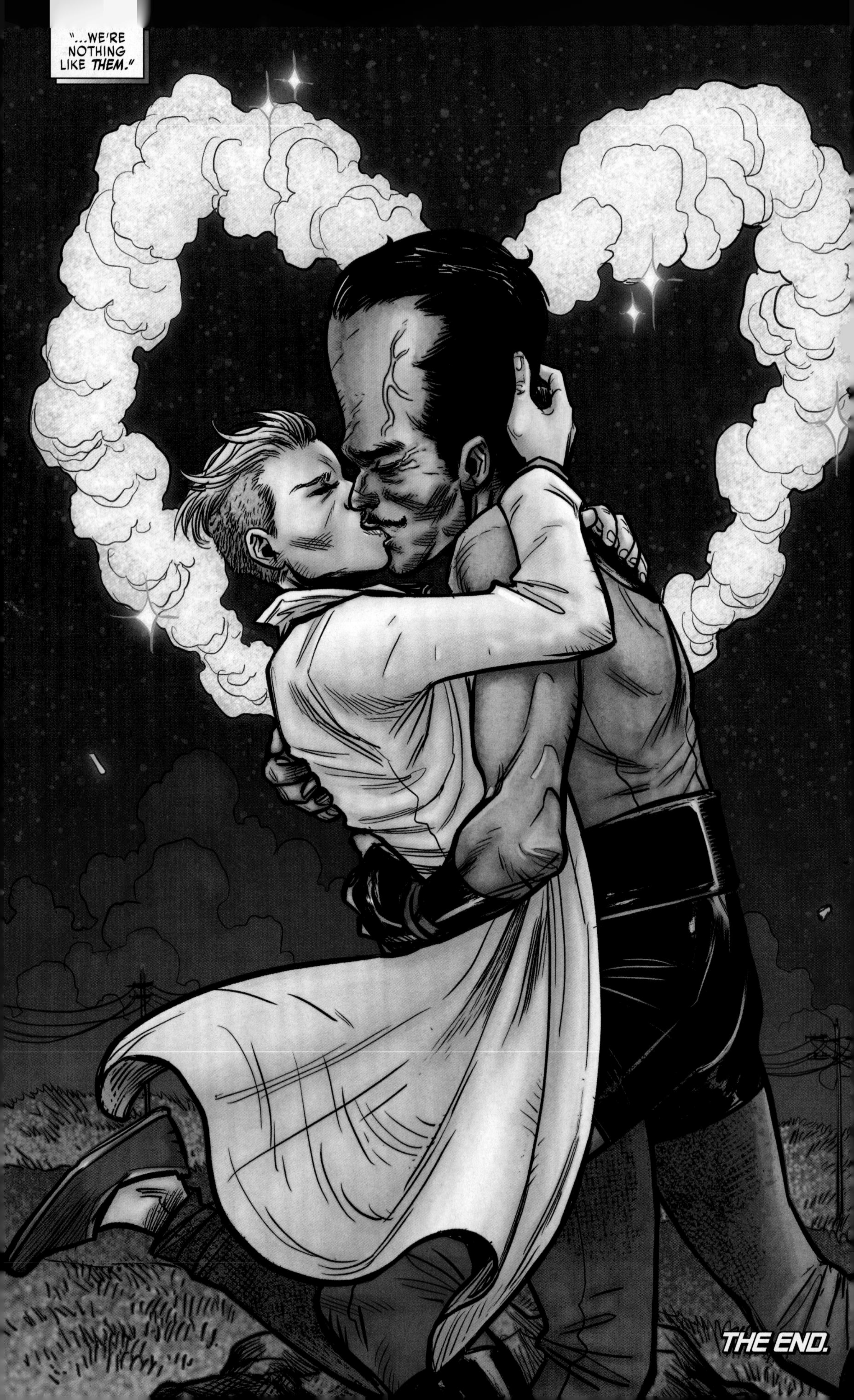
"...WE'RE NOTHING LIKE *THEM*."
THE END.

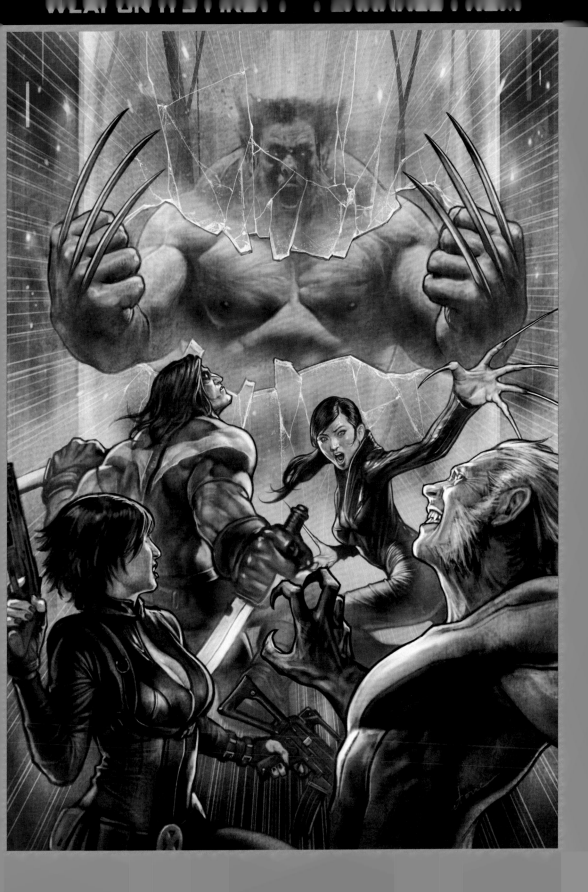

W.M.D.

CONCLUSION

THE TOTALLY AWESOME HULK

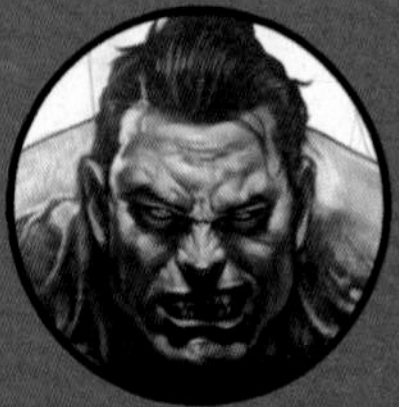

HULK

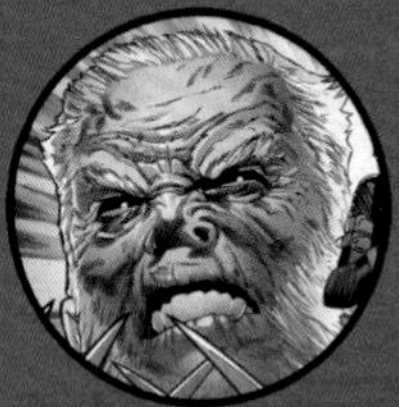

OLD MAN LOGAN

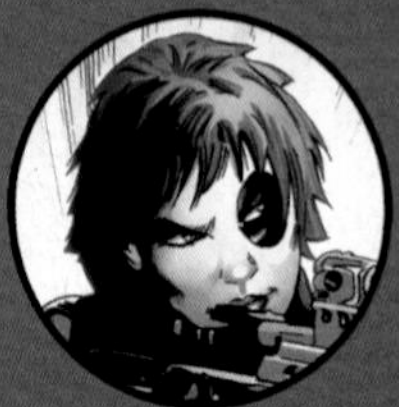

DOMINO

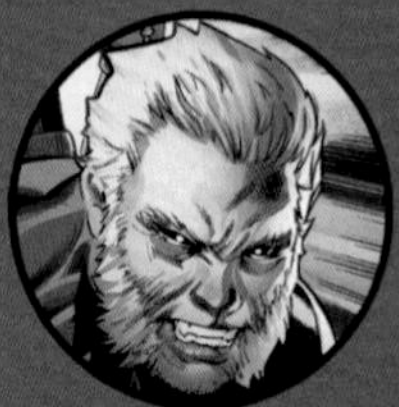

SABRETOOTH

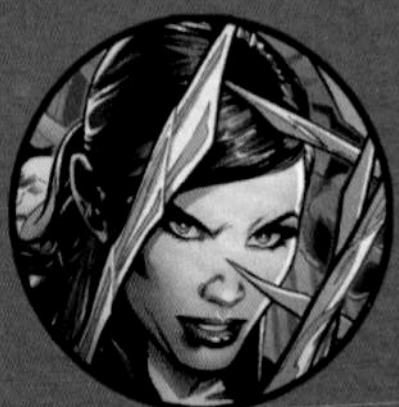

LADY DEATHSTRIKE

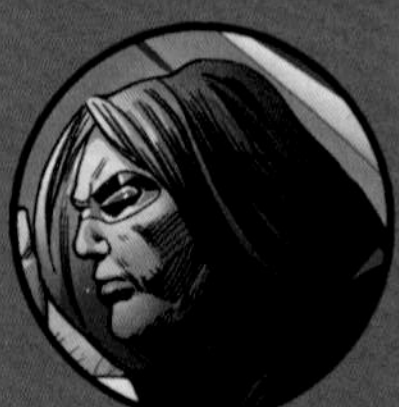

WARPATH

SUPER-GENIUS TEENAGER AMADEUS CHO CURED BRUCE BANNER AND TOOK ON THE POWERS AND MANTLE OF THE HULK!

PREVIOUSLY IN ***WEAPONS OF MUTANT DESTRUCTION...***

USING ADAMANTIUM CYBORGS CONCEALED WITHIN HUMAN SKIN, WEAPON X STOLE DNA FROM THE MOST DANGEROUS MUTANTS ON EARTH: LOGAN, SABRETOOTH, DOMINO, WARPATH, LADY DEATHSTRIKE AND AMADEUS CHO (A.K.A. THE HULK). CLOSE TO ACHIEVING THE COMBINATION OF THE HULK'S AND WOLVERINE'S GIFTS, DOCTOR ALBA HAS ALMOST PERFECTED WEAPON X'S DEADLIEST EXPERIMENT, BATCH H—THE SUCCESS OF WHICH COULD MEAN THE ERADICATION OF MUTANTKIND.

AMADEUS, LOGAN AND THE REST OF THE MUTANTS TARGETED BY WEAPON X RACE TO STOP HER, BUT AS DOCTOR ALBA'S TRIAL SUBJECTS H-ALPHA AND H-BETA REACH THE FINAL STAGES OF GESTATION, THEY MAY ALREADY BE TOO LATE....

WRITER GREG **PAK**

ARTIST ROBERT **GILL**

COLORIST NOLAN **WOODARD**

LETTERER VC's CORY **PETIT**

COVER ARTIST STONEHOUSE

ASSISTANT EDITOR CHRIS **ROBINSON**

EDITOR MARK **PANICCIA**

EDITOR IN CHIEF AXEL **ALONSO**

CHIEF CREATIVE OFFICER JOE **QUESADA**

PRESIDENT DAN **BUCKLEY**

EXECUTIVE PRODUCER ALAN **FINE**

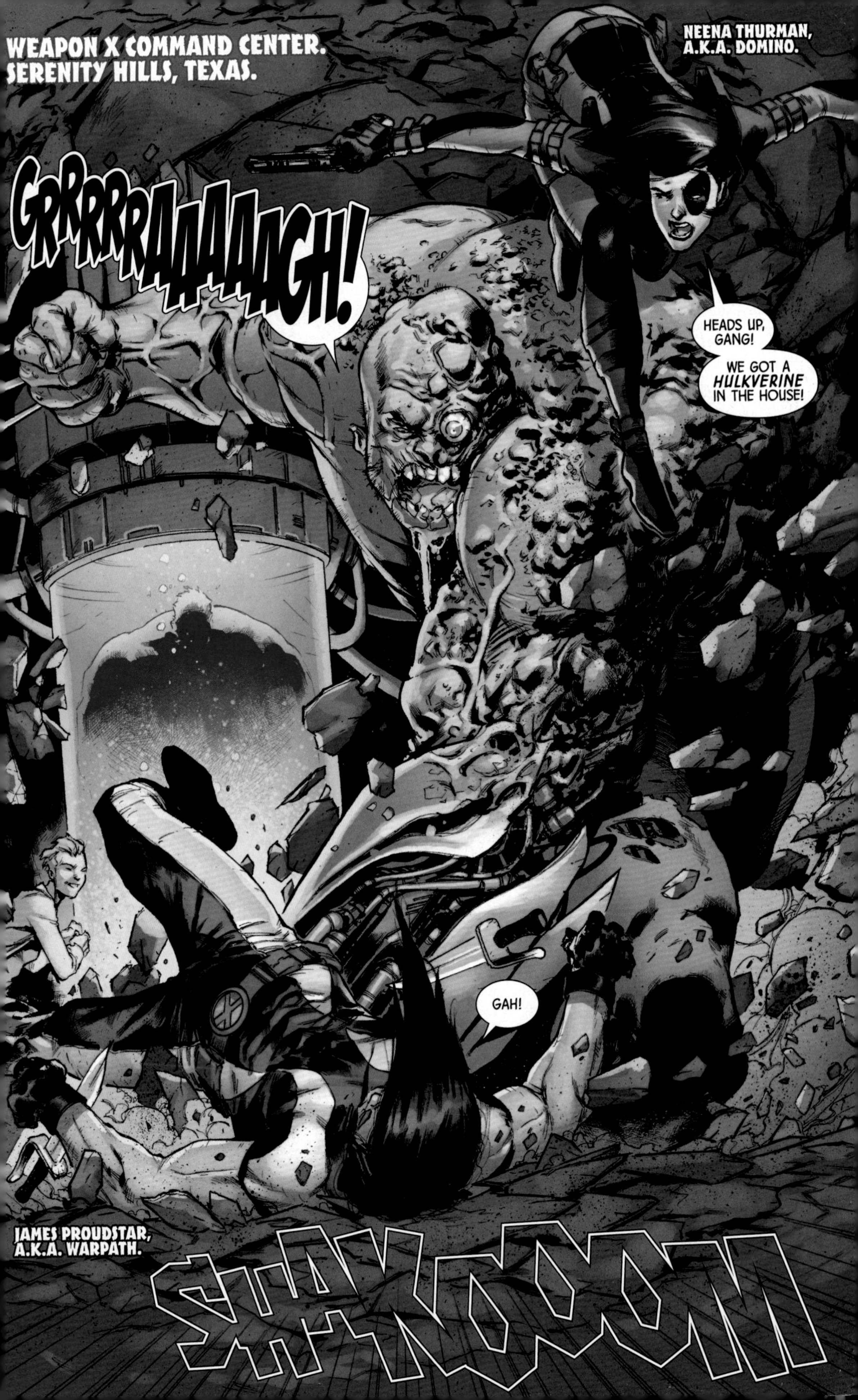

WEAPON X COMMAND CENTER.
SERENITY HILLS, TEXAS.
NEENA THURMAN, A.K.A. DOMINO.
GRRRRRAAAAAAGH!
HEADS UP, GANG!
WE GOT A HULKVERINE IN THE HOUSE!
GAH!
JAMES PROUDSTAR, A.K.A. WARPATH.
SKADOOM

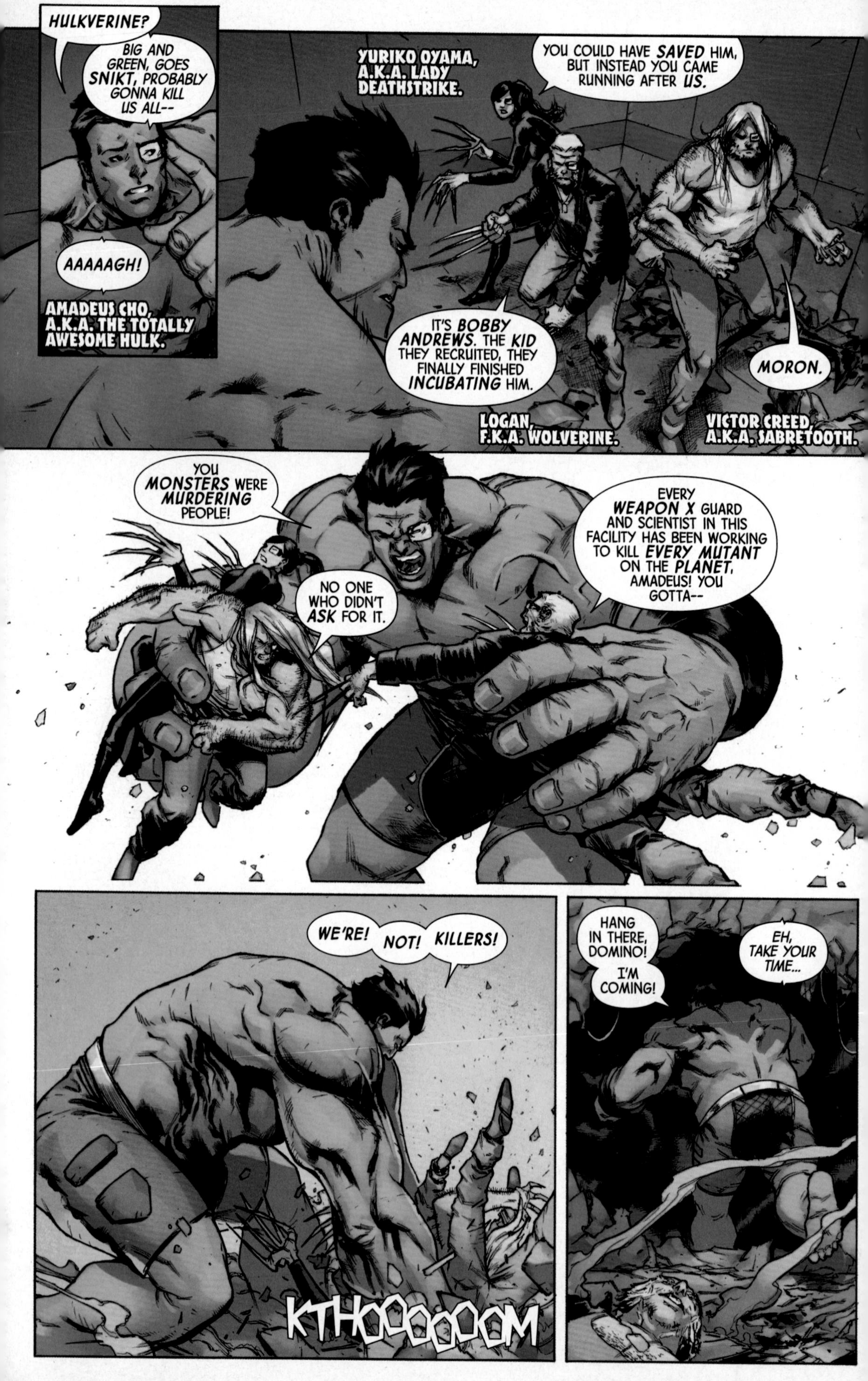
HULKVERINE?
BIG AND GREEN, GOES SNIKT, PROBABLY GONNA KILL US ALL--
AAAAAGH!
AMADEUS CHO, A.K.A. THE TOTALLY AWESOME HULK.
YURIKO OYAMA, A.K.A. LADY DEATHSTRIKE.
YOU COULD HAVE SAVED HIM, BUT INSTEAD YOU CAME RUNNING AFTER US.
IT'S BOBBY ANDREWS. THE KID THEY RECRUITED, THEY FINALLY FINISHED INCUBATING HIM.
LOGAN, F.K.A. WOLVERINE.
MORON.
VICTOR CREED, A.K.A. SABRETOOTH.
YOU MONSTERS WERE MURDERING PEOPLE!
NO ONE WHO DIDN'T ASK FOR IT.
EVERY WEAPON X GUARD AND SCIENTIST IN THIS FACILITY HAS BEEN WORKING TO KILL EVERY MUTANT ON THE PLANET, AMADEUS! YOU GOTTA--
WE'RE!
NOT!
KILLERS!
KTHOOOOOOOM
HANG IN THERE, DOMINO!
I'M COMING!
EH, TAKE YOUR TIME...

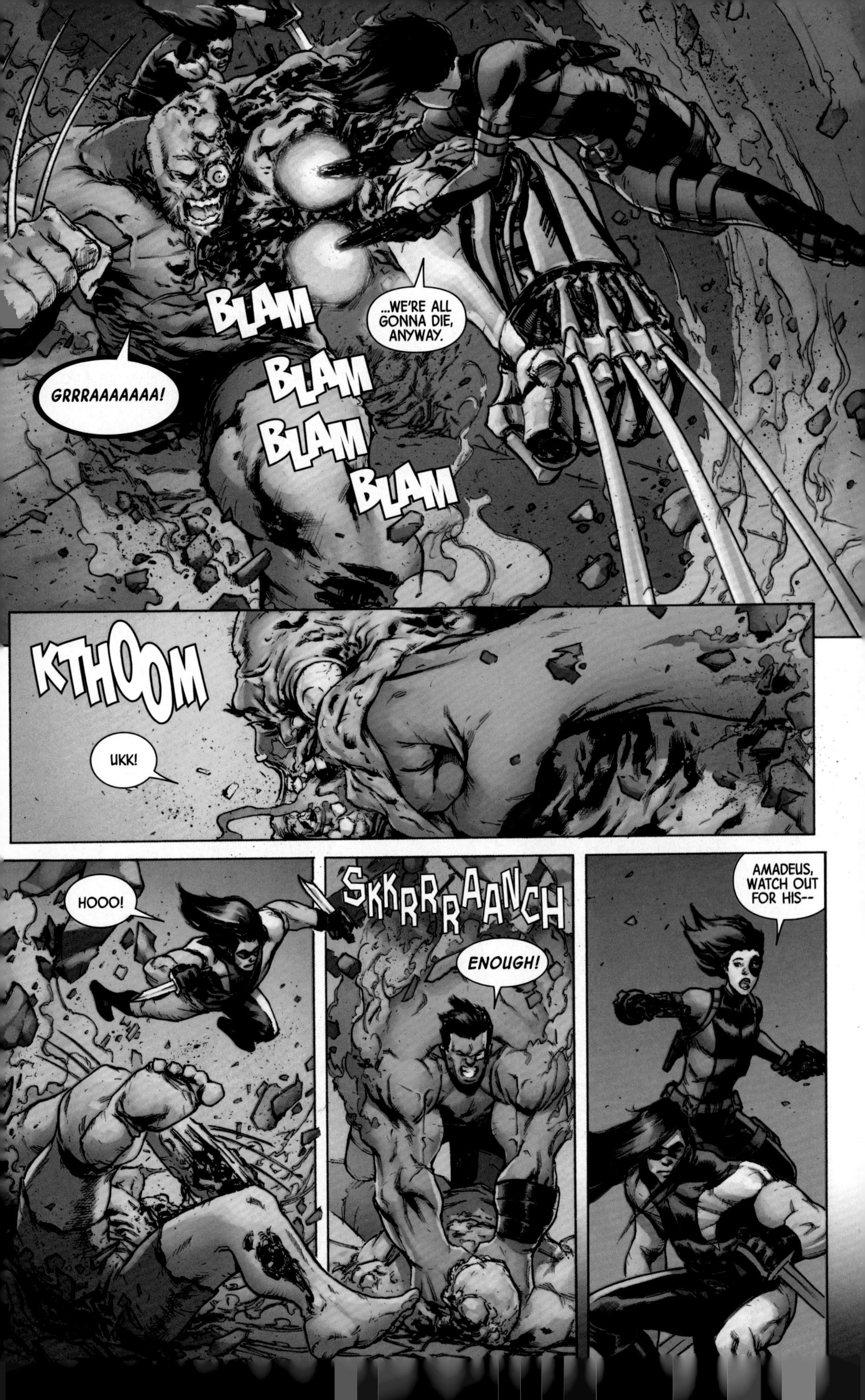

BLAM
...WE'RE ALL GONNA DIE, ANYWAY.
GRRRAAAAAAA!
BLAM
BLAM
BLAM
KTHOOM
UKK!
HOOO!
SKKRRRAANCH
ENOUGH!
AMADEUS, WATCH OUT FOR HIS--

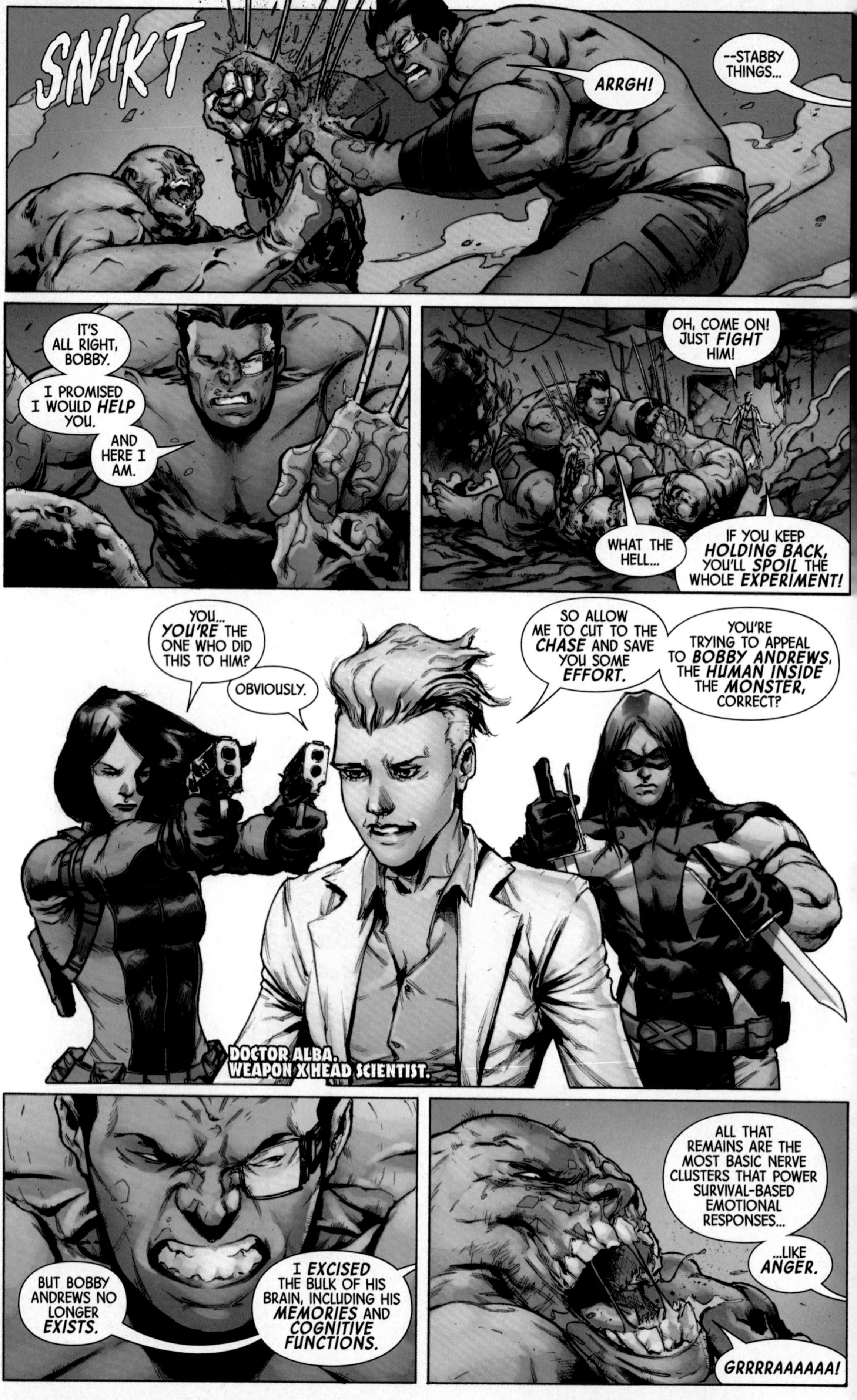
SNIKT
ARRGH!
--STABBY THINGS...
IT'S ALL RIGHT, BOBBY.
I PROMISED I WOULD HELP YOU.
AND HERE I AM.
OH, COME ON! JUST FIGHT HIM!
WHAT THE HELL...
IF YOU KEEP HOLDING BACK, YOU'LL SPOIL THE WHOLE EXPERIMENT!
YOU... YOU'RE THE ONE WHO DID THIS TO HIM?
OBVIOUSLY.
SO ALLOW ME TO CUT TO THE CHASE AND SAVE YOU SOME EFFORT.
YOU'RE TRYING TO APPEAL TO BOBBY ANDREWS, THE HUMAN INSIDE THE MONSTER, CORRECT?
DOCTOR ALBA. WEAPON X HEAD SCIENTIST.
BUT BOBBY ANDREWS NO LONGER EXISTS.
I EXCISED THE BULK OF HIS BRAIN, INCLUDING HIS MEMORIES AND COGNITIVE FUNCTIONS.
ALL THAT REMAINS ARE THE MOST BASIC NERVE CLUSTERS THAT POWER SURVIVAL-BASED EMOTIONAL RESPONSES...
...LIKE ANGER.
GRRRRAAAAAA!

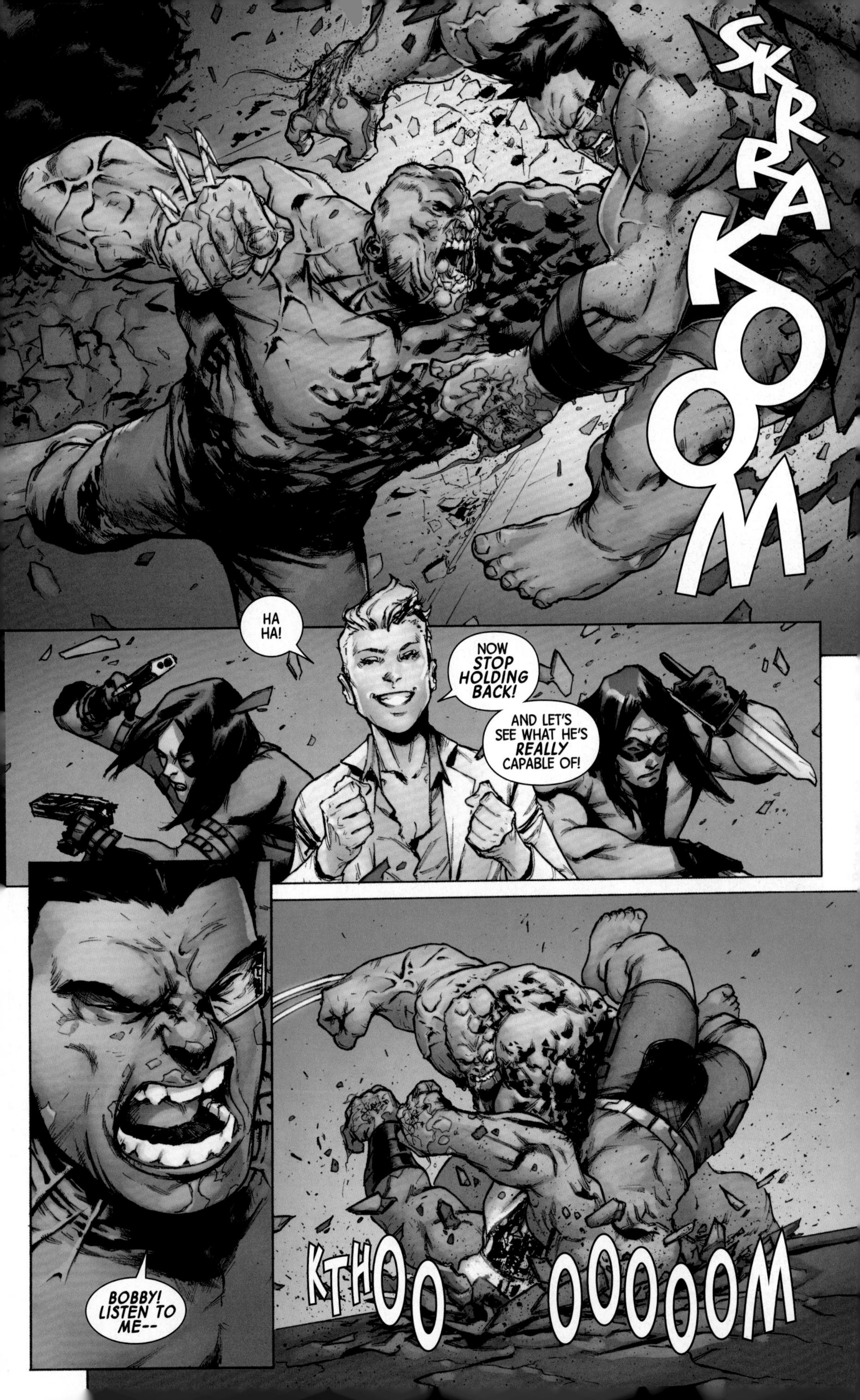
SKRAKOOM
HA HA!
NOW STOP HOLDING BACK!
AND LET'S SEE WHAT HE'S REALLY CAPABLE OF!
BOBBY! LISTEN TO ME--
KTHOO OOOOOM

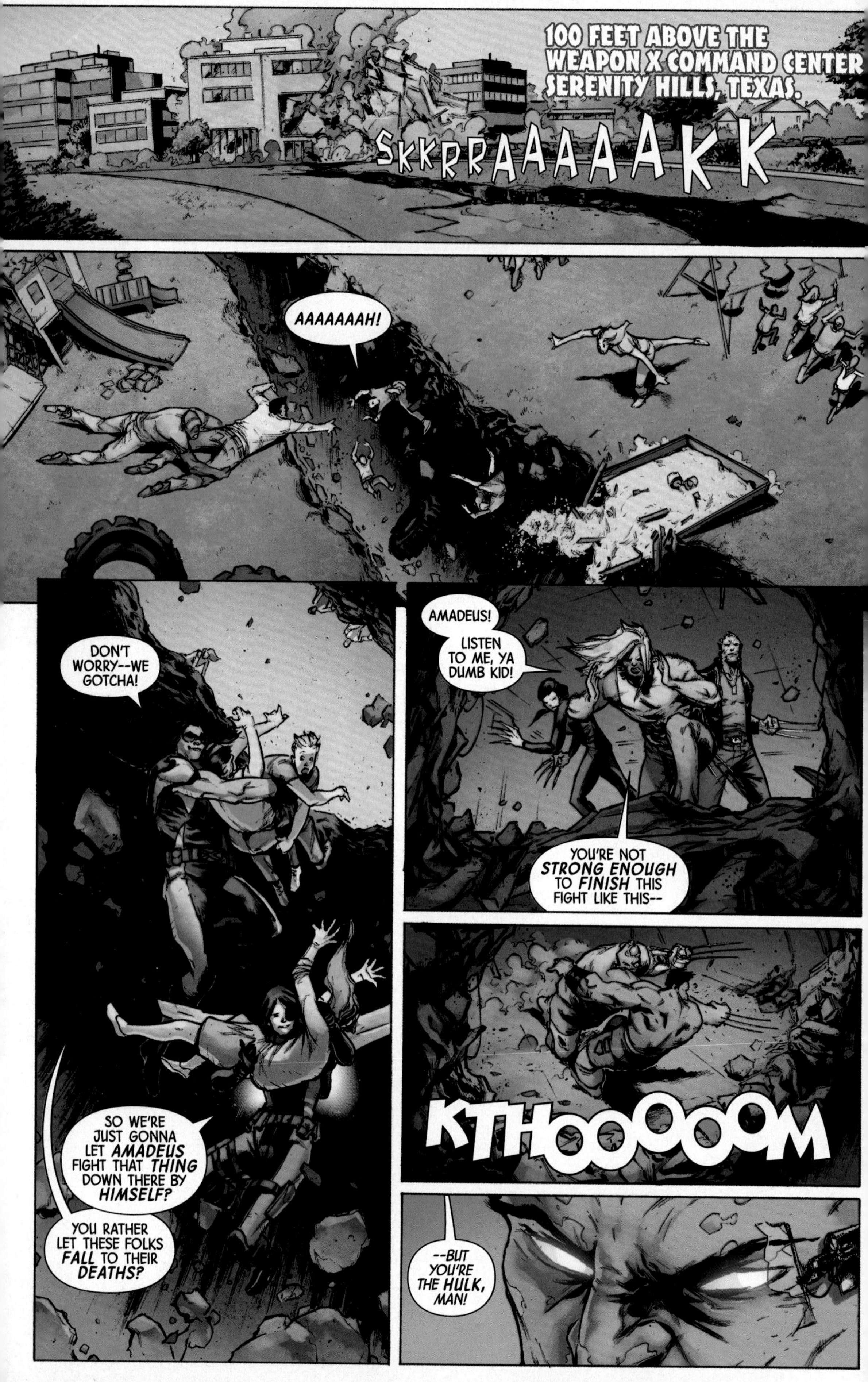
100 FEET ABOVE THE WEAPON X COMMAND CENTER SERENITY HILLS, TEXAS.
SKKRRAAAAAKK
AAAAAAAH!
DON'T WORRY--WE GOTCHA!
SO WE'RE JUST GONNA LET AMADEUS FIGHT THAT THING DOWN THERE BY HIMSELF?
YOU RATHER LET THESE FOLKS FALL TO THEIR DEATHS?
AMADEUS!
LISTEN TO ME, YA DUMB KID!
YOU'RE NOT STRONG ENOUGH TO FINISH THIS FIGHT LIKE THIS--
KTHOOOOOM
--BUT YOU'RE THE HULK, MAN!

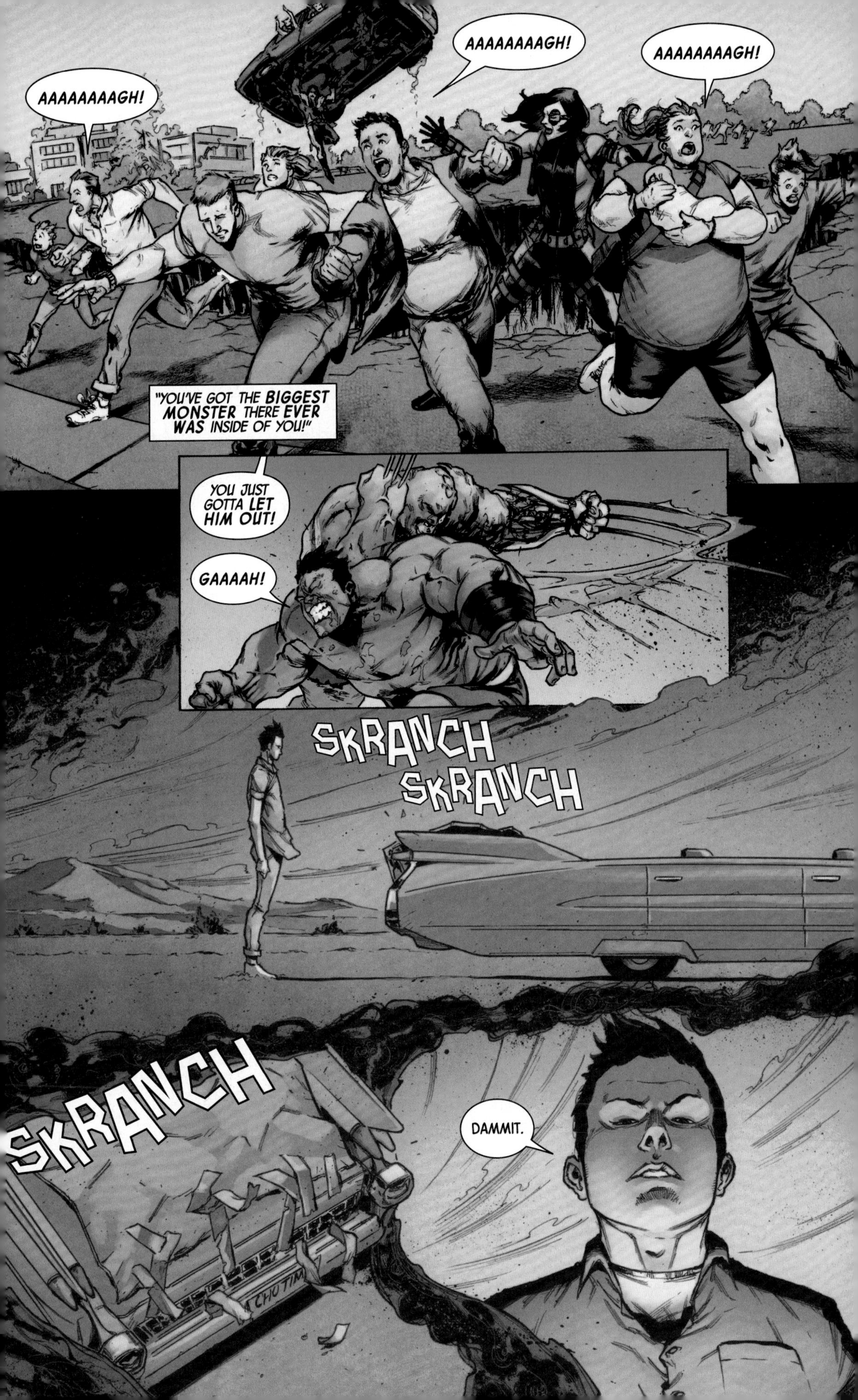
AAAAAAAAGH!
AAAAAAAAGH!
AAAAAAAAGH!
"YOU'VE GOT THE BIGGEST MONSTER THERE EVER WAS INSIDE OF YOU!"
YOU JUST GOTTA LET HIM OUT!
GAAAAH!
SKRANCH
SKRANCH
SKRANCH
DAMMIT.

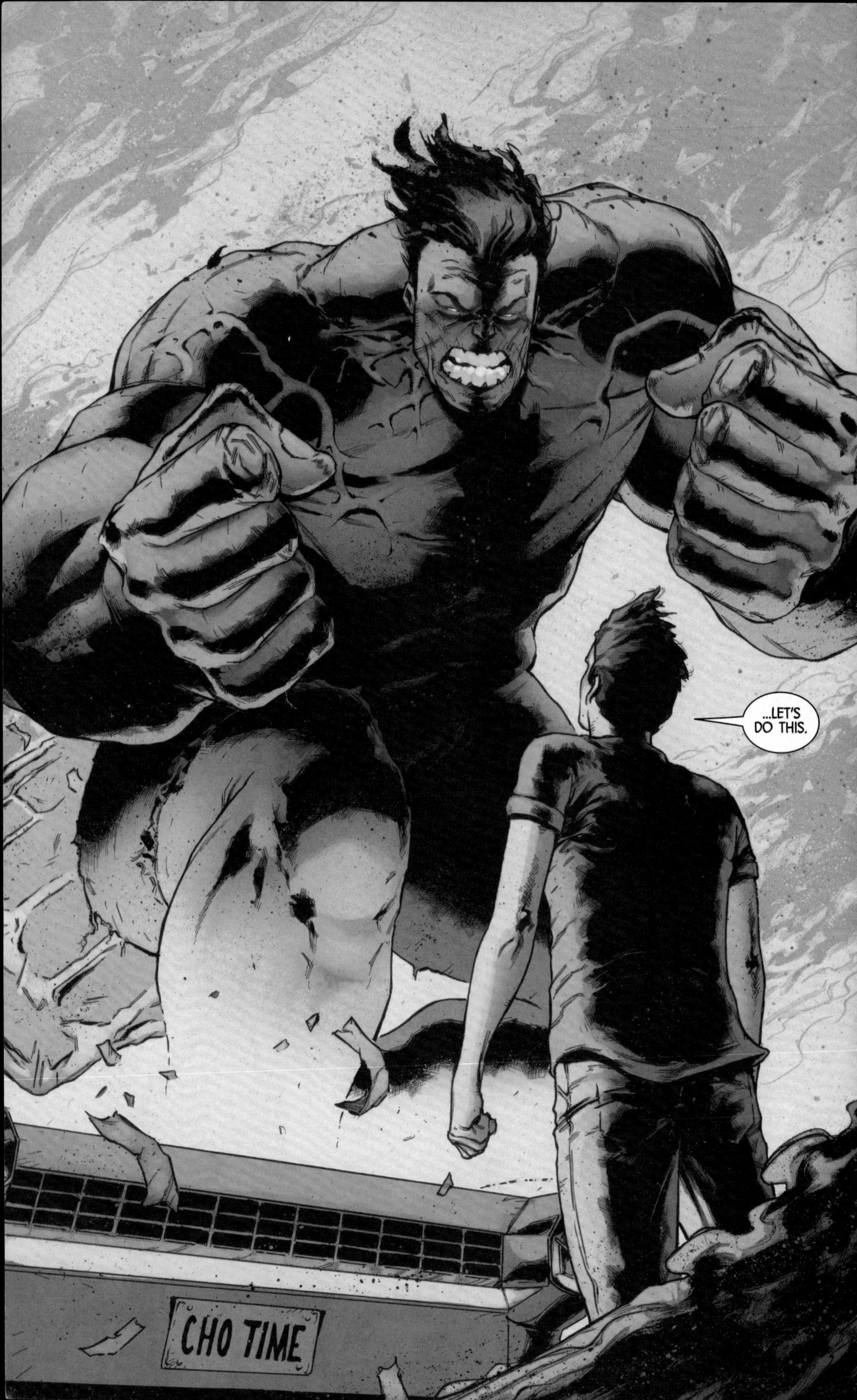
...LET'S DO THIS.
CHO TIME

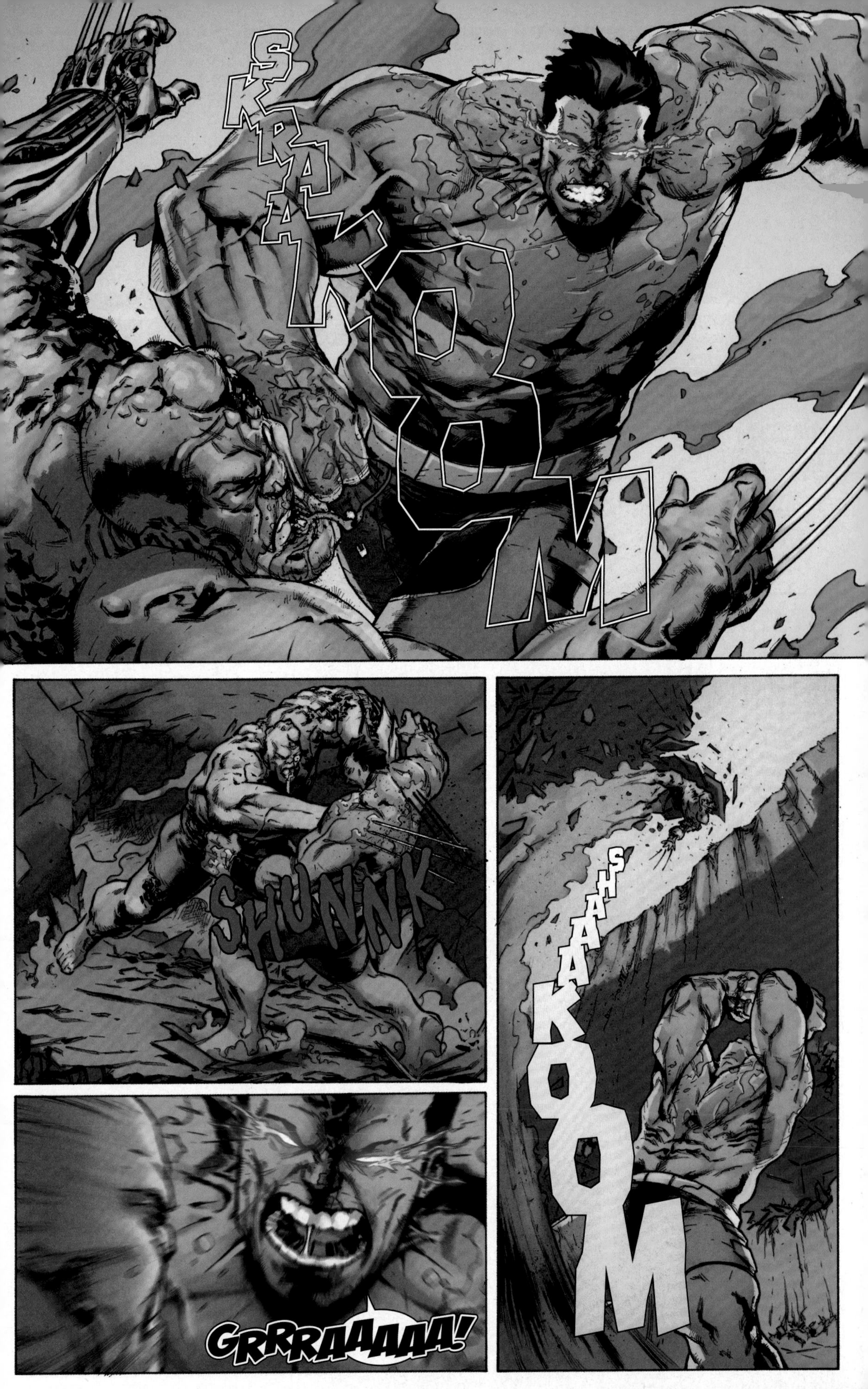
SKRAAKOOM
SHUNNK
GRRRAAAAAA!
SHAAAKOOM

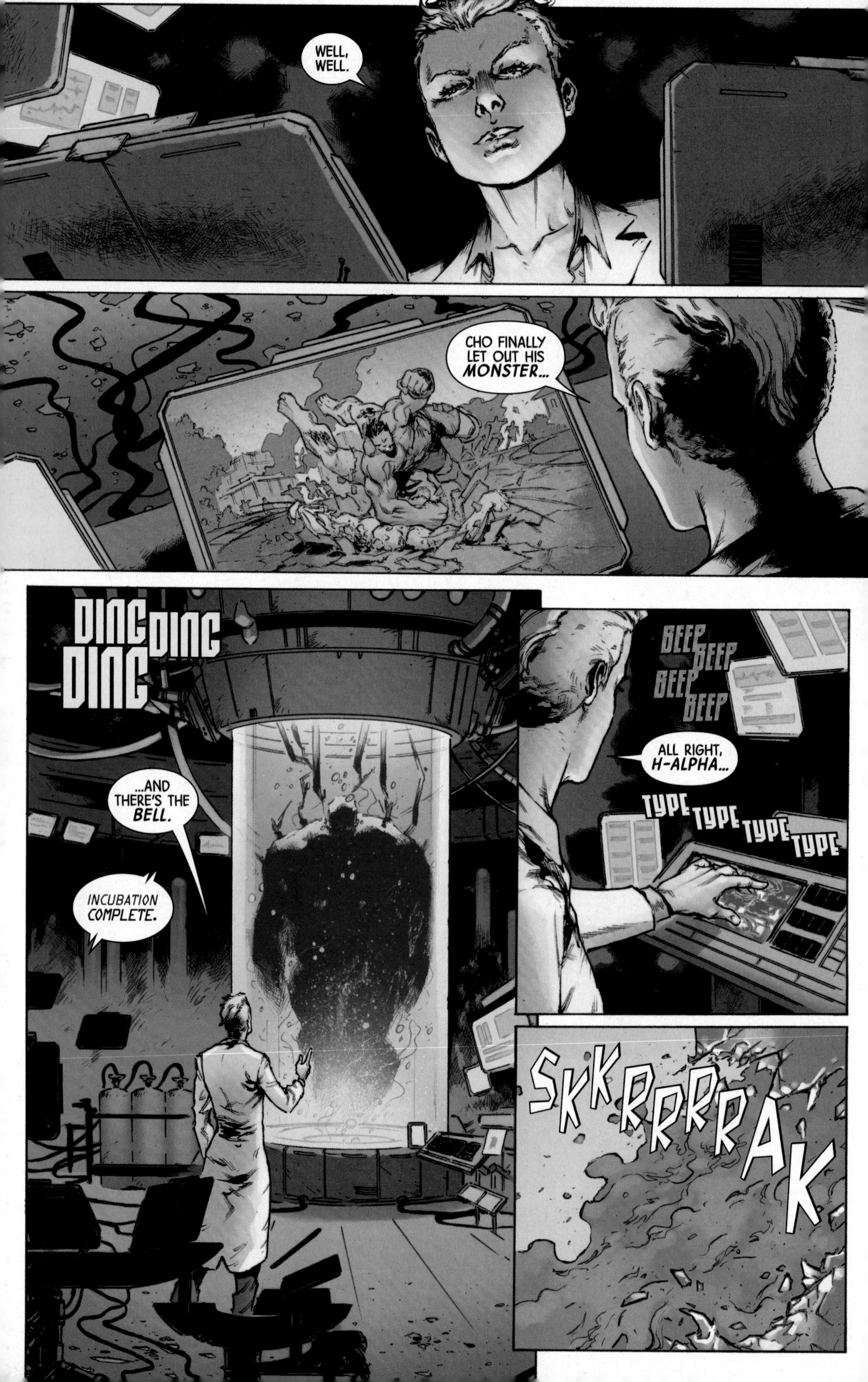
WELL, WELL.
CHO FINALLY LET OUT HIS *MONSTER*...
DING DING DING
...AND THERE'S THE *BELL.*
INCUBATION **COMPLETE.**
BEEP BEEP BEEP BEEP
ALL RIGHT, *H-ALPHA*...
TYPE TYPE TYPE TYPE
SKKRRRRRAK

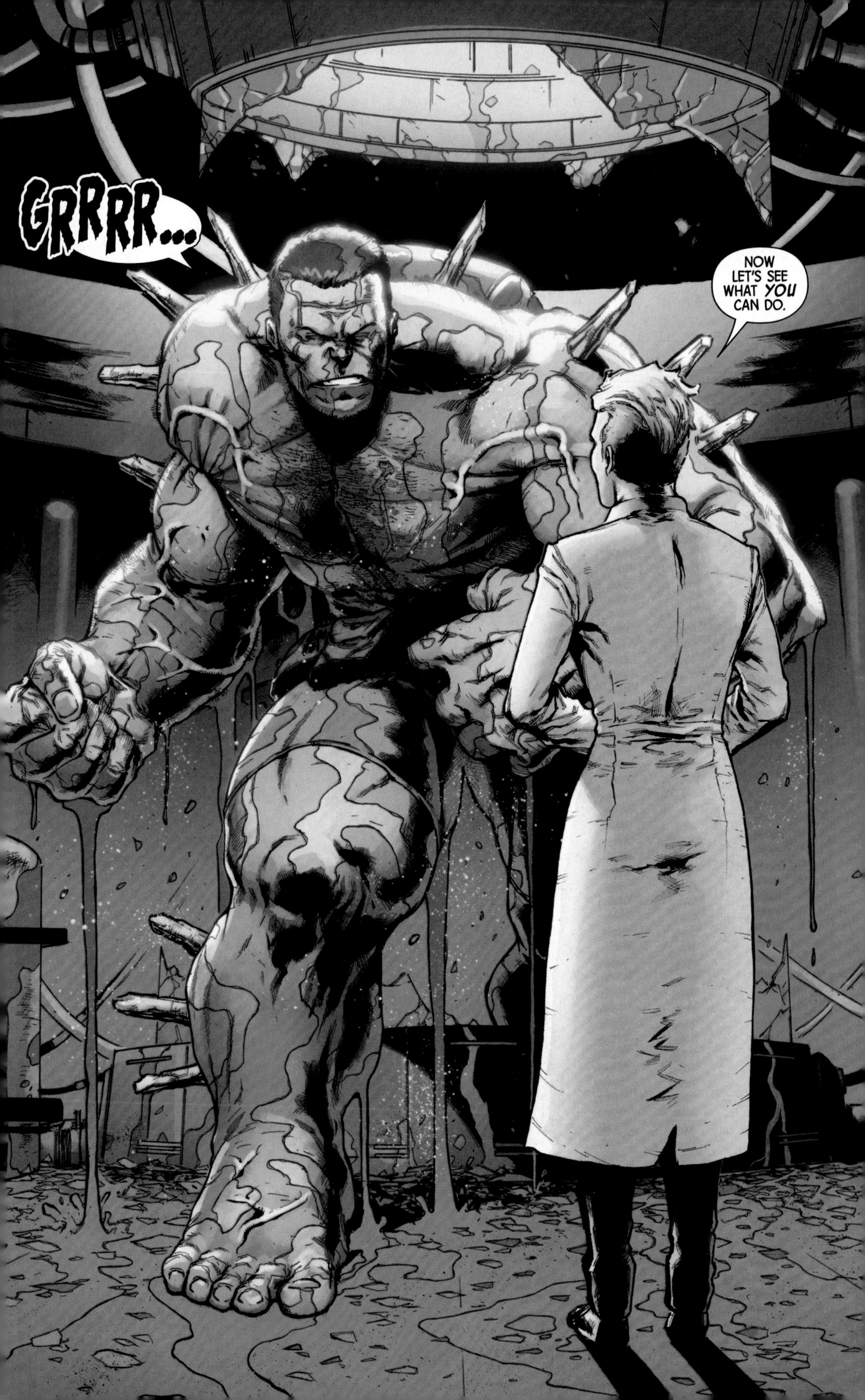
GRRRR...
NOW LET'S SEE WHAT *YOU* CAN DO.

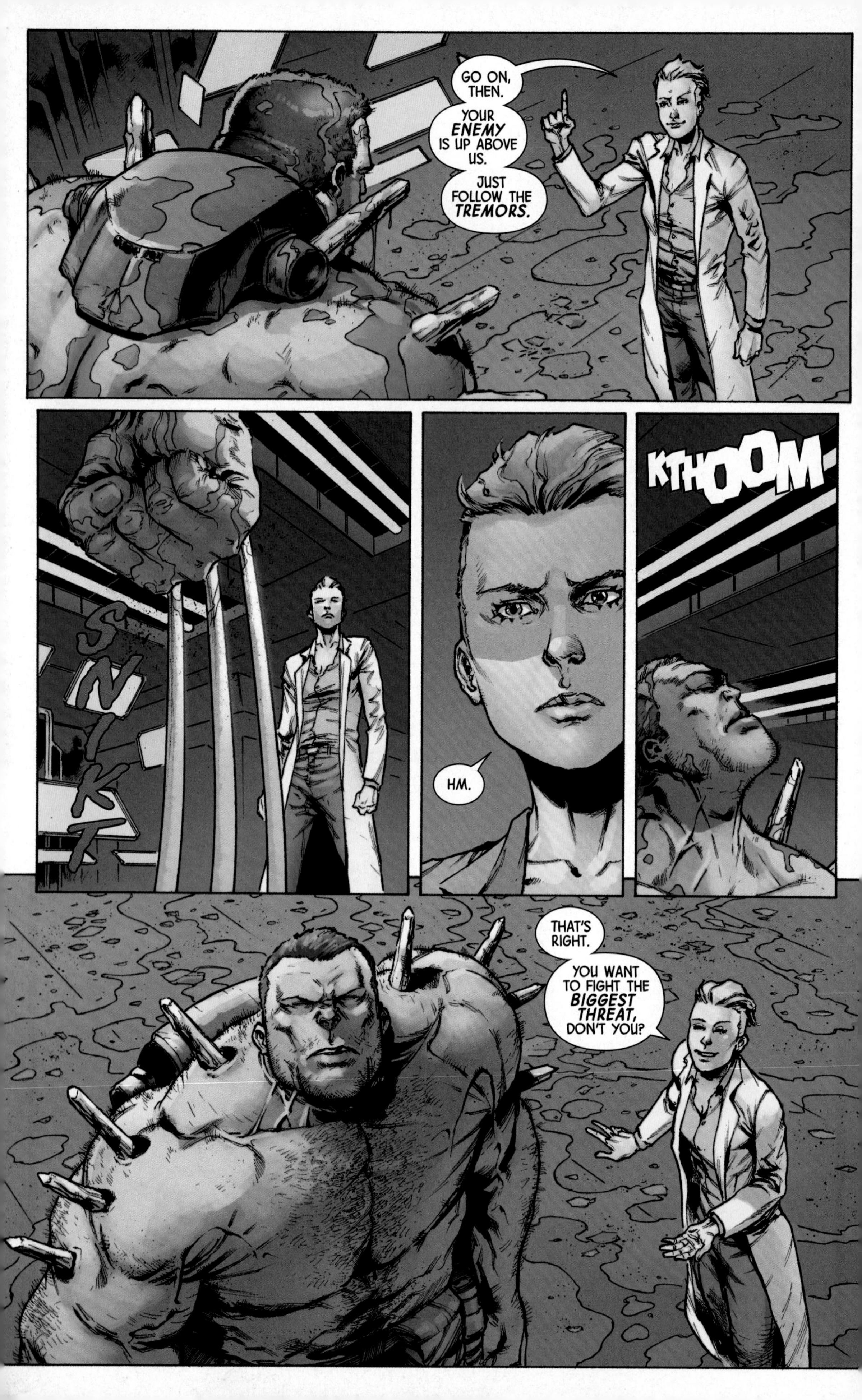
GO ON, THEN.
YOUR ENEMY IS UP ABOVE US.
JUST FOLLOW THE TREMORS.
SNIKT
HM.
KTHOOM-
THAT'S RIGHT.
YOU WANT TO FIGHT THE BIGGEST THREAT, DON'T YOU?

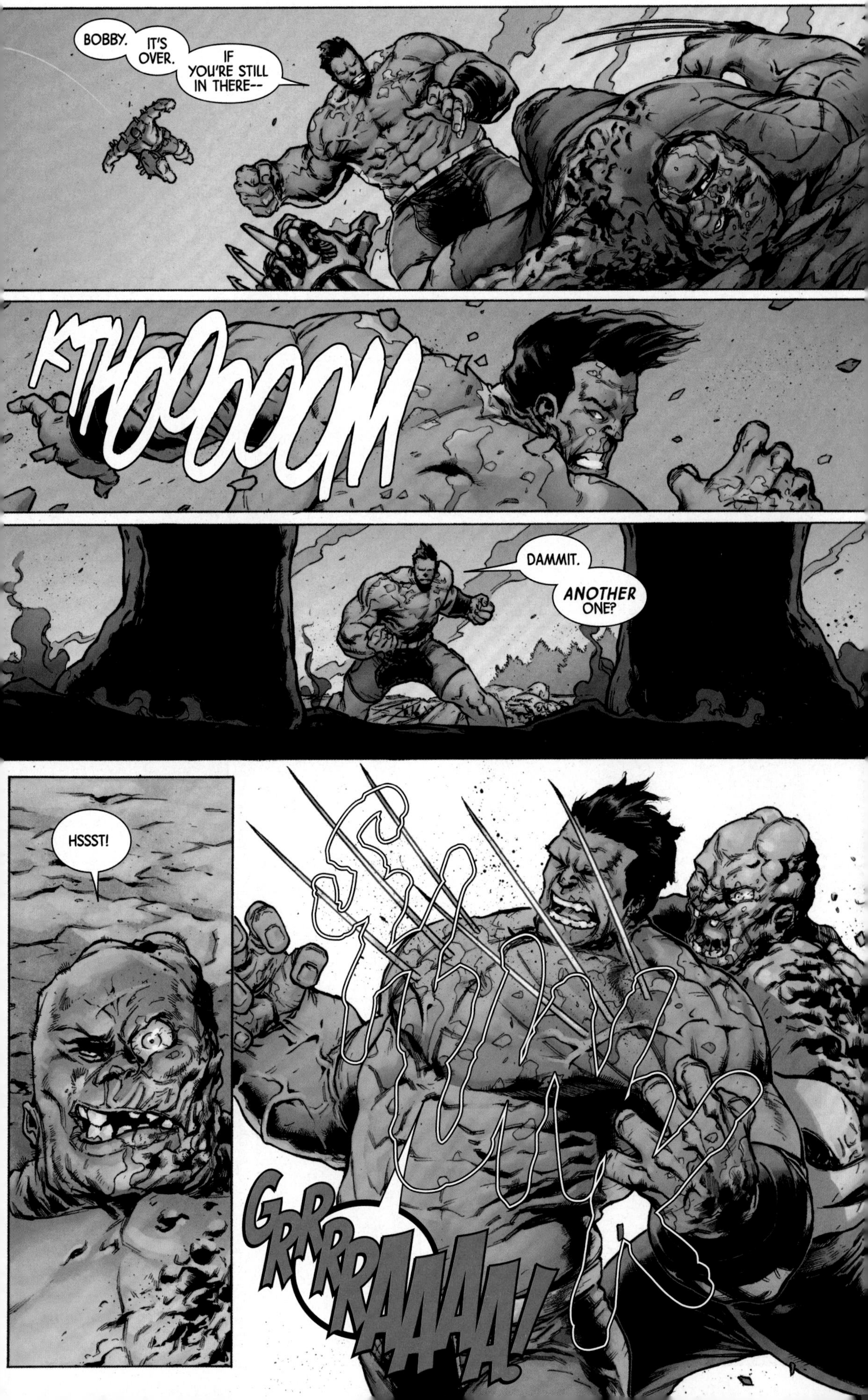
BOBBY.
IT'S OVER.
IF YOU'RE STILL IN THERE--
KTHOOOOOM
DAMMIT.
ANOTHER ONE?
HSSST!
SHNKT
GRRRRAAAAA!

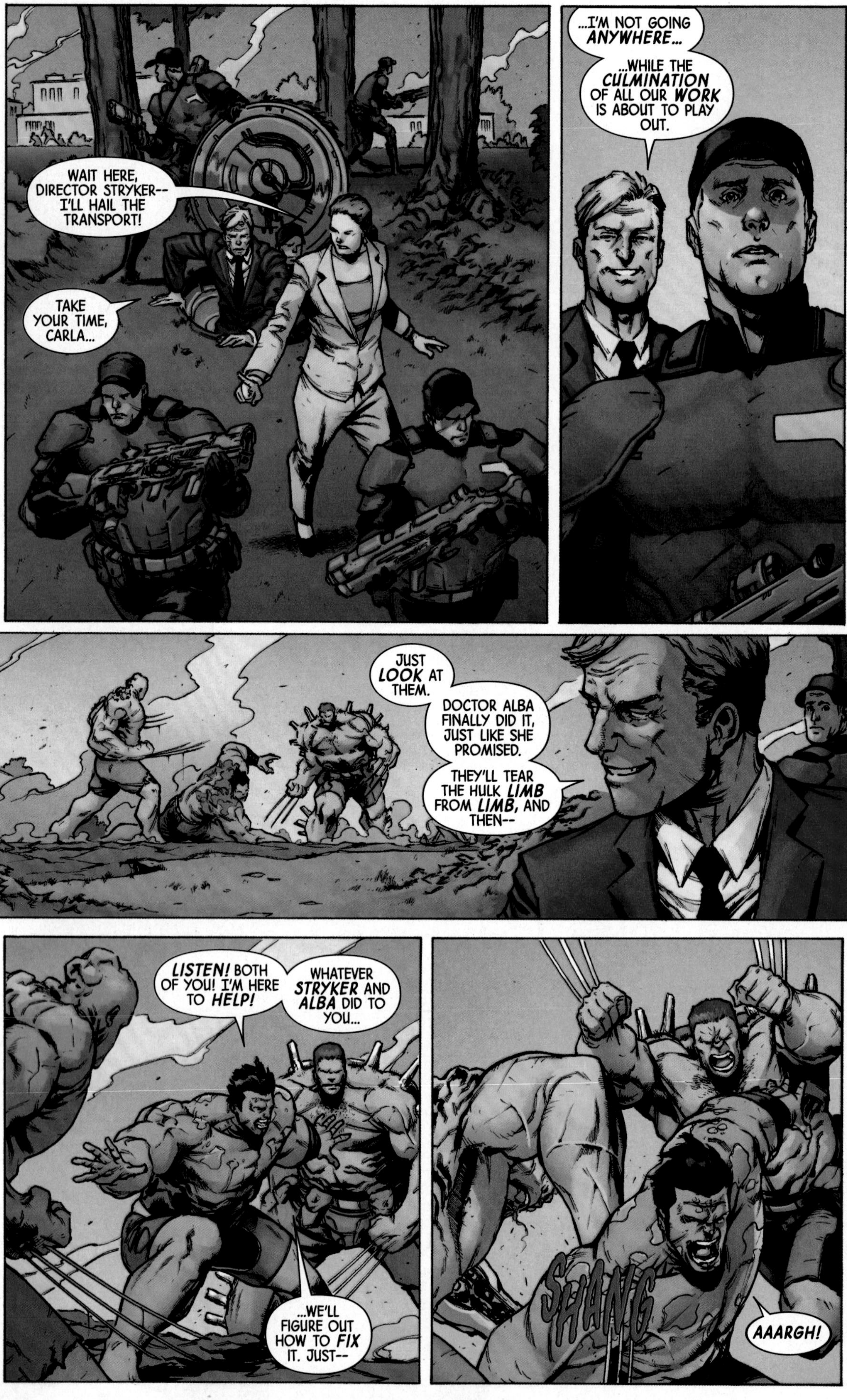
WAIT HERE, DIRECTOR STRYKER-- I'LL HAIL THE TRANSPORT!
TAKE YOUR TIME, CARLA...
...I'M NOT GOING ANYWHERE...
...WHILE THE CULMINATION OF ALL OUR WORK IS ABOUT TO PLAY OUT.
JUST LOOK AT THEM.
DOCTOR ALBA FINALLY DID IT, JUST LIKE SHE PROMISED.
THEY'LL TEAR THE HULK LIMB FROM LIMB, AND THEN--
LISTEN! BOTH OF YOU! I'M HERE TO HELP!
WHATEVER STRYKER AND ALBA DID TO YOU...
...WE'LL FIGURE OUT HOW TO FIX IT. JUST--
SHANG
AAARGH!

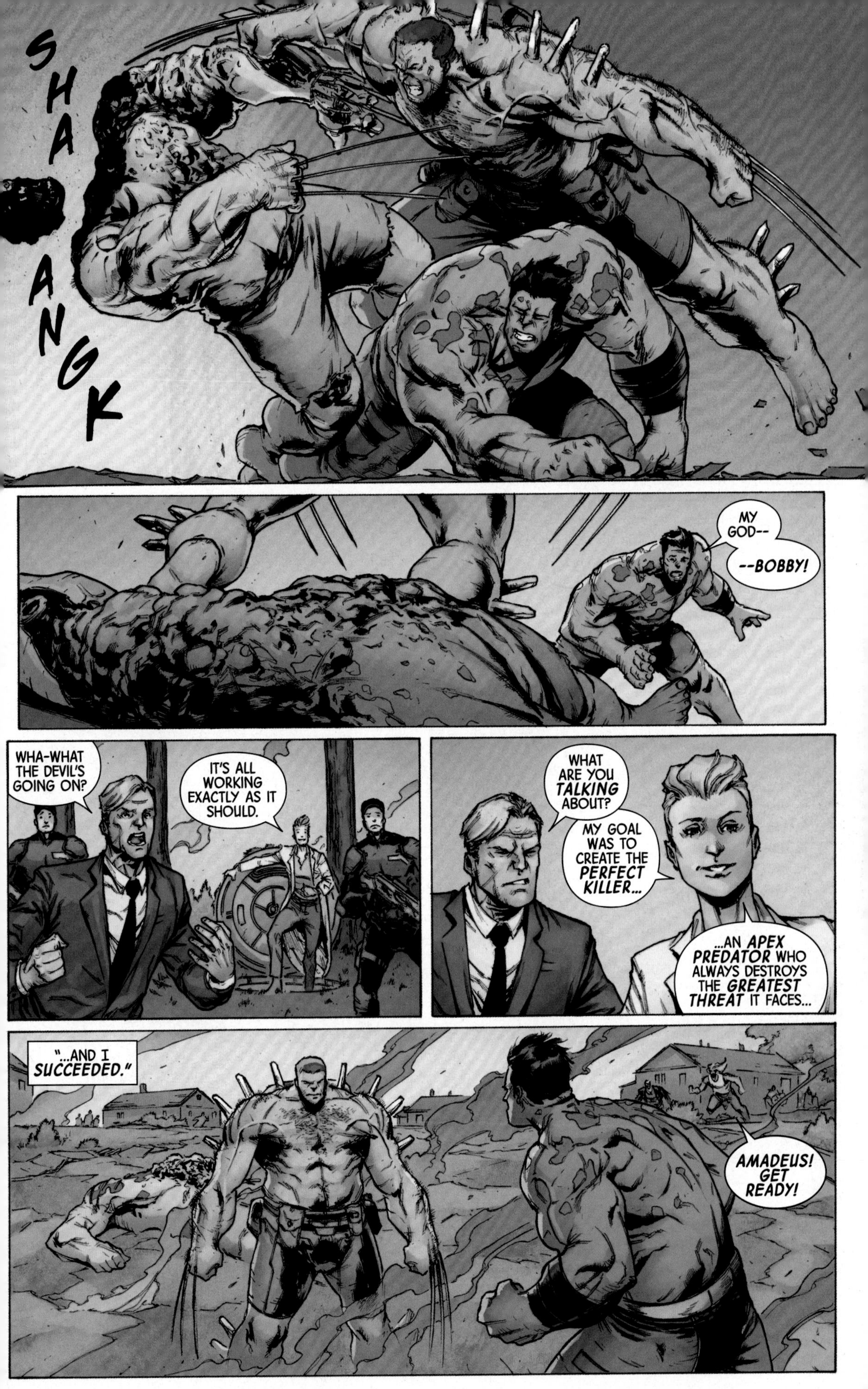
SHHAANGK
MY GOD--
--BOBBY!
WHA-WHAT THE DEVIL'S GOING ON?
IT'S ALL WORKING EXACTLY AS IT SHOULD.
WHAT ARE YOU TALKING ABOUT?
MY GOAL WAS TO CREATE THE PERFECT KILLER...
...AN APEX PREDATOR WHO ALWAYS DESTROYS THE GREATEST THREAT IT FACES...
"...AND I SUCCEEDED."
AMADEUS! GET READY!

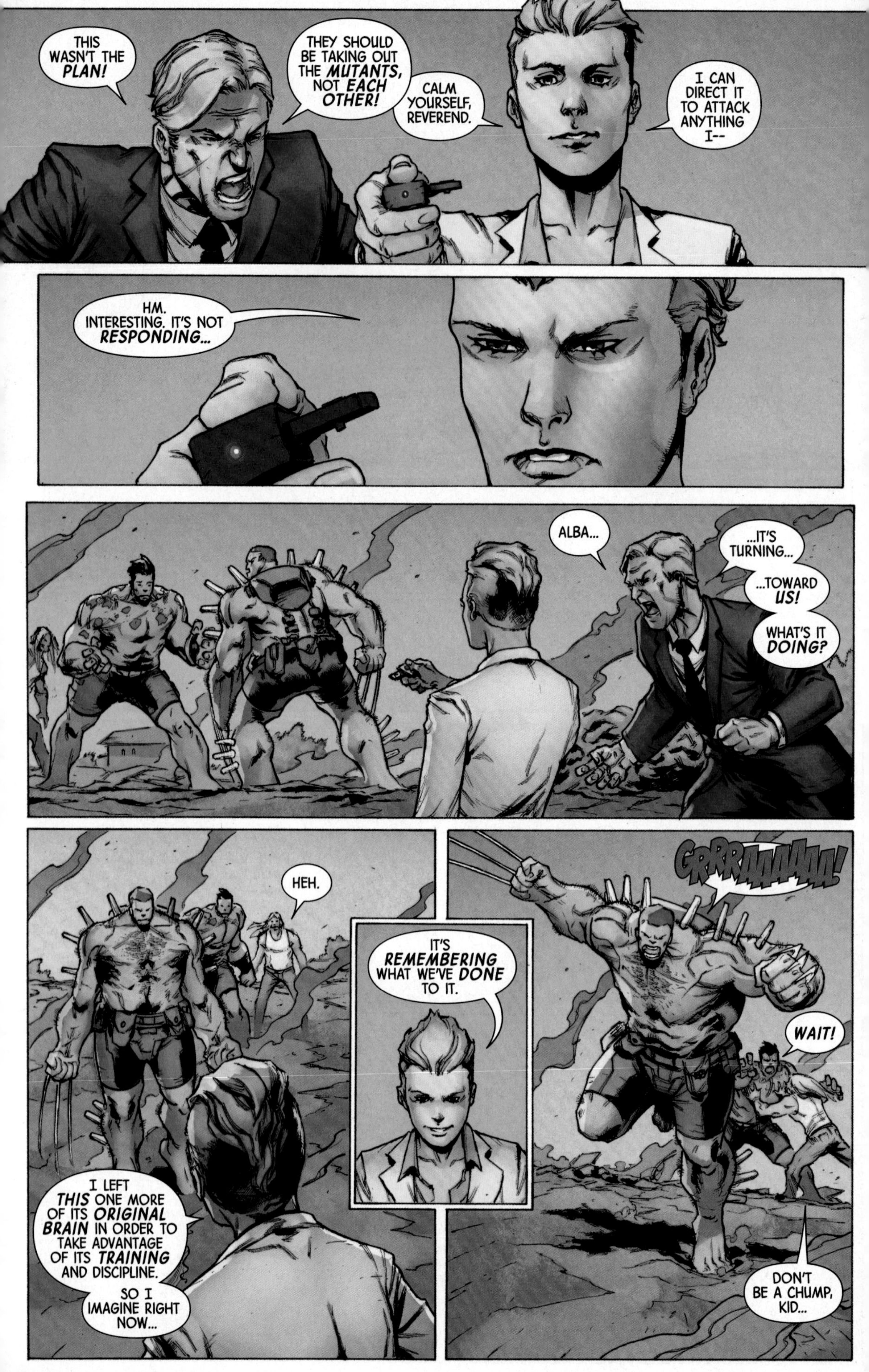
THIS WASN'T THE PLAN!
THEY SHOULD BE TAKING OUT THE MUTANTS, NOT EACH OTHER!
CALM YOURSELF, REVEREND.
I CAN DIRECT IT TO ATTACK ANYTHING I--
HM. INTERESTING. IT'S NOT RESPONDING...
ALBA...
...IT'S TURNING...
...TOWARD US!
WHAT'S IT DOING?
HEH.
I LEFT THIS ONE MORE OF ITS ORIGINAL BRAIN IN ORDER TO TAKE ADVANTAGE OF ITS TRAINING AND DISCIPLINE.
SO I IMAGINE RIGHT NOW...
IT'S REMEMBERING WHAT WE'VE DONE TO IT.
GRRRAAAAAAA!
WAIT!
DON'T BE A CHUMP, KID...

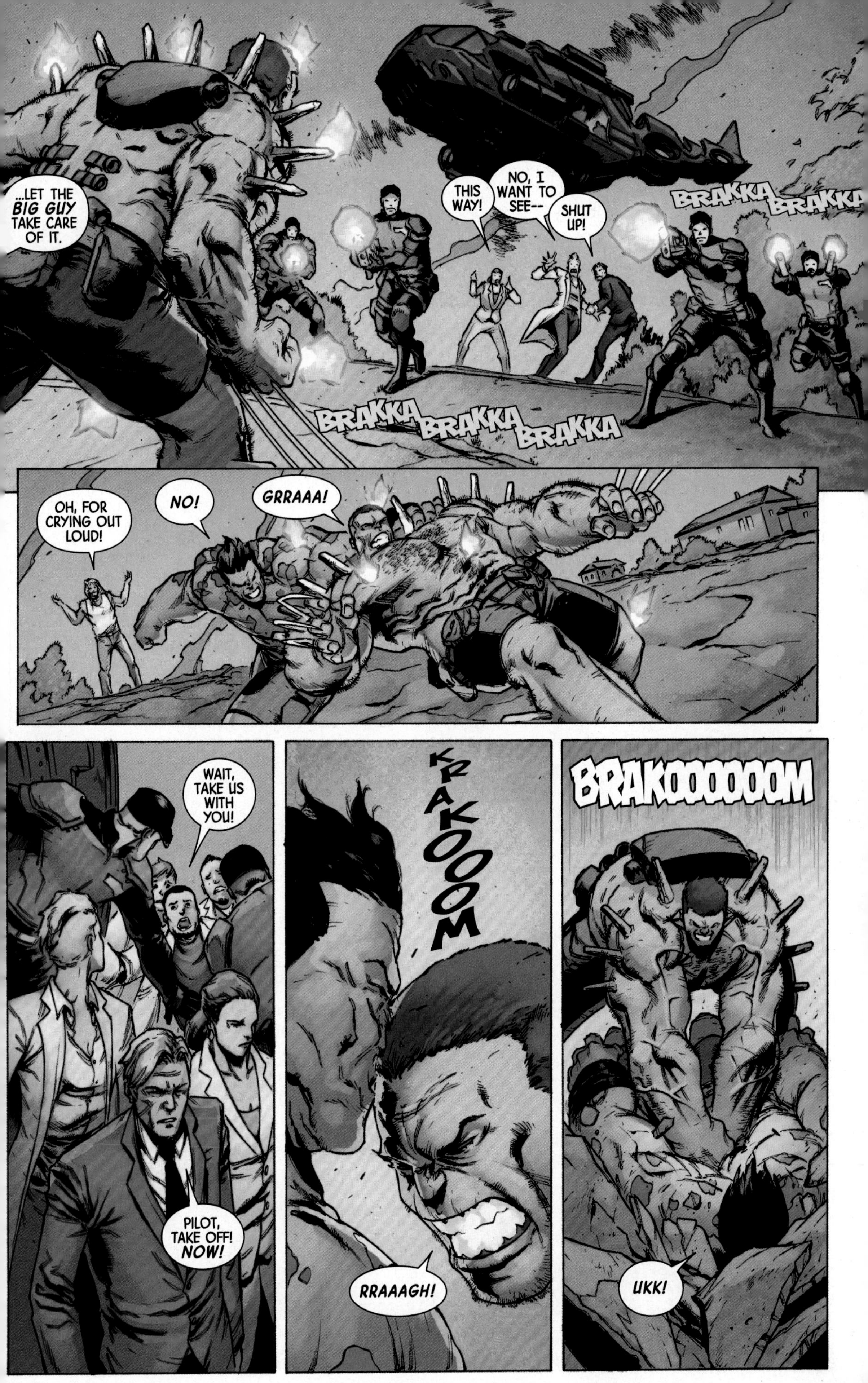

...LET THE *BIG GUY* TAKE CARE OF IT.
THIS WAY!
NO, I WANT TO SEE--
SHUT UP!
BRAKKA BRAKKA
BRAKKA BRAKKA BRAKKA
OH, FOR CRYING OUT LOUD!
NO!
GRRAAA!
WAIT, TAKE US WITH YOU!
PILOT, TAKE OFF! *NOW!*
KRAKOOOOM
RRAAAGH!
BRAKOOOOOOM
UKK!

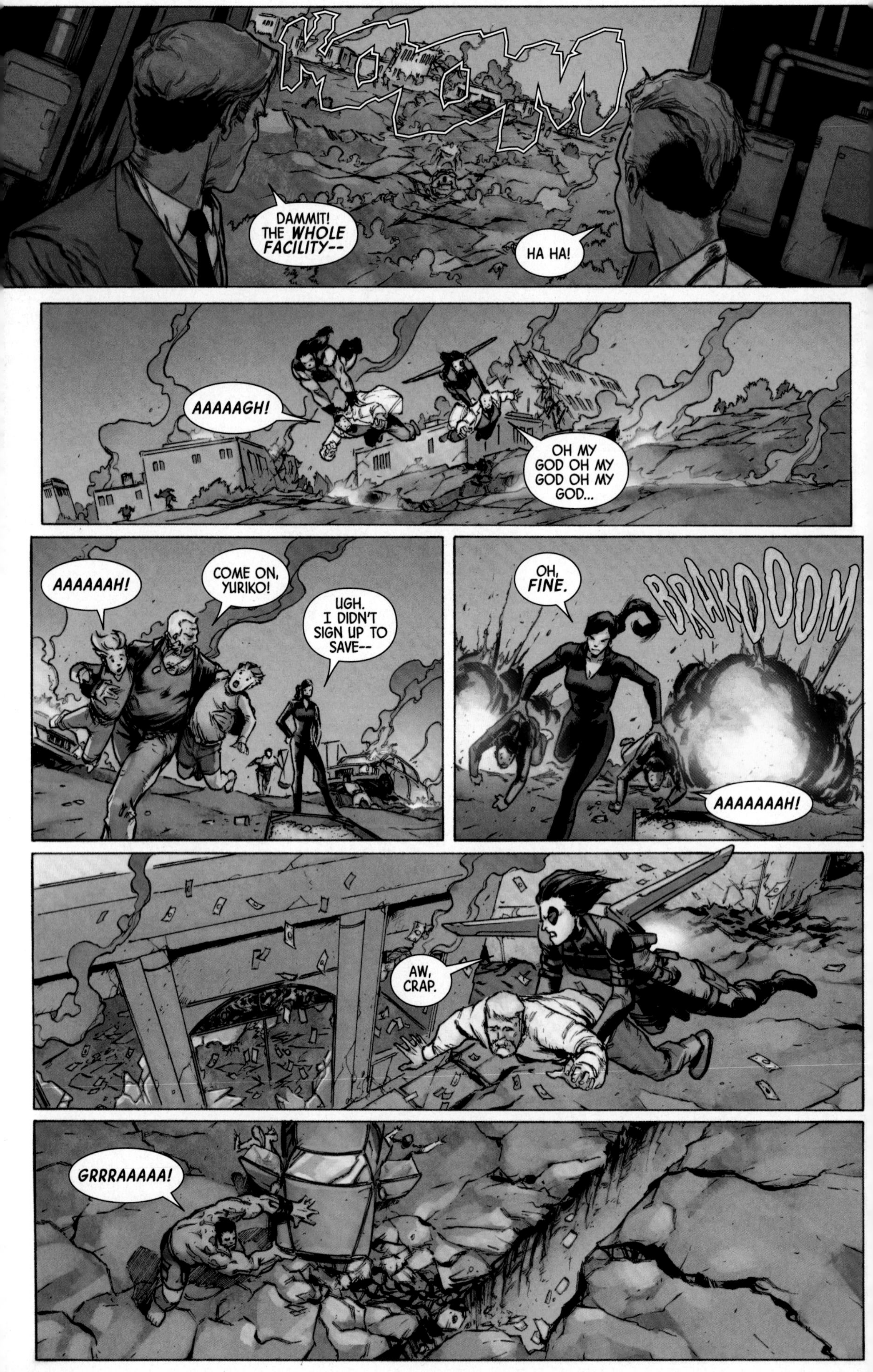
KA-BOOM
DAMMIT! THE WHOLE FACILITY--
HA HA!
AAAAAGH!
OH MY GOD OH MY GOD OH MY GOD...
AAAAAAH!
COME ON, YURIKO!
UGH. I DIDN'T SIGN UP TO SAVE--
OH, FINE.
BRAKOOOM
AAAAAAAH!
AW, CRAP.
GRRRAAAAA!

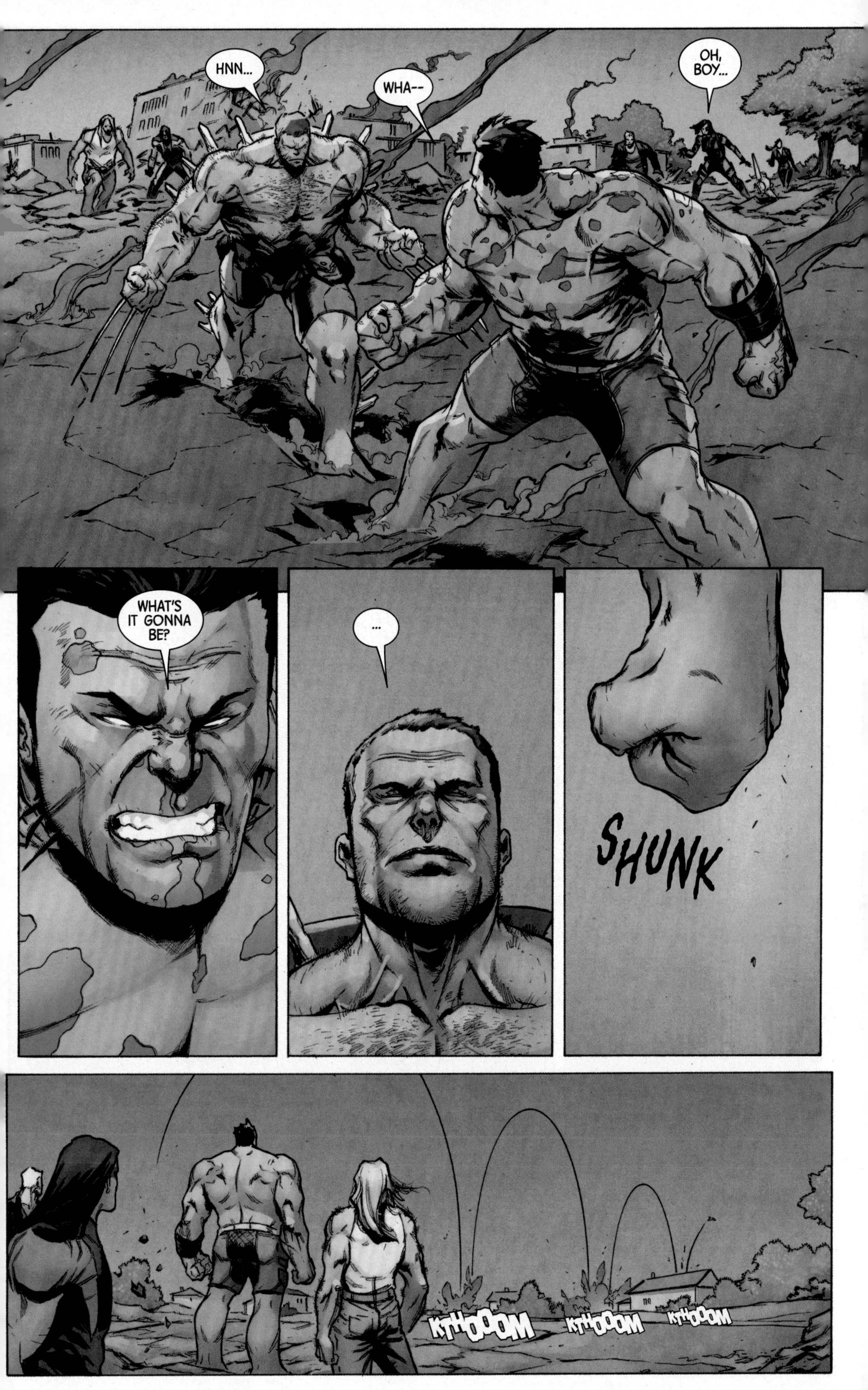
HNN...
WHA--
OH, BOY...
WHAT'S IT GONNA BE?
...
SHUNK
KTHOOOM
KTHOOOM
KTHOOOM

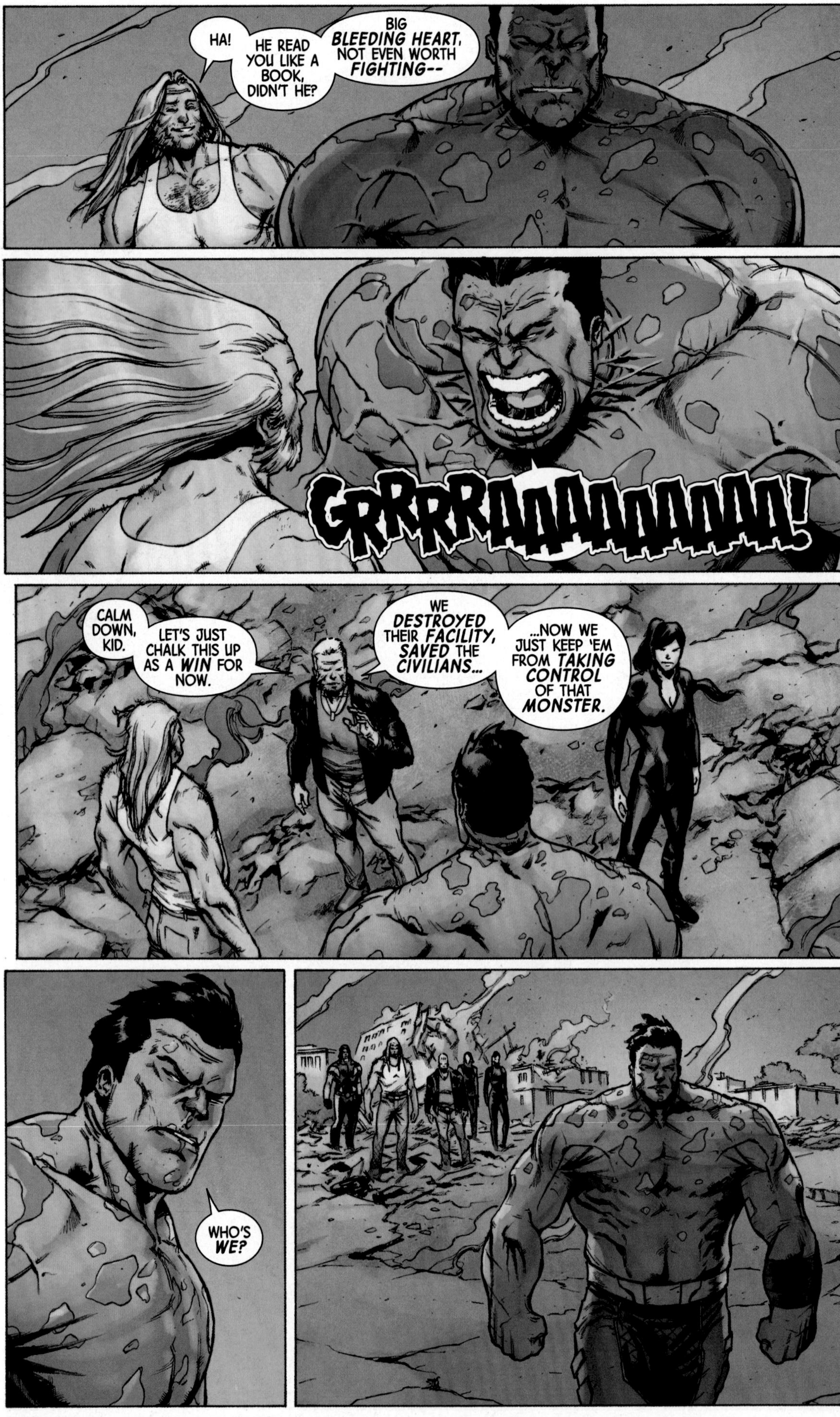
HA!
HE READ YOU LIKE A BOOK, DIDN'T HE?
BIG BLEEDING HEART, NOT EVEN WORTH FIGHTING--
GRRRRAAAAAAAAAA!
CALM DOWN, KID.
LET'S JUST CHALK THIS UP AS A WIN FOR NOW.
WE DESTROYED THEIR FACILITY, SAVED THE CIVILIANS...
...NOW WE JUST KEEP 'EM FROM TAKING CONTROL OF THAT MONSTER.
WHO'S WE?

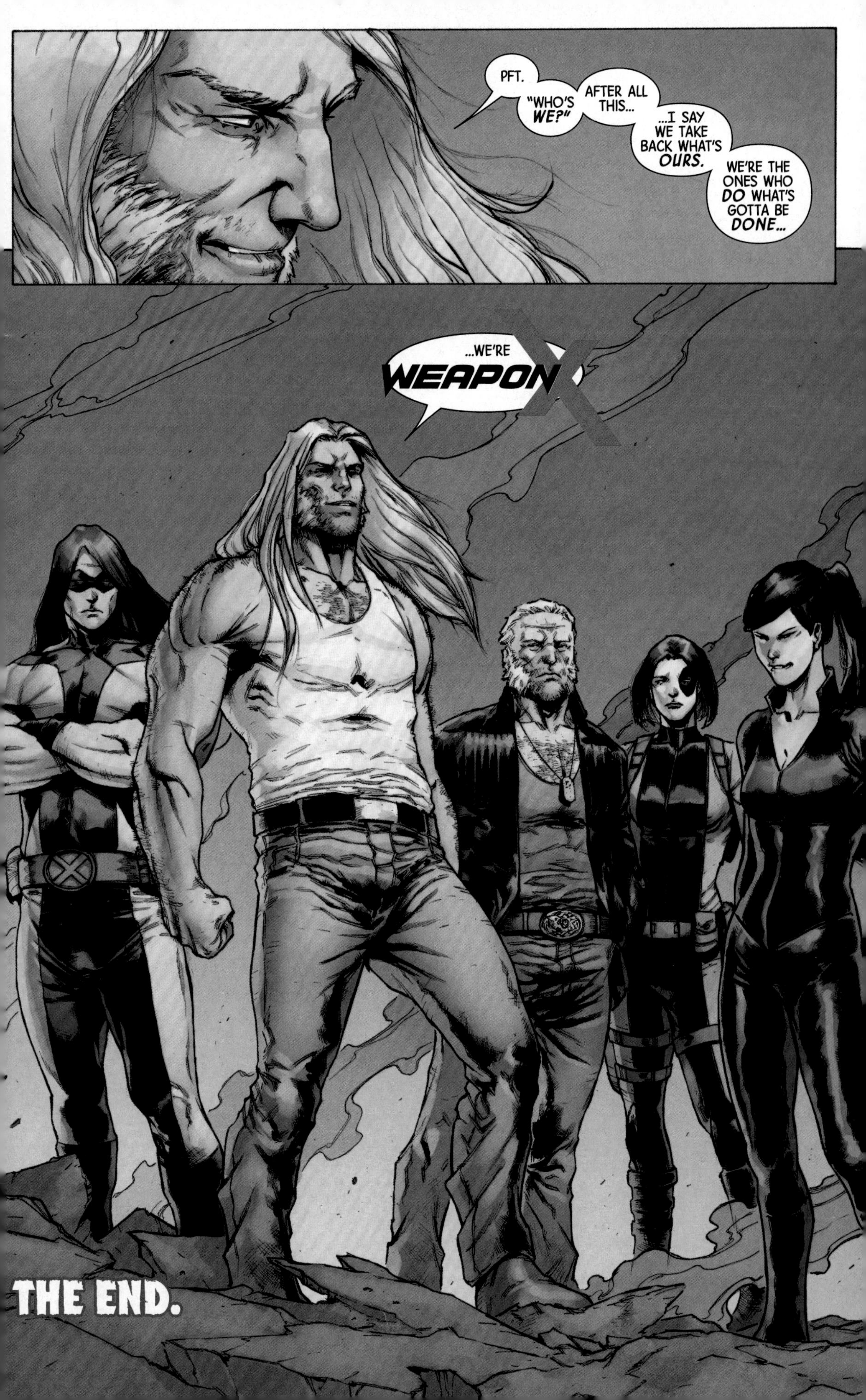
PFT.
"WHO'S WE?"
AFTER ALL THIS...
...I SAY WE TAKE BACK WHAT'S OURS.
WE'RE THE ONES WHO DO WHAT'S GOTTA BE DONE...
...WE'RE WEAPON X
THE END.

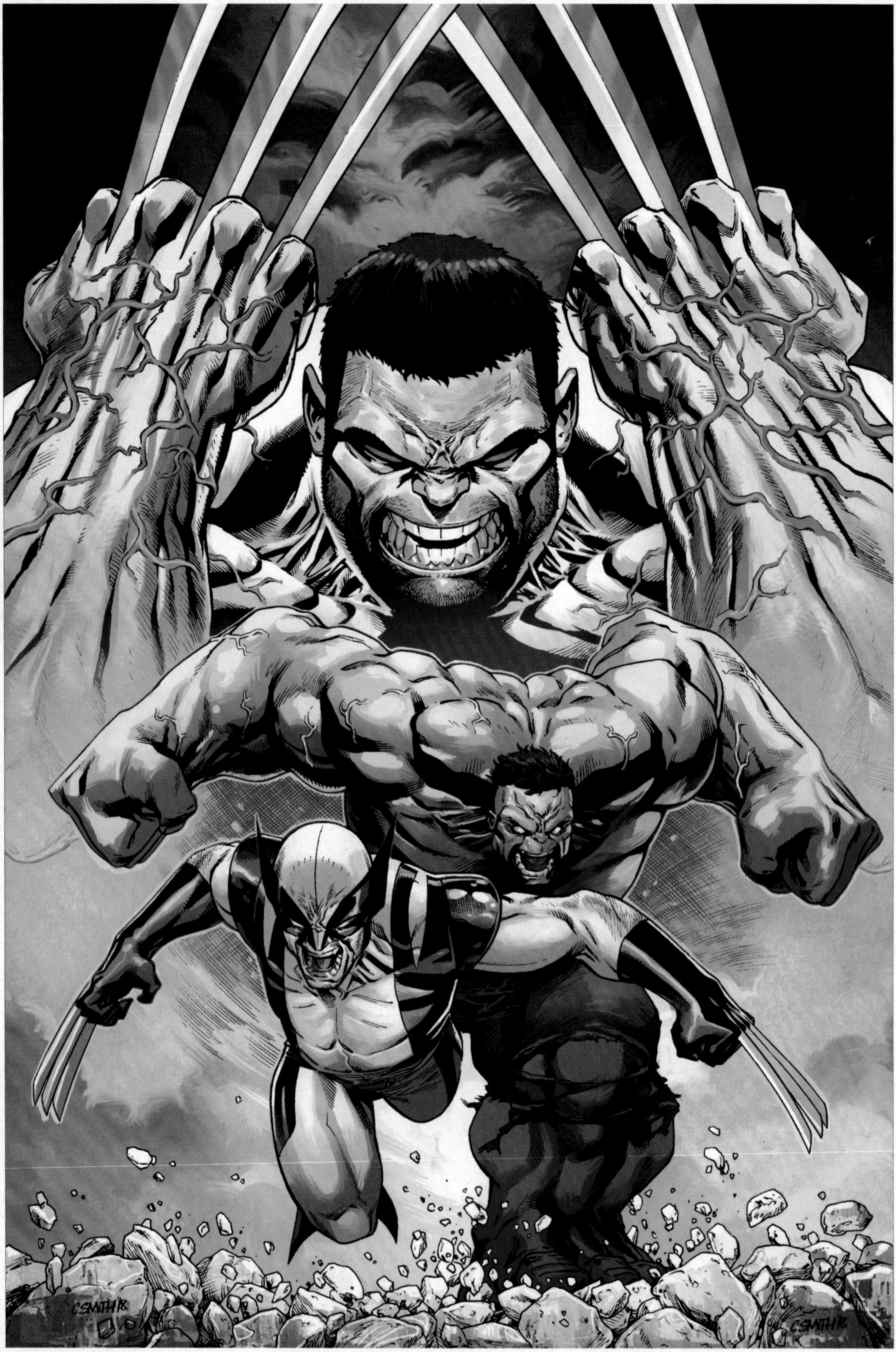

#1 VARIANT BY CORY SMITH & ROMULO FAJARDO JR.

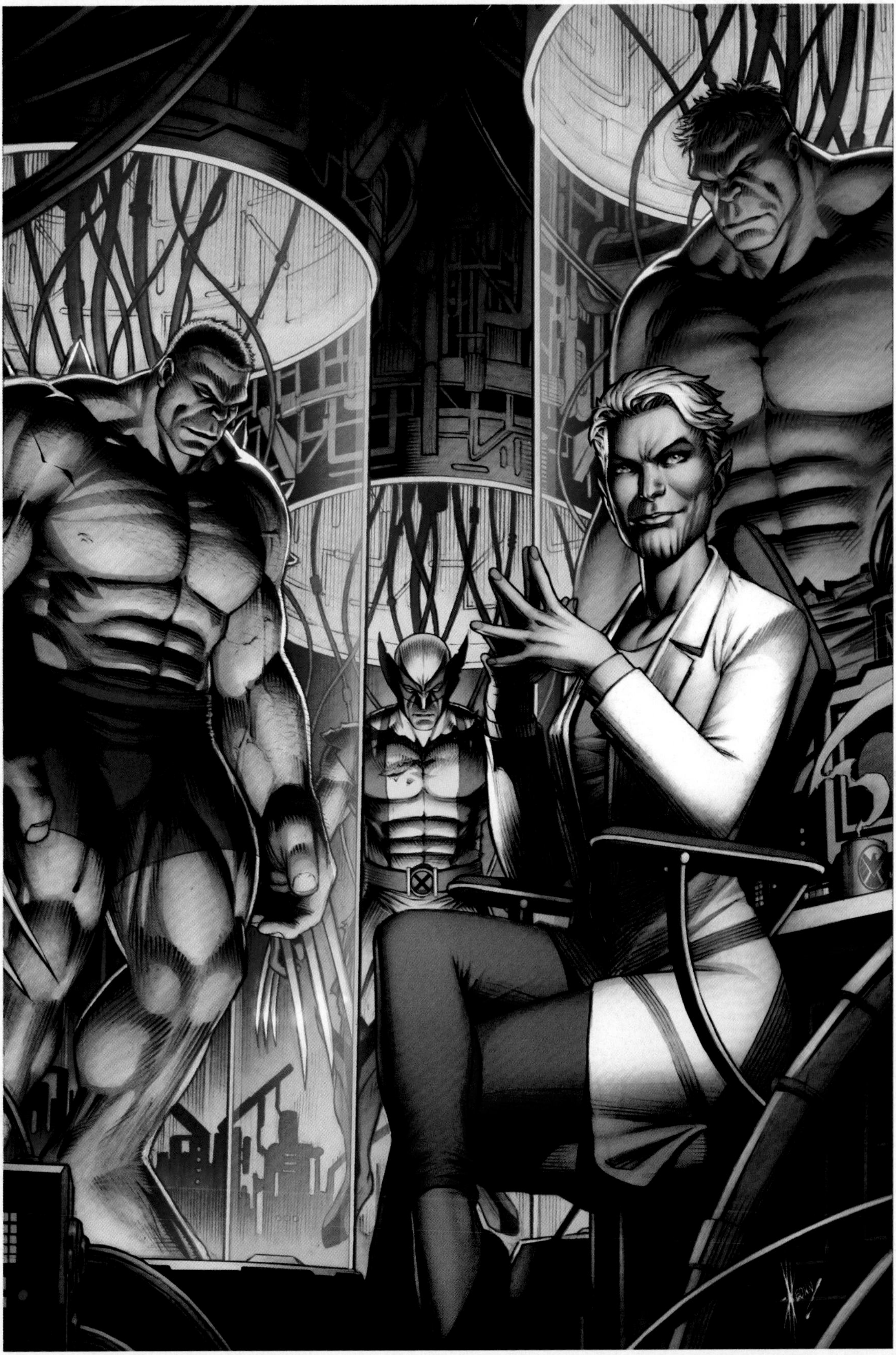

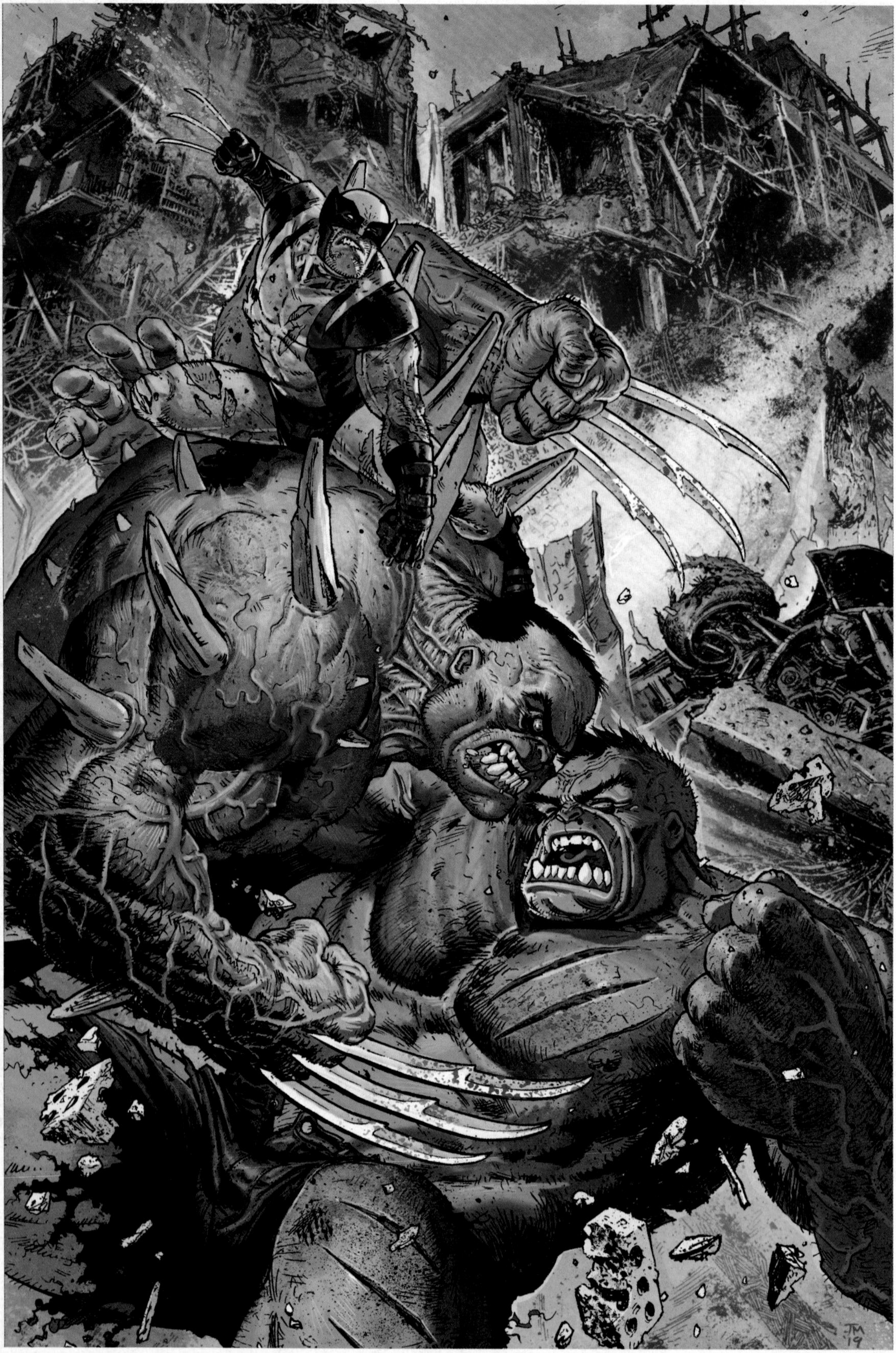

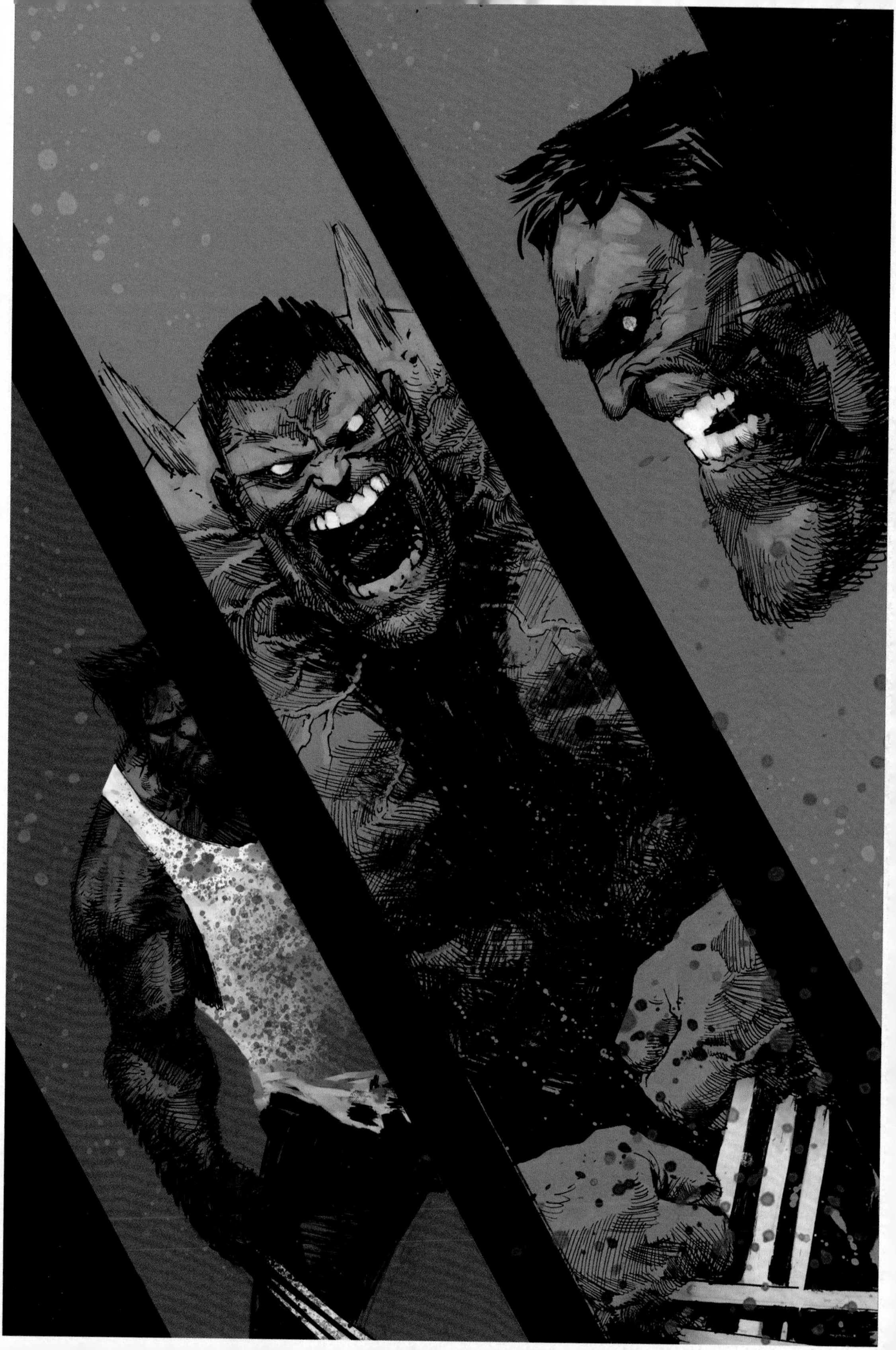

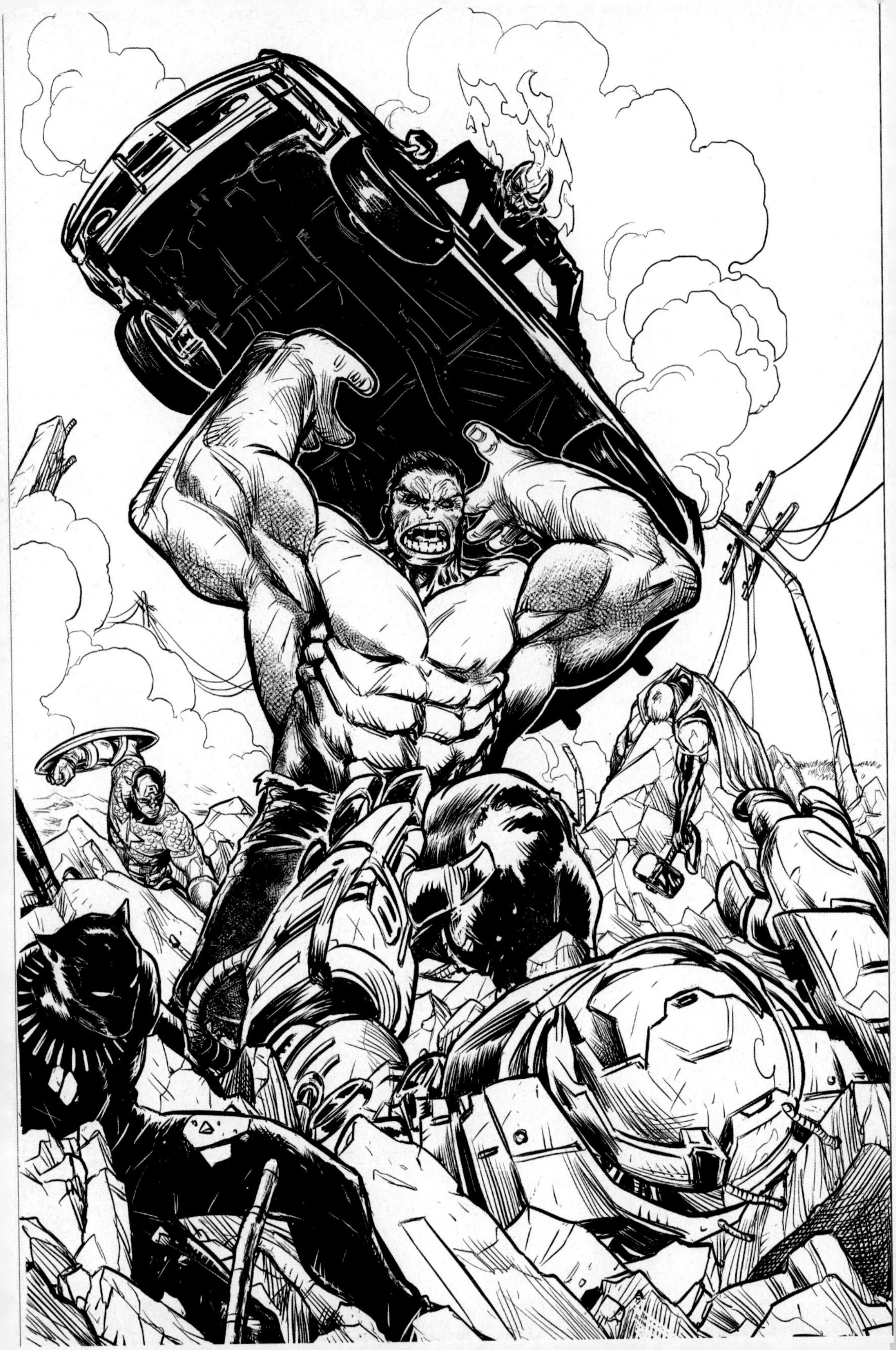

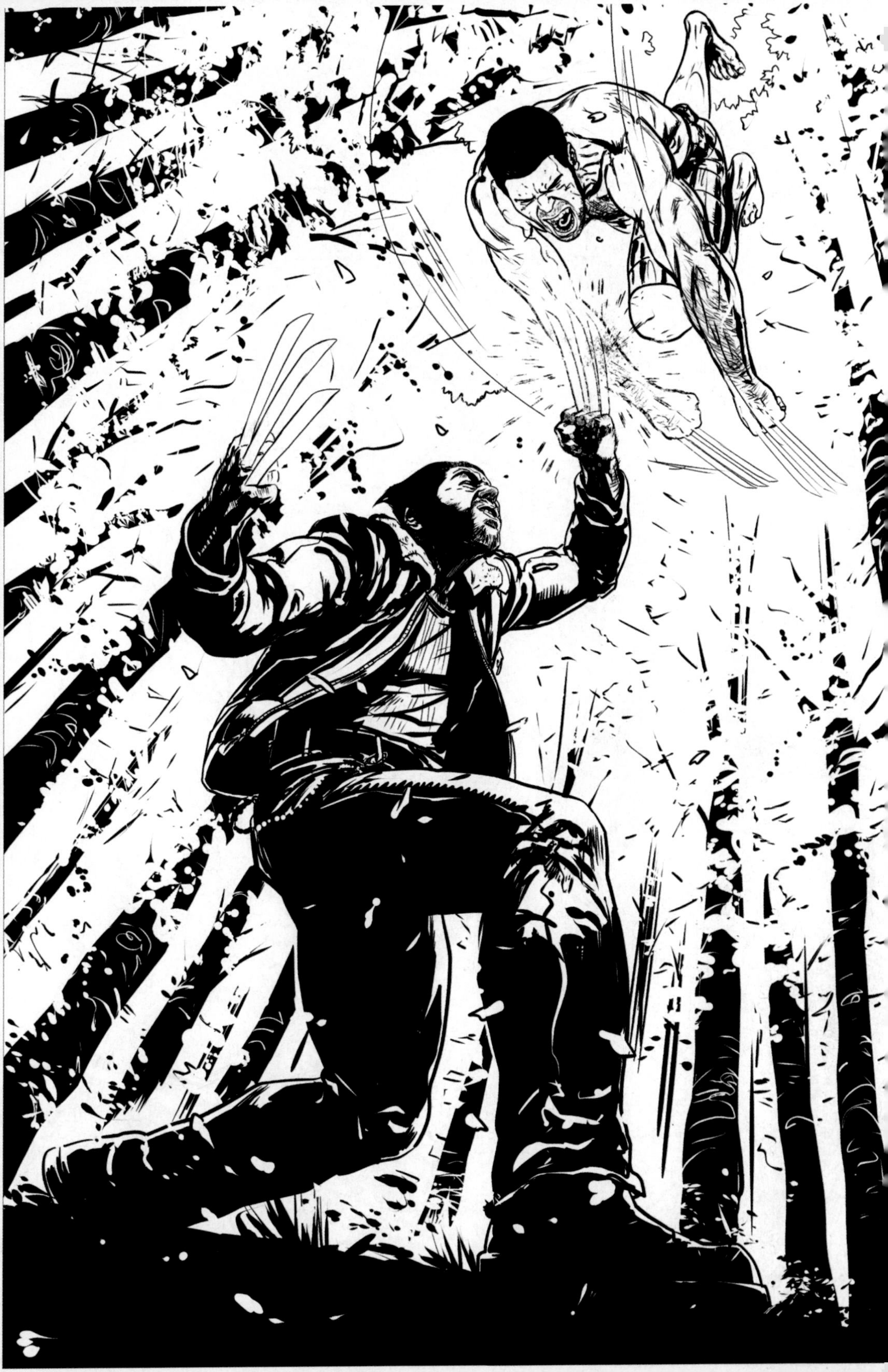

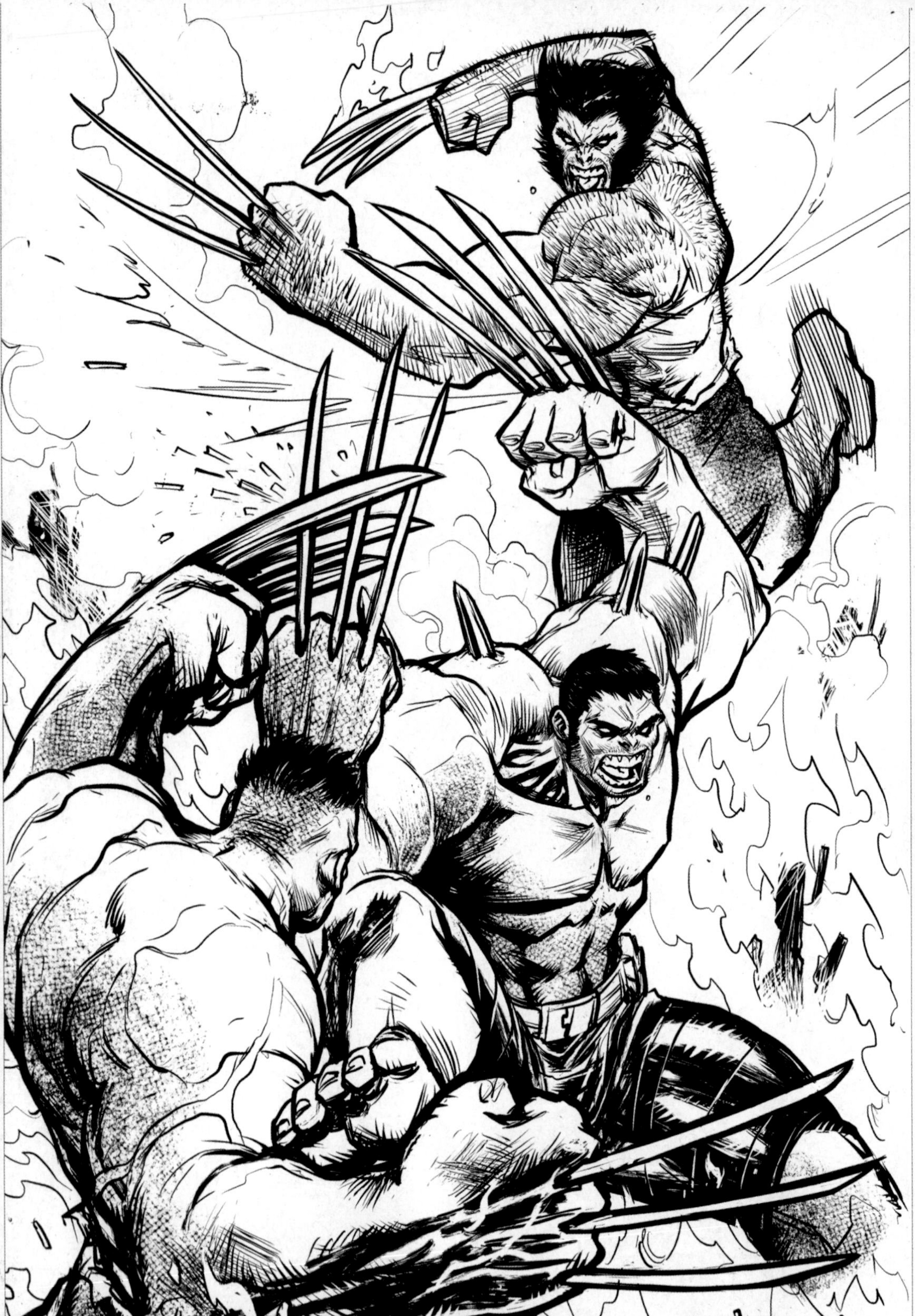